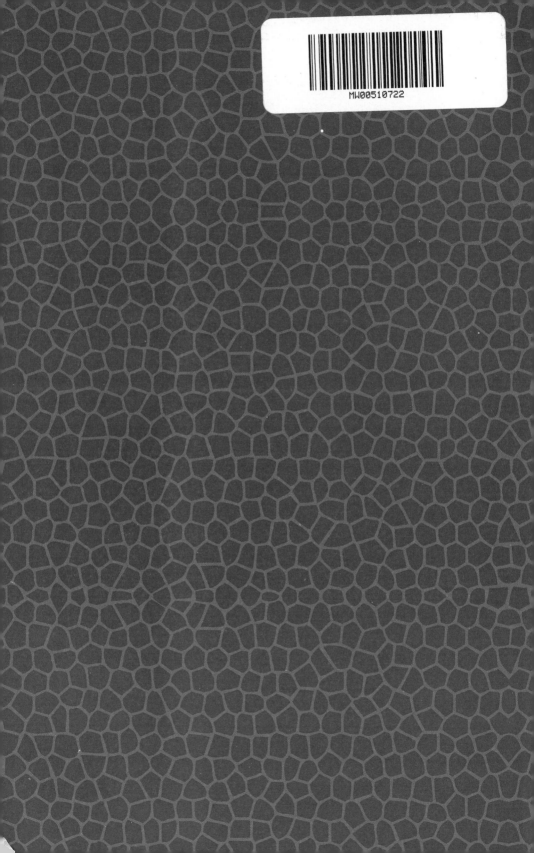

MW00510722

AN AUDIENCE OF
one

MOSAICA PRESS

SARAH SHAPIRO

AN AUDIENCE OF

one

and other stories

Published by Mosaica Press, Inc.
www.mosaicapress.com
info@mosaicapress.com

For Becky and Adam

Matt and Annisa

Dovi and Yani

Yael and Yechezkel

Mimi and Dovy

Yehudit and Nati

Yehuda and Tzipora

and

Lala and Muti

TABLE OF CONTENTS

ACKNOWLEDGMENTS

The author wishes to express her profound thanks to the superbly diligent, dedicated Sherie Gross, managing editor of Mosaica Press; to Rayzel Broyde, its gifted art director; and to their staff: Brocha Mirel Strizower, typesetter; Meira Lawrence, copyeditor; and Daliya Shapiro, proofreader;

to Rebbetzin Hindy Kviat, the artist Elisheva Marshall, the poet Roberta Chester, and Rabbi Yirmiyahu Cowan, who gave of their time to view portions of the manuscript;

to Rabbi Doron Kornbluth, co-founder of Mosaica Press;

to Ami Magazine senior editor Rechy Frankfurter;

and to the Jacobs family, for their generous support.

Sarah Shapiro
Jerusalem

THE FLOWER IN QUESTION

My mother and I were taking a walk one day through the woods behind our house, making our way here and there among wet piles of autumn's brown leaves and clumps of unmelted snow, when she reached for something overhead on a low-hanging branch. "Look at that," she said, as much to herself as to me (who was at the time about eight or nine years old). "Have you ever seen anything as beautiful as this?"

She was cupping carefully in her upraised hands a pale-pink flower—its rose-tinged petals still sealed against the cold spring air—and turning to me with a wondering smile of amazement, certainty, and awe, she then said the words that until today are seeds, sprouting in my mind: "How can G-d create such a thing?"

The two of us were for some unremembered reason by ourselves that morning—or it could be that I've dropped from memory the other child who was there. For usually when we took walks along that path, it was Sunday, when my best friend, whom I'll call Emily, had spent the night. Her mother and father, longtime friends of my parents, lived in an adjoining town, and were the only other Jewish family around.

Emily was long-stemmed and blond, and though just my own age, aspired to sophisticated worldliness, scorning anything that smacked of childish innocence. In school, she was always at the top of the class academically, and her sense of humor was ironic and cutting. She was tutored in such things by her brilliant, cynical older brother, a philosophy major at Harvard and a self-described nihilist. I remember him pontificating to us in their kitchen about Darwin's theory of evolution and the random nature of the accidental universe. It was he—with his shrewdly humorous, proud adherence to the void—whom Emily adored and idolized.

1

Emily and I both were "the baby" in our respective families, and we didn't like that situation one bit. The game we loved to play whenever she came over was "dress-up." We'd furtively plow our way through my older sisters' closets, especially the wardrobe of my sister who was away at college, and would put on the lipstick we'd find in my mother's purse.

Whether or not she was there in person in the woods that day, my best friend's physical presence or absence is a moot point. For Emily was with me in spirit—as she was throughout our parallel childhoods—casting a shadow of skepticism over the path we shared. Even now, decades later, she who is still an artist and a poet—and who forty-some years ago was committed to a mental-health facility—is in thrall to her late brother's intellectual prowess.

Meanwhile, as years hurried by, my mother, *a"h*, and I would enjoy long conversations about the Judaism to which I, as a young *baalas teshuvah*, had recently been introduced, but to which she—raised by a prematurely widowed, impoverished young mother, a Yiddish-speaking nineteenth-century immigrant from Minsk—had never been exposed. My mother would thank me for sharing the Torah I was learning, which was new to us both, marveling again and again at what she called "a whole new world" opening up before her eyes. But she never knew that it was she herself—one long-ago spring—who had planted belief in the Creator in her little girl's mind.

WHISTLING IN THE DARK

One summer night at 2 a.m, in an old second-story studio on Jaffa Street, I was looking over the shoulder of Zehava, a seamstress. We had found her when only two weeks remained until our eldest daughter's wedding, and it was from mercy on her part that she acquiesced to such pressured work: four matching gowns to be fitted and sewn in ten days. As the deadline neared, she'd arrive at her studio at 7 a.m. and leave after midnight. Dark circles appeared under her eyes.

Zehava was a stern woman in her sixties, meticulous and exacting, and we all felt intimidated by her. "You must bring Devorah for a fitting immediately," she would declare over the phone just as I was getting ready for bed, or, "Tell Yael to get here in ten minutes, without the baby this time."

This was the first time I was with her by myself, in the wee hours of the morning, with a June breeze wafting in through the big open windows of her studio, and the stop-and-start of a sewing machine murmuring from another room. (She had hired a Russian girl to help her finish the job.) That's when I noticed something one of my daughters had mentioned, that Zehava talked to herself as she worked, a little smile playing on her lips, though if you looked at her directly, you'd see it wasn't a smile, exactly, as much as an expression of single-minded tranquility and focus.

I was perched on a stool, watching, as without hesitation she measured, cut, and penciled in markings onto her handmade brown-paper dress pattern. With just the two of us present, and noisy Jaffa Street so still and quiet in the darkness, I noticed for the first time that though her lips were hardly moving, she was emitting a low sort of soft whispering—or whistling—under her breath.

I was curious. "Excuse me, I'm sorry to interrupt you, but are you saying something?"

Continuing to work, she said, "I'm saying *Tehillim*."

"Do you always do that when you're working?"

"Always."

"You know all the Psalms by heart?"

"Yes. But sometimes I'm just speaking to *Hashem* in my own words, the way I would talk to my father, or to my mother. You don't need a prayer book to talk to a friend, *nachon*?"

"G-d is your friend?"

She lifted her eyes and looked at me sharply. "You can say more to Him than you can to any friend. You can tell Him everything."

"So just now you were talking things over with Him?"

"No. Tonight I am asking Him to help me make beautiful dresses. I am asking Him to help me succeed." Placing the large scissors deliberately upon her cutting table, Zehava straightened and stood there a moment, regarding me levelly. All at once I felt self-conscious—as if she were sizing me up, too—and it suddenly struck me how exhausted she looked. "You can ask G-d for whatever you need. Don't you know that?"

"Well—"

"You have to know it. That is what we are here for: to discover that we can talk to Him. Don't you like it when your daughter puts her head on your shoulder and says, 'Mommy, please give me this, please give me that?' It is exactly like that."

I tried visualizing this scenario, but saw in my mind's eye the image of my engaged daughter's happy relief upon finding a good seamstress who had agreed to do a rush job on her sisters' dresses. "But wasn't there ever a time you asked for something that wouldn't have been good for you, so *Hashem* didn't give it?"

"Everything I have ever wanted or needed, I asked Him and He gave it to me."

"*Everything?* Really?"

Zehava gazed out briefly into the predawn darkness, one hand on hip, thinking. Then she declared, "Yes. Everything. It's not difficult for Him. He's your Father and wants to give you what you want. He's just waiting for you to ask."

A CHILD'S HOUSE

Not until we are lost, in other words, not till we have lost the world,
do we begin to find ourselves…

Henry David Thoreau

It's ironic that to [leave the culture in which you were raised and]
become a *baal teshuvah*, you have to be somewhat rebellious…and yet
then, after entering the society of Orthodox Jews, you find yourself in
one of the most conformist systems known to man.

Rabbi Yaakov Asher Sinclair, "A Gift from the Wilderness"

They hoped to find something away from the road, if possible, in nature.
With a lot of trees, and grassy space for the children. They'd been shown
one place after another—lovely New England colonial-style homes, and one
or two modern contraptions, pretentious and uncomfortable. But it was the
big old Bennett house—to the real estate agent's ill-concealed surprise—that
they'd fallen in love with, and it fit the bill exactly. Situated at the end of a
long, rocky, winding uphill driveway, and hidden away from the street, the
house was smothered with climbing ivy all over its front, and (depending on
the beholder) was beautiful to the eye. Set upon its hilltop amid forty acres of
wild, unmanicured woodland and overgrown fields, there was nothing else like
it around.

The property had languished on the market for years—no one else wanted
it, and understandably so. For Old Man Bennett was a stubborn, crotchety sort
of fellow, and stood his ground. Anyone who wanted his unkempt house had
to buy in addition the equally broken-down wreck of a barn out in back, and

5

the adjoining long-out-of-use chicken coop. Even the ancient and obsolete iron horse plow was a mandatory, inviolate addition to the selling price.

For her, the barn and the chicken coop were nothing but a plus. Now she'd have room to plant a vegetable garden to feed her family organic food! It was the dream she'd hardly dared to dream of fulfilling anywhere, ever. And in the barn she'd raise chickens to give her family organic eggs! The plow was the plow, and nothing could be done. But she visualized a multicolored rooster with a red comb, perched on the plow to crow each morning, an alarm clock for the hens. (And, indeed, that dream would come true one day.)

And if they moved here, his elderly mother—who had already had a stroke—could move in with them, too, into the bedroom on the second floor. They'd fix up the attic room for the two youngest girls, and the two older ones could each have a room of her own now, for the privacy suitable to their age, not to be crowded in, one atop the other.

For all of them, for the parents and for the children...space...to think, to write, to do homework, to play the piano, to read, to listen to music, to go for walks, to cook, to play, to dream, to have guests, to have friends over...for everyone in the family, and visitors, to enjoy being alive and to accomplish life's proper work and proper play.

The two of them had been looking in this particular Connecticut suburb first and foremost because of its public education, rated number one in the nation. They would never send their girls to some upper-class, exclusive private school; it was against their principles, and their budget. For the two of them believed deeply, with a profound faith, in the ideals of American democracy: the America of George Washington, Thomas Jefferson, Abraham Lincoln, Benjamin Franklin...

The town was fifty miles removed from the city where he'd grown up during the Depression, in a congested, Yiddish-speaking urban neighborhood. His own parents, and hers—all late nineteenth-century immigrants from Minsk and Pinsk and White Russia—had escaped by boat from Czarist Russia, as had thousands of other Jews. And in the goldene medinah of Brooklyn, that's where he'd been forever alienated from Jewish education by the rebbi whose job it had been to prepare the boys for bar mitzvah. They weren't taught the meaning of the Hebrew words; whenever a boy didn't memorize and recite the prayers correctly, or asked philosophical questions that revealed a lack of faith, he was boxed around the ears.

Their daughters would be guaranteed exemption from mind-numbing "education" such as this.

And the town was right on the line of the commuter train as well, just an hour's ride from the Manhattan office of his magazine.

Their old and dear friends, an elderly Jewish couple by the name of Henry and Bertie Myers, lent them the money, on a handshake. They trusted him implicitly. It took twenty-five years to repay the debt.

The good thing about that was that he became a public speaker on the side — to repay the debt. It became an important part of his lifework, after America dropped the atomic bomb on Hiroshima, to speak about the danger to mankind of the nuclear arms race.

The downside was that his incessant traveling — however constructive and productive his lectures proved to be for the rest of the world — took him away from home a great deal.

Decades later, standing on a street corner in Jerusalem, he would tell his youngest daughter (who had moved to Israel by then) that for the last ten years, he hadn't been able to sleep at night. "Sometimes," he said, "I think I should have just given it up, the whole lecture circuit."

"Daddy!" His daughter's heart contracted to hear such a thing from him. "What are you saying!?"

"To be at home more when you girls were growing up. I'm saturated with regret."

"Daddy!"

He died that year.

ONE OF THE THINGS that as a child I hated but as an adult came to love — and love still, in retrospect — was my parents' unconcern for convention. They weren't pretentious or self-conscious about it. They didn't go around town making declarations of independence, or wave integrity like a flag. Together as a couple, and as individuals distinctly different from each other in personality, they were just naturally nonconformists in our middle-class non-Jewish town, and simply remained true to their inner North Stars — the inborn moral code and idealism that they shared, which one day I'd come to recognize as the outward expression of their Jewish *neshamos*.

My priority as a child, though, was *fitting in*. How I longed to belong!

With whom did I want to belong? The boys and girls in my class at school, of course, from first grade through sixth, who from birthday party to birthday party, classroom to classroom, "station to station, encampment to encampment," were traveling alongside me, on our road toward Life.

What was it that I hated?

In that era when the subject of nutrition and natural foods was still in its infancy, and its adherents were looked upon as crazy fanatics (and an oft-aired TV commercial presented America with a stern, bespectacled man in a white coat, stethoscope hung 'round his neck, sagely informing America that nine out of ten doctors smoke Camels), it was my mother's homemade foods that embarrassed me; there was such a contrast to what you could get at other children's houses. Other mothers let their children have potato chips and fries, and hotdogs on white rolls, and ice cream and chocolate chip cookies. They bought their children pink- or white- or blue- or green-colored birthday cakes at the Swiss Chalet, a bakery on Main Street, with its tidy, cold little German-speaking proprietress, while *my* birthday cakes were whole wheat and covered with the so-called frosting that my mother had made herself. She wouldn't use food coloring or powdered sugar, so the frosting was always some kind of strange something or other of unidentifiable beige.

I was so embarrassed.

She forbade anything she dubbed as junk food, and even made the ice cream with fresh whole milk bought from a local farm, no chemical additives.

I was so embarrassed.

Mommy often said that she knew her purpose in life was to keep her husband and children healthy, and she behaved likewise with all of our countless houseguests, as well as anyone who came to our house to do any kind of work. Everyone got the same treatment. All mankind was her family—anyone who stepped foot inside our door. She fed us all. The rich, the poor, the troublemakers and the kingmakers, the old and the young, the relatives and the strangers. Every person who entered her kitchen was her maternal responsibility.

I—and as far as I know, my sisters, too—were never expected to help her with any of the housework, neither the cooking nor the cleaning, and certainly not the gardening. She preferred that we spend our youth doing schoolwork, learning as much as we could, and engaging in the arts: painting and writing, reading poetry and world literature, practicing the piano, learning French and Latin...all the things that as a child she had never had an opportunity to study.

Another terrible embarrassment was that I was the only one in school who didn't go to church. I suspected that people knew I was Jewish, but they were too polite to mention it in my presence, and I myself didn't know much more than they did. I knew we were Jewish, of course, and that our relatives were Jewish. We went to the annual Passover Seder at Aunt Sophie's. My grandmother, after whom I was named, was Jewish. The name Sarah was Jewish. There was an old photograph of my grandfather's long-bearded father, Rabbi Meir Kozin, who was the rabbi of his shtetl, seated with unidentified others before some sort of wooden shack. And up in our attic there was a big book of photographs entitled *We Have Not Forgotten*. Indeed, I wouldn't forget...the kerchiefed, impoverished old lady walking in a line of other poor people, heads down, with a little girl walking behind her. Pictures of dead bodies in piles. Another picture of very, very thin, empty-eyed, raggedly-covered men staring out listlessly from some sort of three-tiered bunk.

Was that what it was, to be Jewish?

I wished so much that we'd go to church too, sometimes. It wouldn't have to be a really religious religion, like the Catholics—whose stern, authoritarian brick-and-stone edifice lorded it over South Avenue. There were a few to choose from, but what I had in mind was something along the lines of the Congregational Church. It was so graceful and pure-looking and modest, standing under the trees with its white wooden steeple. Methodist was also made of wood (not stone like the Catholics) and also painted white. But it wasn't as beautiful. My weekly Girl Scout meeting was held there.

Maybe I could tell people we were Unitarian. My father had given some talks there.

Daddy was seated at our dining room table with his steno pad, pencil in hand, writing his weekly editorial, when I put the question to him at last.

I remember how it caught his attention abruptly. He turned his head to me and stopped writing.

He tipped back his chair.

I was already getting embarrassed.

He was always kind, and was kind now, looking into my eyes with an unusual, hard-to-describe expression—a mix of curiosity...concern...mystification—that somehow evoked my shame.

I became aware in those long moments of a cowardice in myself that I didn't understand.

He gave one small shake of his head.

No.

WHAT EMBARRASSED ME as much as health food and church was our house.

It was so big, and so far off the road. So different from other people's houses.

I did love my room up on the third floor. But after my grandmother died, my sister, who had shared that upstairs room with me, moved into the now-unoccupied bedroom on the second floor.

So Mommy helped me decorate it exactly as I wanted, with yellow daisy wallpaper on the slanted attic ceiling, and a white bedspread, and a frilly white lamp by my bed. And there was a tree out my window.

With Scotch Tape, I put up a lot of postcards all over one wall, of Impressionist paintings from the Metropolitan Museum of Art. I thought that this would make my sister—and maybe her friends, and some of the other people who passed through our home—want to come up and spend time with me up there.

But it didn't.

Each week all the kids in sixth grade went to dancing school at the country club, and we had to learn the steps. You were to put your white-gloved hand upon the shoulder of your dancing partner, and do this, and do that. There were rules.

I asked my parents if we could have the shutters painted white. And at some point, they agreed. But by then it was too late.

I was already outside the box. The box, and its rules, had no meaning.

FOR MY FIRST GRANDSON'S third birthday fifteen years ago, one of my friends—who was apartment-hunting at the time—gave him a card game called "Take Them Home!" Half the deck consisted of pictures of animals: a grizzly bear, a polar bear, a lion, a giraffe. A hippo, a bird, a frog, a snake. A dog, a bumblebee. A cat and a whale, a horsefly and a gorilla. A spider. A butterfly. A goldfish. A turtle.

The point was to match up each of these with a card from the other half of the deck. There was a picture of a dark cave, and another of a sunlit jungle. A nest holding three speckled blue eggs. A swamp, and a spiderweb. A fish bowl filled with water. A hole in the sand, a honeycomb. A flower in bloom, a doghouse, an ocean. An ice floe, a pink pillow. A horse's tail. A turtle.

"They want to go home," said three-year-old Elchonon as the game progressed, and it struck us that every living creature has a home tailored to its particular needs and particular nature: the desire to go home is imprinted in all of us; it's genetically programmed.

When I got married in Jerusalem in the 1970s, my sister—who had never been here before—was bothered by a persistent sense of being at home in the city. That in itself wasn't unusual: millions of Jews down through the centuries, including me, have felt the same way. In my case, the feeling had come over me inexplicably not long after I arrived for a summer visit, and it has kept me here through thick and thin—through all kinds of perils I would have never encountered in my hometown. How far-fetched it would have sounded—given my agnostic upbringing—if anyone had ever predicted, back then, that one day I'd be drawn to the land of Israel, and that that's where I'd marry and raise children.

But when it came to my sister, the sister with whom I had shared an attic room, the attraction was especially unsettling. "I feel so at home here," she kept saying as the wedding day approached. "I don't really want to leave," she repeated, boarding the plane back to California.

Being Jewish, she said, had always been one big mystery anyway.

WHILE ON A VISIT to family in America, a few of us rented a car and took a drive out to Connecticut to see the house I grew up in.

As I turned into our rocky old driveway, I realized with a start that it wasn't rocky anymore, and that—to my horror—a totally unfamiliar house was standing imperiously right there where trees should have been, at the entrance to the driveway. Most disorienting of all, this tidy black-topped driveway didn't continue on through the woods toward our ivy-covered house, but simply came to a stop a few yards from the street. Where in the world was our driveway? My daughter asked if maybe I'd made a mistake.

"Of course not!" I snapped. I backed out, drove up and down the street a few times to see if some other entryway had somehow come into being, then pulled back in to the now-truncated driveway. "Wait here," I said, getting out of the car and slamming the door.

"Mommy, wait!"

Into the woods I ran, determined. "Don't worry! I'll be right back!"

I have no idea how long the following episode took; my sense of time dissolved as I set foot into those woods. The world I knew so well, the world I knew like the back of my hand, had vanished! I was instantly enclosed in the dappled sunlight and silence of woods both familiar and unfamiliar. Vegetation had grown up over and obliterated the driveway that once was.

I saw all around me the poison-ivy leaves that had been the main danger of my childhood, but I didn't care, I just kept plunging on desperately through the underbrush. Was there nothing left at all of the kingdom in my mind?

All at once there was a clearing, then another unfamiliar house, which I couldn't bear to look at. I was standing on the curb of a street, a new street altogether! I was in the middle of a housing development! A house here, a house there! I kept going forward in the direction I knew I had to go…something familiar was drawing me…when something told me to look straight up, and all of a sudden, framed on one side by the long branch of an oak tree and on the other side by a towering pine, there was a piece of sky I knew so well, and the very same clouds—my clouds!—floating overhead! I was standing under the tall, old oak tree where I used to swing.

SOON WE'LL BE SITTING in our sukkah in Jerusalem, with its walls made for dismantling, and its roof not meant as a permanent refuge from rain, sun, or the passage of time. Had I known what Sukkos was when we lived in that big, big house in Connecticut…and if out in front of our big house we had built on the grassy lawn a little house whose proportions were suitable for a child, constructed according to strict rules, some of them understandable to the rational mind and some not—then I as a child would have looked up through the wooden slats at the stars and had an inkling that the world I lived in every day was not the one that's made to last.

Sitting all together with my mother and my father and my sisters and our guests, in one little space, crowded all together as we ate, knowing with whom and to whom I belonged, there would have been room for everyone. The child wouldn't be alone. I would have known that G-d is all around us, holding us all securely and steadily in His Hands.

For the bear or the bumblebee, home may be a material thing. But it's precisely because the sukkah, in all its bright loveliness, is insubstantial, temporary, flimsy…that the truth surrounds us when we're within its walls.

WORLD HISTORY,
ANCIENT AND MODERN

For world history, ancient and modern, in tenth and eleventh grade respectively, I got Mr. Lewis. Mr. Lewis was a drolly humorous, laconic fellow whose heavily-lidded, half-closed eyes mirrored the boredom of his teenage charges. *Pass the weekly quiz, kids,* his expression confided conspiratorially, *review for the midterms, and I'll get you outta here with Bs in June.*

The history curriculum mandated by the Board of Education started with the cavemen, continued into the so-called Fertile Crescent, took us up the so-called Ladder of Civilization (not necessarily in the following order) from Babylon and Mesopotamia to the pyramids and the Pirates, the Vikings and Ancient Greece...Rome, the Dark Ages, the Middle Ages, the Inquisition...The Crusades were in there somewhere, and the Renaissance. This king and that king. Communism and Socialism, Democrats and Republicans, World War I, World War II...That war. And this war. The rise and fall of empires.

The present, meanwhile, in which we sat entrapped at our desks like insects under glass, waiting for the bell to ring, would remain immune to the onrushing tides. We were the wave of the future; we were Breaking News. History—an irrelevant string of facts and dates that we had to memorize in order to graduate—could never catch up. Our own lives would defy that randomness. We weren't going to get old, the way all the adults did. We'd unlock the meaning of life on our own, by deciphering carefully the song lyrics of the Beatles and Bob Dylan, by traveling to Europe during summer vacation, and marching in peace rallies.

13

Never did we dream—nor could Mr. Lewis, then in his own Middle Ages, ever have dreamed—how fast our twentieth century would turn gray-haired and slow, as quaintly obsolete as George Washington's wig. To borrow from some other unremembered high school textbook—maybe the one we used in English with Miss Sherry, it was all "a lot of noise, signifying nothing."

I DAYDREAMED THROUGH MOST of this, but every once in a while, some detail in class would catch my fancy, and I'd be roused to attention. I remember, for example, the rhythmic, poetic singsong (if not the correct names) of King Ferdinand and Queen Isabella's ships: Niña, Pinta, and the Santa Maria, in which Christopher Columbus sailed in search of a new route to India, but instead would make possible Connecticut suburbs such as ours, with our Main Street and Elm Street, a choice of three different country clubs, four different churches, two large supermarkets—Grand Union and Safeway—as well as the comfortable high school classroom in which Mr. Lewis droned on and on, good-naturedly, 'till the end of time: a cog in the wheel of what was reputed to be our town's excellent educational system, rated number one in the state.

One of the things that stayed with me from the twentieth-century unit was the image of white-mustachioed, white-maned Albert Einstein, with his exotic mane and name. No one, neither in the textbook nor in class, mentioned that his was a Jewish name. In fact, from first grade through twelfth, in our top-rated educational system, no mention was made—at least not in my presence—of Jews at all. No mention of the word, or what Ancient Rome did to their Temple. I remember learning that the Roman Colosseum, an architectural triumph, is one of the Seven Wonders of the World, but not whose murder it was that the Ancient Romans enjoyed witnessing, as sport, in the Colosseum's arena. No mention of the Greeks' persecution of the Jews, or the Inquisition's, or Russia's. No mention of the Holocaust in our time.

For me, a Jewish child growing up in the 1950s, that immense silence silenced me. If six million murders can go unmentioned, then burying one child's identity isn't much of a stretch.

Silence was the form that hatred for the Jew in America could take in those days. No one wanted to be associated with the evil of Hitler, *yemach shemo*.

Nowadays, political opposition to the State of Israel's existence is the hatred's acceptable cloak. I can tear my hair out, trying to comprehend and prove, to an imaginary audience, the irrational inaccuracies and recurrent blood libels, generation after generation. If it were up to me to draw up a history curriculum for secular American high schools, I'd entitle it "What We Don't Want to Address: The Pivotal Role throughout History of Mankind's Hatred and Fear of the Jew."

The antidote to my disquiet is an awareness that hatred for the Jew is a G-d-given phenomenon. "Eisav hates Yaakov," as was written in the Torah at civilization's dawn.

"It is precisely in the fact that in every generation enemies rise up to destroy us," Rav Yitzchak Tuvia Weiss recently declared, "that our salvation lies."

SIGNS OF LIFE

Dr. Avraham Bauer, originally from Chicago, graduated from Harvard in 1987 and got his PhD in biochemistry from the University of Wisconsin. He moved to Israel in 1992, married in 1994, and four years later founded the Israeli biotech company BSD, whose research lab he directs in downtown Jerusalem. The Bauers have four sons, of whom Yehonathon is the eldest.

In the remodeled Jerusalem home in which Avraham's Yemenite wife was born and raised, we take seats at the dining room table. Passing in and out between their kitchen and the rooms in back, Revital Bauer, petite and quick, apologizes with a flash of a smile for not joining us; she's getting the kids ready for a family wedding tonight. "And actually," she pauses long enough to add, "*b'emet*, I don't like going back there."

The boys show up fleetingly in the dining room, one after the other, to eavesdrop on the conversation for a few seconds before moving on. Their playing was rambunctious and noisy out in the courtyard, but their dark eyes are shy and smiley when warily appraising the stranger who's writing something about the *pigua*. I wonder which one is Yehonathon, but none of them seems the right age—he must be about thirteen by now. I ask Avraham if he's here.

"Yes, he's around."

"Can I speak to him, too?"

"Well…Yehonathon doesn't talk about it."

"Does he know why I'm here?"

Avraham rolls his eyes and smiles. "Oh, yes."

One son, introduced as Yehudah, about five, climbs up onto his father's lap and turns to regard me with a mix of curiosity and boredom. No sooner does our conversation resume than Yehudah starts fiddling with Avraham's ears, playing with his shirt buttons, carrying on a running monologue all the while. He's not an English speaker, this little boy, but his determined interruptions tell me he knows what we're talking about. His father keeps lifting him off his lap, telling him to go find Ima, and finally Yehudah does depart, whereupon the story unfolds.

"IT WAS A COLD, miserable winter day, the week before Pesach, and Yehonathon hadn't been feeling well. That's how this whole thing started—he had strep throat, and he could hardly speak. I'd just taken him to the doctor and had a prescription in my pocket—I was going to stop off at the pharmacy to have it filled—and the two of us were on our way home, walking hand in hand along King George.

"The guy blew up three feet behind us.

"I didn't see Yehonathon fall down. I was pushed forward by the shock wave. Picture someone pushing you powerfully from behind and you have no control. I was thrown like a sack of potatoes about five meters forward, and, the next thing I knew, I saw that my arm was bleeding.

"I knew what had happened, it didn't take much to figure it out.

"I got up and turned around.

"The initial experience was of a complete, total silence. And perfect stillness. Everything was in smoke, like a fog, and I couldn't see anything. Nothing was moving. It was surreal. There was no sound.

"People around the corner had heard a massive explosion, but in the immediate zone of the bombing, where all the air was blown out, there was no sound. We had heard nothing.

"I looked for him and couldn't find him. Then I saw him, lying facedown on the sidewalk. I lifted him under the arms and held him up high in front of me, his legs dangling, to look at him. He was moaning. That was the first sign of life.

"I ran with him away from the site of the bombing and put him down on the sidewalk. Two policemen were already there, and a group of people had gathered around, wanting to help. Yehonathon was moaning but not fully responsive. I saw that they were taking care of him, so I ran back to get my bag with my cell phone so I could call Revital. Everything was upside down. I couldn't hear, and I was screaming into the phone. I told her we'd been in the bombing and they were taking care of us. When I was kneeling next to Yehonathon, trying to speak to her, there was a man—I still don't know who he was, though he's in one of the pictures—who treated my arm for me.

"They put him on a stretcher. He was the first one to be put in an ambulance—it was the first ambulance to arrive on King George. I started to climb in, but they closed the door and started pulling out—they didn't know who I was. I screamed, '*Ani ha'aba! Ani ha'aba!*' and they stopped and let me in, and we took off for the hospital.

"In the ambulance, the medics stripped Yehonathon down but couldn't find anything wrong. There was no outward sign of anything on his body. He was oscillating now between being totally quiet, and flailing his arms around and screaming, but the medics still couldn't find anything wrong, so that's when they checked the towel under his head.

"It was totally drenched with blood.

"It was a lifetime, that ride in the ambulance. All of Jerusalem passed by me through the window. I remember how the glass was speckled with rain.

"I had to call Revital again—I had to tell her where they were taking us—but all the lines were down. All over Jerusalem people were calling their loved ones. So from the time I made that first call to her from the site of the bombing, until I called her from the hospital, Revital went through twenty-five minutes of not knowing what the situation was.

"At Hadassah, the CT scans showed that Yehonathon had suffered a severe brain wound. A piece of shrapnel had passed through the right occipital lobe of the brain and had lodged itself in the front cranial bone. They determined that Yehonathon was paralyzed on the left side and that he was blind."

Revital stops on one of her trips through the dining room to remark that from their house, they'd always heard all of the bombings that took place downtown. "When Sbarro was bombed, we saw the smoke. Moment Café, we also heard it. We heard the bombing of the Machaneh Yehudah *shuk*. We don't know why I didn't hear anything this time. *Min haShamayim.* I was trying to call Avraham back and couldn't reach him. I didn't know anything. I didn't know what to do, where to go. My brother rushed right away to King George Street but couldn't find them. When I finally arrived at Hadassah, our *rav* was already there. He was in shock."

One week before the bombing, explains Revital, she had asked this *rav* a *she'eilah*: should they move to the States? "Most of the bombings had been downtown, where my husband works. From the house to Avraham's lab on

Rechov HaRav Kook, every single path had had bombings, so we wanted to know: What should we do?"

Avraham points out that it is halachically forbidden for a Jew to intentionally put himself in danger, so they had sat down with their *rav* to go over the relevant laws.

"In the hospital," says Revital, "they took me to see my husband—they were preparing him for surgery. Then they took me to see my son. He was already anesthetized, and they'd put a brace on him, so I just gave him a kiss. Then I was waiting for the surgeries to finish. For a few hours I was jumping back and forth between the two of them."

I ask Avraham about his own injury, and he shows me an oddly disfigured forearm. "Two screws went through my left arm. One went in here and passed through fully, coming out here, and the other one lodged in the wrist. Each one knocked out one artery. The bombing was at 4:20 in the afternoon. My surgery, which involved two skin grafts and a vein taken from my left leg, started about 6 p.m. and lasted about six hours. At 2 a.m., they presented me with this."

He holds a rusty screw on his palm for a moment, looking upon it with wry thoughtfulness, as if at some ancient archaeological find that never fails to amaze. He appears to be remembering something, with an expression that's somewhat akin to a smile, and relates that Friday morning, the day after the bombing, he got a voicemail message from his optometrist. "He didn't know we'd been in the *pigua*. He called to say my contact lenses were ready.

"On a normal day that would have been important to me: my contact lenses were ready. Now it had no meaning. No meaning at all.

"That's when I realized: we were in a new world now. We were speaking a new language. And using a new currency. Where we were now, the lenses were worthless.

"Everything had already changed."

AVRAHAM TRIED DURING THIS period to maintain an internal balance between objectivity and hope.

"The morning after the bombing, when I saw Yehonathon for the first time after his first surgery, his eyes were completely gray. His head was terrifying to see. I sat next to him and said *Shema*. Then I went outside and cried.

"When they took me to my ward after my own surgery, there was a young soldier in the bed opposite mine who had suffered a penetrating head wound, very much like Yehonathon's. His condition is definitely better now, but at that time he was close to a vegetative state. During the week that I was in the ward to receive medication and recuperate, I had a hard time interacting with him and his family. I didn't want to graft his situation onto Yehonathon's developing condition.

"Any conclusions I could have come to, or was frightened of coming to, based on the condition of someone else who had gone through a near-identical event, would in fact have had no meaning. What *Hashem* plans for one person is by no means a sure indication of His plans for anyone else. *Hakadosh Baruch Hu* decides each person's fate. But I was trying not to equate 'brain injury' with 'vegetative state,' trying with all my might to keep my distance from that conclusion.

"For the first three days, Yehonathon was unconscious, and was medically sedated to allow the fluids in the brain to drain and the fluid pressure to return to normal. When the doctors decided to bring him out of the sedative, the entire staff came in to watch. They wanted to see how he'd react to questions, and to some general commands—to see what he could and couldn't do.

"First they asked me to interact with him.

"Then they asked Revital to say something, and at the sound of her voice, Yehonathon opened his eyes and said, '*Ima sheli. Ani ohev otach.*'

"Everyone in the room started crying.

"That was the beginning of the recovery."

FOR THE NEXT FEW WEEKS, Yehonathon was bedridden and blind, and unable to move his left side. "He had tremendous head pain," says Avraham. "He cried. He'd scream from the pain. We didn't know if it was part of his healing process or if this was something going on inside that needed medical attention. So they would run tests on him, and did CT scans almost every day. They couldn't tell what was going on in his brain.

"One of my roommates at Harvard had become a brain surgeon. A week and a half after the bombing, he heard about it and got in touch, and offered to look at the X-rays and all the medical material. And from then on, he stayed in touch with Yehonathon's doctors. After looking at the pictures, he said to me, 'His vision is going to come back—his left side function is going to come back. And he'll walk again.' Now, Revital and I knew this was no guarantee. We knew my friend wasn't a prophet, and he said himself, 'I'm not G-d.' But we knew, too, that he wasn't saying it to make us happy. He made his prognosis according to the path of the screw through the brain, and it gave us tremendous hope. Hearing a positive report was tremendously helpful. On the other hand, we didn't know how significant it was, how seriously we could take it. Maybe it didn't even mean anything at all. There was no way of knowing.

"You try to look at your child objectively, but you see him suffering. You can distract him. You can read him stories. We spent time, hours and hours, reading stories to him. But when your child can't see and is writhing in pain...there's a limit. A limit to how much comfort you can provide.

"Months later, someone told us that a well-respected medical expert had come by the pediatric ICU during those first hours, and after examining Yehonathon said one thing: '*Ein mah la'asot*.' [Nothing can be done.] *Baruch Hashem*, it's a good thing no one mentioned it to us at the time.

"And *Hashem* had the last word. After three and a half weeks at Hadassah, he could be made to sit up in a wheelchair. That's when we brought his brothers to see him for the first time since it happened—they were ages six, four, and one. Then Yehonathon was transferred to Alyn Hospital, and on his first night in Alyn, I was sitting by his bed, when all of a sudden he said to me, 'I see it says "Spring" on the juice bottle.'

"I was in shock. It was overwhelming. From then on, more and more, he liked to describe the world around him. And shortly after that, he started walking again.

"A month or so later, prior to the operation to remove the shrapnel from Yehonathon's brain, the brain surgeon, Dr. Constantini, was reviewing the CT scans and said, 'You know, if I had to put a bullet into someone's head, this is the exact path I would have chosen—it missed the blood vessels and critical regions.'"

At this point in our conversation, a fawn-like, almost ethereal boy—something about his hesitant step tells me instantly this is Yehonathon—passes unobtrusively through the dining room with a lowered glance in my direction. He proceeds to devote his attention—from what I can gather—to setting up a trick he wants to play on his brothers, which involves draping some sort of large paper contraption over the front door that's going to fall down when someone walks in. I realize that what I saw as hesitancy might actually be a slight limp, and ask Avraham about it. "Yes, a little. He's still in rehabilitation to bring back feeling and movement on the left side. And his vision is not complete. He doesn't see the extremes of the visual field. But he's fine, his mind is completely fine.

"These days we have to decide how much rehabilitation to insist upon. He comes home from his Talmud Torah and wants to play. He doesn't want to go to a clinic for exercises, and we have to remind ourselves, he's a child. We have to let him be a child.

"We are tremendously grateful to *Hakadosh Baruch Hu*."

I ASK AVRAHAM BAUER if he ever asks *Hashem* why they had to go through this. He thinks for several moments, then replies: "In any situation such as this, you ask, 'Why did this happen?' And you can answer it in one of three ways. The first answer is, 'It was a random event. I was in the wrong place at the wrong time.' The second is, 'It happened because of the Arabs; Arabs have the power to hurt people.' Now, if you believe either of these two, you're repudiating the Torah. The Torah is full of *pesukim* that say there is no such thing as chance, and that there is nothing separate from *Hashem*. Would anyone say, '*Hashem* was out having coffee when this happened'? And if you believe that the Arabs possess power independent of *Hashem*'s Will, you're denying *hashgachah pratis* and that *Hashem* is One.

"There's only one other possibility: that everything is from *Hashem* and *Hashem* is only good. Everything evil in the world is under *Hashem*'s total control. The *Ramchal* writes this, and a person has to see this very clearly, that all is controlled by *Hakadosh Baruch Hu*. Even though we may not understand it, this is the foundation: everything that happens is for the good. Even though it was very painful and we did a lot of crying, what we went through was only from *yad Hashem*. On this, there was never a moment of doubt."

"Never a moment of doubt? Really, Avraham?"

"Look, in daily life I can miss a bus. Someone can dent my car. Do I believe these events are too insignificant to have been directed from Above? Faith is always needed in our lives, but sometimes it's challenged to the nth degree—the physical, emotional, and spiritual challenges associated with life-and-death issues. Let's say a person has a fire extinguisher in his house. It can be there for years, but it's only when fire breaks out that he runs to use it.

"When something like this happens, either your faith is going to get tremendously strong, or you will fall apart. You either start having all kinds of questions and all kinds of doubts, or you throw yourself on *Hashem*. There is no middle ground. In a five-second event, our lives were turned upside down. If you don't have faith, you can jump out the window.

"We knew that whatever would be with Yehonathon, either *Hashem* runs the world—or *Hashem Echad* is not true.

"There were a lot of crucial decisions to make every day—there are still a lot of decisions—and the only thing we could do was turn to G-d to show us the right path. For example, the hospital wanted to perform a certain surgery and was pushing us very hard to do it, but other people had advised against it. The decisions were ours and ours alone to make. No mortal could give us the answer.

"The most difficult decision we had to face arrived two months after the bombing, when the time came to remove the shrapnel from Yehonathon's brain and we had to choose a brain surgeon. The enormity of this decision overwhelmed us. We didn't know where to turn. The person widely known for his expert advice on medical matters was the one who had said, '*Ein mah la'asot.*'

"That day, as we were struggling with this question, Revital's sister was waiting on line at a local copy shop and heard the man ahead of her in line talking about his daughter's successful brain surgery. She asked him who the surgeon was and he said, Dr. Shlomi Constantini, of Ichilov Hospital in Tel Aviv.

"We called Dr. Constantini, went for an appointment, and decided to take him as our surgeon. Had we undertaken an international search for the right surgeon, had we sought the best possible advice from experts all around the world, the operation couldn't have had a more success-ful outcome.

"We derive from our faith a perspective on the event, not only on what happened to us but on how to go forward. Ultimately it is a great challenge to be a Jew, to take the principles we affirm both in our *davening* every day and in our learning, and actually apply them to life. A person goes through an experience like this and has to decide: Am I going to abandon what I be-lieve? Am I going to throw my fate onto the doctors and the politicians? Would the values and ideals imbibed comfortably at home or on a padded seat at *shul* stand up to challenges of this 'new' world?

"Our lives were no longer that which they had been, and as is always the case during crisis or tragedy, the ability of other human beings to under-stand and empathize is limited, giving rise to a new awareness of one's aloneness with *Hashem*.

"For example, at one point during those weeks, a little Arab boy was brought in, along with a lot of security people. He'd been a passenger in his father's car when Israel tried to assassinate the father—a known terrorist—with an Apache missile. The car burst into flames, the father leaped out and ran away, and the boy, whom the father left behind, was burned over 90 percent of his body. Security staff was running around the unit, and one fellow said that there was concern his father—the terrorist!—might come to see him! Would we be in danger? What were the risks?

"I witnessed what many others have witnessed before and after me, that the Hadassah staff treated that Arab child with precisely the same professionalism as they do everyone across the board, Arab and Jew. Doctors Without Borders, however, brought a reporter in to the hospital to publicize what Israel had done to a Palestinian child. Yehonathon was right there in the same room, but Doctors Without Borders wasn't interested in him. They didn't even ask how he was doing.

"Sometime after the bombing, I came into contact with Gal Shemesh, the brother of the young father who was killed, Gadi Shemesh, along with his pregnant wife Tzipora. They were in their twenties and had two little girls. The Shemesh family sued the Palestinian Authority for financial support for the children, but the case has been hung up in the High Court for four years due to the State's indecision regarding the legality of suing the PA in Israel. How did this delay come about? Because of an objection raised by a Jewish lawyer. To this date, theirs and similar cases remain in legal limbo in the Israeli court system.

"One of the most terrible experiences in the early days after the bombing: the hospital we were in was a teaching hospital. A professor came in with a group of medical students and said, 'Don't mind us, we just have to do some tests,' and he proceeded to administer what's known as the Glasgow Coma Scale, designed to measure the degree of a person's consciousness on a scale of three to fifteen. The lower the score, the worse the situation. If the patient doesn't respond to his name, it's, say, number five, if he doesn't respond to a pinprick, number four, etc. Lower than three and the person is not in this world. As I stood by the bed, he unhesitatingly recited all the low numbers.

"For that doctor and his students, Yehonathon was a teaching opportunity.

"You can lose your mind—if you believe in reality. I learned that the thing to do at such moments is to block out the world and focus on *Hakadosh Baruch Hu*."

I RETURN TO THE QUESTION of whether Avraham ever asks *Hashem* why this had to happen, and he replies: "I'll put it this way. When something bad happens, you should look around and say, 'What is G-d trying to tell me?' On *Tishah B'Av* we do ask 'Why?' It's not forbidden. This doesn't mean, though, that we'll get the answer. The *Chaftez Chaim* says, 'We can't understand.' But we can try to understand what we did that could have helped bring this about, to cause us to be tested in this way.

"There are two ways to relate to G-d. You can see Him as Omnipresent and Omnipotent, the Creator and Ruler of the entire world, and I'm a little thing in His Creation. Or you can say, 'I'm a genius, I can understand.' In our bombing, there were eighty-something people injured, and if you were to interview all of them, you'd get a lot of different perspectives on life, different answers. Maybe there are some who would say, 'If I'd only been walking a little faster, I wouldn't have gotten hurt.'

"In a moment of truth such as this, a person finds out where he hangs his hat."

"So, Avraham," I ask, "aren't you and Revital glad to see where you hang your hats?"

He thinks this over, then replies: "A person can't give himself a report card. Only *Hakadosh Baruch Hu* knows how we're actually doing. We hope that we're better for the experience, because you either come out better from something like that, or you come out more detached from Him. No way to come out as you were. No way you're ever going to be the same person."

"What would you say to the rest of us, as a result of what you've experienced?"

"I'm the last person to give advice, but what I'd say is, strive for *achdus*. It was a horrific event, but we saw it bring out tremendous *ahavas Yisrael*, and in other circumstances we wouldn't have been *zocheh* to see it.

"In the case of the horrific number 2 bus bombing, perhaps you'll recall that most of those injured were *chareidim*, but after it happened, someone from the anti-religious Shinui Party came to visit the wounded at the hospital. He must have felt, 'Human beings have been hurt, I want to go see them.' That's what I would hope for. That we should do more of this for each other. To recognize our oneness with one another without the fire, without shrapnel. *Achdus* without terror.

"Our family received a tremendous amount of *siyata d'Shmaya*. The families here in Shaarei Chesed cooked food for us for two months, every single day. They gave us meals for Pesach, for Shavuos, and for every Shabbos.

When I told them they could stop, they said people had already cooked and frozen meals for the next two weeks—the people who organized it arranged meals two weeks ahead of time—and would feel bad if we didn't use them, that it meant a lot to them.

"People babysat for the kids at home so my wife and I could be at the hospital. Others slept at the hospital so we could be with the children at home. For Revital and me to be able to get some sleep like normal people…and the fact that our kids at home could see both their parents…. They gave us financial assistance. Clowns and magicians came in to do free performances for the kids….

"I wouldn't wish what happened to us on anybody, but I must note that my wife and I were so overwhelmed by the true warmth and sincerity, the help we received from friends, and from complete strangers.

"One boy from Yehonathon's class said he wouldn't make a birthday party until Yehonathon could come. Each child gave him a note saying how much he missed him, and presented him with a gift—something new or something dear. One gave Yehonathon his own little toy hammer. For a seven-year-old boy, it was extraordinary. My wife and I were in tears, watching the sincerity of the kids. They cared very much about him. They said *Tehillim*. On Shabbos they came all the way on foot to see him here.

"When we were truly in need, people came through *mehadrin*. We were the recipients of *glatt kosher chessed*.

"On Pesach we say *Hallel* to praise *Hashem* for our deliverance from *Mitzrayim*, but we ignore the fact that it was He Who sent us there. If someone locks you in a closet for three days, you're not going to hug and kiss him when he lets you out. So why are we so grateful?

"One answer that's given is this: it says in the *pesukim* that when we went down to *Mitzrayim* we were seventy souls, but when we left, it was as one, a united people.

"That's what happened with this bombing. We all came out better than we came in."

Revital, dressed up now for the wedding, has come back in and sits down by her husband. "Years before the bombing," she says, "our *rav* told us, 'A person should feel the Hand of *Hashem* on his shoulder.' He told us to feel that *Hashem* is with us in times of distress. After the bombing, people would say to us, '*Hashem* is with you.' But we really did see it. *We felt it.* I want to feel this sweetness of closeness with *Hashem* without the suffering."

JERUSALEM, 10 A.M.

The post office was packed this morning, as usual on Friday. I took a number (noting with glum stoicism that there were around fifty people ahead of me) and found an empty seat up front, in the first row.

On the chair to my left, a little boy about a year old stood facing backward, toward the crowd. His mother occupied the next seat over, inclined subtly toward him, one protective arm extended tentatively, ready to spring. Around the same age as my own baby—twenty or twenty-one—her hair covered carefully with a scarf, she projected whatever it is that American Jews project: that elusive quality that distinguishes them instantly from Israelis, even before they open their mouths. A quick glance had also categorized her in my mind as a *baalas teshuvah*. However some of us might try to pass as the real thing, born and bred in Boro Park, there's something indefinable—maybe some brand of naive idealism, at once problematic and praiseworthy—that our faces broadcast.

Her *bechor* (with no siblings on the horizon to challenge his sovereignty on top of the world as the most beloved ruler on earth) was gripping the rim of the orange plastic chair and jumping noisily up and down on sturdy legs. In the hush of this crowded roomful of strangers—about two-thirds secular and *chareidi* Israelis, the other third Arabs; a number of men absorbed in their *sefarim*, women here and there in chadors, and all of us resolutely enclosed in our solitary silences—the jumping little boy was babbling exultantly and eloquently into the void, nonstop, in a wordless, sibilant, gurgling monologue.

One of his socks kept slipping off, and his mother—with eyes downturned, her face tinged softly by amusement, embarrassment, and pride—kept placidly putting it back on again. Having to keep still a moment as she held his pink little foot, he turned to examine me, the new person who'd just materialized next door.

Clearest of sky-blue eyes, uninhibitedly alight with curiosity, he possessed the serene fearlessness of a highly intelligent, mischievous Jewish cherub.

I stared back but sensed myself contracting involuntarily, like a turtle pulling in its head. Was I shy? Of a baby? Self-conscious in front of his mother (she, too, in my book, was a child; the two of them the purest of children)? I pretended to be focusing past him at some nonexistent spot. Actually, I wanted to watch her, too, watching him. I know that joy, when all you have to do is look at your baby to be suffused with happiness. I remember.

Suddenly I felt like an interloper from some alien zone, spying back through the light-years at the colorful planet of young motherhood—so profoundly familiar yet so far away—over which I, too, had once reigned, queen of the realm.

The little boy let loose a long burbling giggle, throaty and tinkling, and turning my head slightly to see what he was seeing, I was a little startled to be confronted by three wrinkled faces all in a row. Three women who must have come here together to pick up their mail—their Friday morning outing from the neighborhood old people's home...but no, that narrative didn't stay put: they seemed incognizant of one another. The one on the right I have no recollection of, but the pale and happily mugging, smirking oblong suspended in the middle comes back to me now with cartoonish oversimplification: a powdery-white old clown-face with no eyebrows and a rubbery-lipped, toothless grin, daffy and jovial; feathery long wisps of white hair providing sparse cover for the shiny baldness peeking through. Was she all there? I felt myself almost cringe, and wondered why. She was absolutely absorbed in her enjoyment of the little boy and had no problem playing the fool, winking and nodding and wagging her head uninhibitedly from side to side, seemingly anything to keep getting a rise out of him.

Though they were just inches away, the three didn't appear to notice me looking at them.

The woman on the left, in a navy-blue suit and pearls, was somewhere in her eighties, with inward-looking, veiled eyes and fine-lined, aristocratic features; her loosened skin intricately creased, folded and refolded, and rendered in a style so unlike the broad strokes used to draw the clown that it was as if the two women inhabited different pictures. She too was transfixed, but from a carefully maintained distance, and against her will and better judgment, by the small person bursting with life, utterly delighted with himself and the world, and too close for comfort.

The instant I sensed her sensing me, my line of vision ricocheted off and landed in the mass of standees at the rear of the post office.

What a motley, floating congregation of disembodied faces, of all ages, traveling single-mindedly in the same direction, like heat-seeking missiles through the dense silence, toward mother and child, the primeval light where we all began.

ALL THE WAY HOME

"You have to honor your parents."

These words were delivered in a thick foreign accent by the rabbi—a diminutive, olive-skinned, white-bearded stranger dressed in black suit and hat—in a kosher luncheonette on Forty-Seventh Street. If I had to pinpoint one event, aside from being born, that divided my life into *before* and *after*, those six words would serve as the turning point.

I'd met the rabbi ten minutes before, while waiting on line for a phone booth outside the New York Public Library. Something about his appearance (I'd seen pictures somewhere of religious Jews—maybe *National Geographic*?) had vaguely rung a bell, and I'd turned to say, "You're Jewish, aren't you."

He stared, taken aback. *"You* a Jewish?"

So that's how my life began, and now he was introducing me to my religion over a slice of poppy-seed cake. *(Poppy-seed cake?)*

In memory, all this occurred around a thousand years ago.

The so-called "dairy" restaurant *(something to do with dairy farms?)* was on an upstairs balcony inside the Diamond Exchange in midtown Manhattan, and the Diamond Exchange was the huge room down below on the ground floor, full of busy men in black and white who all looked like him, and shining glass jewelry cases beneath bright lights, and talkative women in silver and gold, trying on necklaces and diamond rings. In nearly two decades on earth, I'd never seen anything like it. Who were these people? If these were Jews, what relation could they possibly bear to me, whose childhood was spent on the fringe of a genteel WASP suburb, gazing in hopelessly at sedately well-mannered country clubs, and community carol sings on the snowy village green?

Across the Formica tabletop, the rabbi had taken a ballpoint pen from a black briefcase and was laboriously spelling out something in capital letters on a paper napkin (he hadn't had much practice writing English, that was obvious), mouthing out the words as he went along. He announced that these lines were what Jews say in Hebrew before eating various foods. (*What they say? You mean, like grace?*) He'd already said I should transfer to college in New York, live with my parents (*You must be kidding!*), and work for my father at his office. (*Ha! For my father? An office job?!*)

"Yes. Days, you work. The nights, night school. Will be very good. Your father," he said, "will be so happy."

"Yeah, but I—"

"You have to honor your parents. You come to us for Shabbat."

"What?" I'd never heard that word.

"You will meet my wife. You will be friends. You see them?" I followed his glance to the right. At the lunch counter were seated two annoyingly pretty girls around my own age, giggling and chitchatting in typical teenage fashion. They were in long-sleeved, calf-length dresses, their glossy hair pulled back smoothly into ponytails. "Those girls, they are Orthodox."

Something in me recoiled with distaste, scorn, bafflement, and—unbeknown to my own self—an envy in the marrow of my bones. Those girls—examples, supposedly, of my own people—were card-carrying members in a universe as weirdly inscrutable to me as China, a club even more off-limits to someone like me than...my own hometown. Who did they think they were! *Holier than thou!* What made this man think he could just come up and pontificate to me like this—it was ridiculous, such quaint, old-fashioned ideas! I should get up and walk out! *Get up and walk out!* But...it was interesting, in a way, being bombarded by all this nineteenth-century stuff (and on some strange level, it was striking a deeply resonant chord, familiar and unfamiliar at the same time). To go work for Daddy—as if I needed my father's approval!—that would be exactly the opposite direction from where I had to go in life. The whole point was to become independent. That was the most important thing—to think for yourself. My whole way of seeing things was totally different from that of my parents. They were middle-aged! I had to find my own way in life—even they would agree with that.

And anyway, who said that Daddy would even want me there, in his office? What would I wear?

He'd be embarrassed.

And I couldn't touch-type, or do shorthand.

The rabbi glanced nervously at his watch a few times and signaled the waitress for the bill. So I gulped down my coffee and, with a mental nod to my diet (*I won't have lunch*), finished off the cake. He pointed to the table napkin he'd written on and gestured for me to take it. "Remember, before you eat. *Le'at, le'at.* Will be a blessing for you."

Outside again in the blazing heat, amid the rushing lunch-hour crowds of midtown Manhattan, he stopped a few moments now on the sidewalk to give directions to his home on the East Side. On Friday night, he informed me, his wife would be lighting at seven. I should get there by quarter of.

Lighting?

"And now you go, tell your father. Maybe you start tomorrow."

With quick, determined steps he scurried toward Forty-seventh and Sixth, and for lack of anything better to do, I guessed I would walk over to my father's office a few blocks uptown. Waiting on the corner for the light to change, I was standing aside the rabbi (he couldn't have been more than five foot two) whose mind now was obviously on other things, when my eyes crossed the street and alighted on a fat, squat grandmotherly type on the opposite curb. Long sleeves, buttoned collar. Some sort of round little hat atop her head. With a small flicker of satisfaction, I recognized the whole get-up—I was an expert already—and gestured in her direction. "She's Orthodox, too, right?"

"Yes," the rabbi replied curtly. Then, as the light turned green: "One day, *you* will be Orthodox."

"Ha!" I shot back with a tart laugh. The warning bells were going crazy. "Never!"

SO FOR A HUNDRED DOLLARS a week I got a job in the Classified Ads department of the *Saturday Review*, a position that required knowledge of the ABCs and how to open and close a filing cabinet. I signed up for night classes to finish my degree, moved back in with my parents, and spent the weekends with them at home in Connecticut.

And an amazing thing happened: my mother and father were so happy about all of this. So, so happy. I hadn't known they would feel this way.

Even more amazing, *I* was happy. Happy to be making them happy. I didn't have to think my way into it, this happiness, it just sprouted by itself, like grass, or wildflowers.

Happy like the rain, as natural as the relationship between earth and sky.

Not since I was a little kid in elementary school, or maybe even kindergarten, had this kind of happiness, plain and simple, been mine, day after day. It didn't go away. Every once in a while, I'd turn around to see what I'd left behind, and there, stretching into the distance, was a huge, convoluted gray maze drifting away into the past. I realized now that I'd been wandering around in there for what seemed like centuries. Until a pint-size stranger had appeared out of the blue, pointing to the exit and ordering: "Thaddaway!"

I could have just ignored him—it would have made sense to ignore him; I came very close to ignoring him. Instead, I found myself in a landscape, green and hilly, fed by streams of water and light from some long-ago era. As if I'd entered a garden that had been right outside my door all along, but which I hadn't visited since the beginning of time, and had then noticed that my name—in Hebrew letters—was inscribed on the gate.

A door had opened before me to another dimension...larger than myself, a vast...something or other, and it belonged to me. I recognized it.

A DAILY RHYTHM ESTABLISHED ITSELF. On weekday mornings, I'd get up early and join my father for breakfast at the hotel across the street, ordering coffee in a Styrofoam cup and enjoying vicariously Daddy's daily two eggs over easy, two slices whole wheat. I myself was eating kosher now, a form of abstention that dovetailed nicely with my diet, and made me feel spiritually elevated amid the consumers of bacon and sausages at the surrounding tables. Then the two of us would catch a cab to the office. Like two colleagues.

I'd never had so much time alone with him.

Nor had I ever seen him at work, up close. It was a revelation. He worked so hard, I'd never realized. There he was, responsible for getting out the magazine every single week, week after week. But all day long, people didn't stop knocking on his door, complaining, beseeching, imploring, demanding. He was a kind father to his staff as he was kind at home, kind to a fault. On one occasion, the head of advertising told me that in thirty years as editor of *Saturday Review*, my father had never fired anyone. "And believe me, he's had his share of jerks on staff, but your father—he can't bring himself to do that to anyone. Did you know that?" I shook my head meekly. If anything, while growing up, I'd averted my eyes from my father's professional self, harboring a hazy resentment toward all those people out there with whom I was obliged to share him. I didn't read his editorials, or his books—this was a point of pride, almost; a matter of personal policy. In some way I couldn't articulate—and had never tried to figure out—ignoring his public persona seemed to offer some kind of protection.

"Well," the advertising head continued, "you should be very proud. I'll tell him, Norm, get rid of this clown, he's not worth the trouble. And your father just gets that look in his eyes, like he's thinking about his next editorial, and changes the subject. He's a prince, your father."

Lucky for me, because by this time (though no one said it to my face) the boss's daughter had messed up some crucial details of a Classifieds column, and upon arrival at the office one morning, I discovered I'd been promoted. My new position, two cubicles over: assistant for the Annual Photography Contest. My job: to number the submissions as they came in and keep a running list of the photographers' names and addresses.

Eventually, to my lasting shame (even to this day), I messed up in this department, too, even more extravagantly than at Classifieds. Finding it a challenge to keep up with the hundreds of incoming contest submissions, I decided one evening to take a few hundred of them home with me in a Macy's shopping bag, and finish numbering them on my parents' dining room table. Call it the Mystery of the Missing Pictures—only a genuine space cadet could have achieved such a stunning sleight of hand—but somewhere on the subway, between Fifty-second and Thirty-fourth, that bag got away from me.

While Mommy and Daddy must have realized that all these harmonious developments (not including the lost bag) were related to my becoming religiously observant, our new arrangements were not without strain. They'd never stoop to say such a thing, but I could tell they looked forward to the time I'd get through this phase, just as I'd gotten through my Zazen meditation phase, and the transcendental meditation phase, and the Nam Myoho Japanese chanting stage, shedding the successive spiritual disciplines, one after the other, like so many flaking sunburns. For although I'd taken on the mitzvah of honoring my mother and father as part and parcel—or to be more exact, as the central pillar—of my Torah observance, almost everything I did religiously seemed perfectly calibrated to worry them and give them pain.

First of all, the silverware. I recall standing in front of the stove in my parents' rented Manhattan apartment, waiting for some of my mother's knives and spoons and forks to come to a boil in her stainless-steel frying pan. I'd waited for an afternoon that neither of them were expected home, but I suddenly became aware of someone's presence behind me and spun around.

"Oh!" I exclaimed cheerily. "I didn't know you were here!"

My mother was looking at me with slightly narrowed eyes; lips parted as if to speak, but no sound came out.

A couple moments passed.

"Sarah...," she said quietly. "What are you doing?"

"Oh! I'm just koshering some silverware! You have to boil it!"

"I see." She was still looking into my eyes. More silence. Then: "You really think G-d cares?"

The question pierced me.

All I knew, at that point, was that *I* cared, for reasons I couldn't yet identify. Did G-d care? *Really?* My mother's opinion was obvious—she whose opinions and tastes and beliefs had always laid the foundation for my own.

So what was the answer? I wanted truth, the whole truth, and nothing but the truth. Five years later, I would have explained that separating milk and meat is the Torah's way of encouraging ethics and compassion in human beings, based on the prohibition against cooking a kid in its mother's milk. Ten years, and I would have said, "This is how a human being can connect to that which is eternal and infinite, precisely because it's beyond rational explanation." Twenty years, and it would be: "G-d gives us physical mitzvos as a way of making His Presence a reality in our lives."

Thirty years, and it would be: "Yes, Mommy, G-d cares."

But by then, she wasn't around.

Then there was her cooking. It's only now, as a mother of grown children, that I can imagine how disheartening, how aggravating it must have been for her each time I politely declined to partake of something she'd made. "No, thank you," to her vegetable chicken soup, from her organic garden, and to her homemade herb bread that I'd always loved, and to her cabbage salad.

"Would you like some of these string beans? I didn't put anything in them, just a little butter."

"I'm so sorry, Mommy...I..."

Or on Sunday mornings: "How about some scrambled eggs? What could be wrong with that? Look, I'll make them in your kosher pan."

But then I'd have to stand over her like a hawk, checking that she used the kosher utensils, the kosher *milchig* utensils. And what about checking for blood spots? She raised her own chickens, so fertile eggs were common, and I didn't want to rock the boat by presenting yet another prohibition. To her mind, all these rules and regulations were no different from superstitions—the irrational mumbo-jumbo her own mother had escaped by fleeing the pogroms of her Russian shtetl.

Above all…Shabbos.

Whenever Friday afternoon rolled around and the three of us would pile into the car for the drive home to Connecticut, they in the front seat and I in the back, talking and talking, singing our old family favorites all the way to New Canaan…it was a joy, it was wonderful.

But my two little fake-silver candlesticks, that I'd bought from a kiosk on Seventy-second—where could I light them to ensure that they wouldn't get blown out or inadvertently moved? And why did I have to make such a big deal about lighting exactly on time? I imagined they were thinking, *You really think G-d cares?* And unscrewing the light bulb in the refrigerator, how could I do that without inconveniencing her? And the lights I'd leave on in the kitchen and living room, which someone inevitably would switch off without thinking. The chicken giblets I'd bought from Meal Mart on Seventy-second, and the yummy chopped liver, and the broccoli quiche…I wanted to share it all, of course! Nothing would have made me prouder! But nine times out of ten, someone would end up using a *treif* knife or fork, and I wouldn't be able to eat it, and they would be distressed.

The trouble increased as winter came on. When Fridays grew short and they'd set out for Connecticut too close to sundown, I'd stand at the door and bid them sadly farewell. "But Sarah, you'll be all alone!" I remember my father's worried eyes. "Can't you come? You're not doing the driving!"

I'm so sorry, Daddy. So sorry, Mommy.

And indeed, I felt like a wandering Jew, a wondering Jew, a Jew in my own personal desert—those silent Shabbosos all by myself, staying behind in their rented apartment in New York City. Friday night and all day Saturday, with a container of coleslaw and cold Meal Mart chicken to keep me company, along with the *New York Times*…unable to take the elevator up or down nine floors…Regarded as a weirdo by the hotel employees as I'd get trapped yet again behind a locked security door…

Take the key with you, miss, the clerk would advise.

But you see, I can't carry it outside…

Oh, all the strange looks, and lonely times!

But once, one cold and rainy Friday afternoon, as my two little candles already flickered on the windowsill and my parents in their overcoats were taking their leave, my father suddenly stopped at the door. "Ellen, I almost forgot! Where's the neckla—?"

"Oh! Right here!" She reached into her purse.

It was from a jewelry store, and when I lifted the lid of the tiny box, looking up at me was…a Jewish star.

THERE WEREN'T ANY *BAAL TESHUVAH* yeshivas in those days, at least not that I was aware of. I hadn't even heard that term, *baal teshuvah*. So I just made my way through a big black volume that I'd found in a bookstore somewhere. Just now, for the purpose of writing this story, I searched through my bookshelves—I've seen it around from time to time—and lo and behold, there it was: the old black spine with the dull gold letters: *JUDAISM*, by Meir Meiseles. Translated from the Hebrew and published by Feldheim, no date listed.

I have it opened before me, here in our home in Jerusalem a lifetime later. Precious treasury—this was the real diamond exchange. I recall sitting by myself at my desk in the Classifieds department (or, excuse me, the Photo Contest department) with my Dannon yogurt or tuna fish sandwich…how I used to prop up my big old black book against the Selectric typewriter to read during lunch hour, when all the other employees would have gone off merrily to the nearby steakhouse. And I'd read:

> *Honor your father and mother, that your days may be prolonged upon the land which the Lord thy G-d giveth thee.*
>
> > Exodus 20:12

> *You shall fear, every man, his mother and his father, and my Sabbaths you shall keep; I am the Lord thy G-d.*
>
> > Leviticus 19:3

> *Cursed be he that holds in light esteem his father or his mother, and all the people shall say, Amen.*
>
> > Deuteronomy 27:16

How could it be? My heart's desire, above all, was to do two things G-d wanted—to honor my parents and to observe Shabbos—and the two seemed mutually exclusive.

I must point out that this was the 1970s, when making your parents happy wasn't on anyone's New Age agenda. To be a self-respecting adult meant becoming your own man, I mean, woman. You had to be proud to be a woman, and not act subservient. Women didn't want to be men, of course, just have the same pay, and be respected like men, and wear mini-skirts and pantsuits. And not be in charge of dishes and laundry.

Rabbi Meiseles wrote:

> There are three partners in the creation of man, the Holy One, blessed be He, his father, and his mother. The Sages taught that whenever a man honors his parents it is as if he had brought down the Divine Presence to dwell with them and honored G-d Himself. But whenever a man grieves his parents, G-d withholds His Presence from among them so that He might not, as it were, be grieved as well.

I'D BEEN WORKING at the office about six months when my father was sued. A longtime staff writer had recently died, having stipulated in her will that what remained of her pension should be returned to the company. Now her son was claiming that his elderly mother had (G-d forbid) been pressured to surrender what was due her, thereby depriving him of his rightful inheritance.

I learned from my mother that Daddy—much to her annoyance and mine—didn't wish to challenge the man's claim. This was the case, she confided, in spite of the fact that in the legal opinion of *Saturday Review*'s lawyer, the unfounded charges would be swiftly disproved in court with my father's testimony, and the magazine would prevail.

On the day of the hearing, on our way downtown in a taxi, Mommy and I were still trying to change Daddy's mind as we made our way through the cross-town traffic. But he just listened thoughtfully, un-budged from his position, and upon arrival in the courtroom, was immediately summoned off to one side by the lawyer for last-minute consultations. So Mommy and I, amazed by this unjust world, went ahead and found seats up front, grumbling to each other under our breath.

The courtroom proceedings had yet to get underway when a tall, lanky man around forty (as far as I was concerned, anyone middle-aged was around forty) slid into the row ahead of us, and draping one arm over the empty seat to his right, swiveled around with a friendly smile. "Hi, Eleanor," he greeted my mother pleasantly. "How are you?"

My mother's posture stiffened. "Just fine!"

"And the family? Everyone OK?"

I sensed my mother bristling speechlessly beside me, and from the side could see her green eyes' electric glare. I realized that this must be the guy who was suing Daddy! He proceeded to shoot the breeze about this and that, but Mommy—her face as incapable of concealing her feelings as an open book—sat there in strangled silence.

"You know, my mother...she wasn't the easiest woman to get along with," he said finally, as if to acknowledge the elephant in the room. "Even before she was ill."

Mommy managed some sort of grunt.

"So it's...you know, a difficult situation, for everyone. No hard feelings, I hope. She kept Bob, my brother, on the up and up, what was going on, but...me, you know, I'm out on the West Coast, and...you know how it is, sometimes, with family. How it gets. She and I were estranged." There was a long pause. "She hated me."

Out of the corner of my eye, I saw my mother's mouth fall open.

"She was so attached to the magazine. Always saying, those people, they're like family. They visit, they do this, they do that. And she liked that Dr. Shriff, Shiffman, that Norman got, the oncologist. Don't get me wrong. We appreciate it, everything Norman did, you all did, for her. But you've got to understand...it's my money. *Was* my money, until this...break happened." With one arm still draped casually over the back of the court bench, he wore an oddly wavering half-smile, and was beseeching with his eyes. "I have to get something back, Eleanor. You understand. This was my only option. I'm sorry it had to...be like this, but...I'm..." His voice trailed off.

For some reason I remember the sight of his long, pale, nervous fingers curved tentatively on the back of the wooden bench, emerging from the cuff of his navy-blue jacket. But I can't recall where the conversation went from there, only that he must have switched seats (small wonder), whereupon my mother sprang to her feet, with me close on her heels. We darted over to where Daddy and his lawyer were still in a huddle.

The lawyer's open briefcase, full of papers, was perched upon his lap.

"Norman!" my mother exclaimed in a whisper, hands clasped over her heart. "Paul! You won't believe what [of course I'm censoring the name here] just told us." She proceeded to excitedly repeat all of it, then turned to the lawyer. "That's the proof we need!"

My father sat there, not responding as I deemed appropriate. "Daddy!" I chimed in. "It proves he's lying!"

He continued sitting there without speaking.

"Please, Norman," my mother entreated, to which he stated calmly: "You can't do that."

"What do you mean!" I demanded, sensing what was coming. "Can't do *what*?"

"To make something like that public. You can't repeat something like that, that a man tells you about his mother." My father gave one slight, decisive shake of the head, *no*.

It wasn't a jury trial. First one lawyer spoke, then the other. The judge rose; retired to his chambers; emerged a quarter of an hour later; instructed plaintiff and defendant to stand before him. And then...

In my mind's eye, I see the image of my father, awaiting the verdict in those moments: he stood upright, chin slightly lifted, hands clasped behind his back, with a matter-of-fact, quietly cheerful expression on his face of consciously chosen serenity. And I see Daddy's expression as the judge delivered his ruling: the rock-solid equanimity befitting a man who has emerged victorious over a deceitful legal claim.

Except that actually, my father's company had just been ordered to pay the plaintiff twenty-five thousand dollars.

I remember my father's uncomplaining, amicable nod to the judge before turning to depart, and his courteous smile as he said, "Thank you, your honor."

True love involves a complete identification with one's fellow man, I had read at my desk one day in the Photo Contest department, over my tuna fish sandwich, with the big black book propped open before me, *a full understanding of his needs and difficulties. He who benefits from his friend's dishonor forfeits his share in the hereafter. As Rabbi Moshe ben Maimon, the Rambam, commented, love of one's fellow man means being as careful about his honor and money as if they were our own. We are taught that no price is too high for protecting a man from shame.*

Afterward, on our way back to the office, the three of us were riding along without talking in the back seat of a cab, when my mother said quietly, "You were right, Norman."

He reached for her hand.

THE YEARS WENT BY. My parents got older. And so, of course, did I.

I moved to Israel, got married, had children, and the conversation with my parents about Judaism went on and on. We had angry arguments about evolution and the Chosen People, disagreements over the roots of anti-Semitism, clashes on the subject of ritual and superstition. But our dialogue continued, our love grew, and our mutual respect deepened. And one day in 1988, I got a letter:

> *Dearest Sarah,*
>
> *In the course of tending to matters in connection with my will, an issue has arisen I feel compelled to share with you. I don't want you to think anything is pending or that I have premonitions, it's simply prudent to take the necessary steps to avoid as much confusion and misunderstanding as possible.*

My father then informed me that he was planning on being cremated, and told me what he intended to do with the ashes:

> *I would like—given the concerns that have dominated my work these past thirty or forty years—for my ashes to be scattered over Hiroshima.*

The reason for this is that my father had been involved deeply, since the end of World War II, with providing aid to survivors of the Hiroshima Bomb.

> *I realize that there may be sensitivities for you on this point, but I hope you will agree that, given my philosophical bent, this is an appropriate and acceptable choice.*
>
> *Your feelings and responses matter more to me than I perhaps have ever been able to convey. I do not wish to make this kind of decision without discussing it with you. It means much to me to know that I have your support and understanding.*
>
> *Love,*
>
> *Daddy*

I called Rav Noach Weinberg for advice. "How should I answer?" I entreated. "What can I say?"

Rav Weinberg asked: "Would your father ever want to hurt you?"

"Never."

"Tell him that if he does this, it would hurt you, and you know he wouldn't want to do that."

My reply was as follows:

Dear Daddy,

Your asking me about this beforehand is a gift for which I cannot thank you adequately.

I have to just go ahead and say that I think sprinkling your ashes over Hiroshima (sounds like the song: "Stars Over Alabama") is a horrible idea, and if my vote carries veto power, I vote NO. Giving up your presence so frequently during my childhood to the people of Hiroshima may well turn out to have been my chief contribution to world peace, but giving them your physical remains, as well, is absolutely out of the question. A child must certainly learn to share her toys, but I see no reason at all for her to share her father's body.

More to the point: cremation is forbidden by Judaism. Don't ask me why, because obviously I don't know—but it's not something I want to fool around with. Though years ago I might have dismissed tradition as meaningless in and of itself, now I would say: Even if this is just a matter of tradition, come on, join the club. When our time comes, let's join the thriving, growing community of the happily dead throughout history whose bodies have graced Jewish cemeteries from time immemorial, from ancient Egypt to Levittown, right on down to our very own familial haunting grounds in New Jersey. Mount Lebanon Jewish Cemetery may not be my idea of the best spot to spend eternity, though I'm grateful that the Miller Family Association had the foresight to guarantee us all our very own plots, well-tended and reasonably spacious; and even though Mom and Pop and the whole mishpachah would surely appreciate my company. Let us go from dust to dust, not dust to ashes. And if indeed—inscrutably so to us mortals—a spiritual relationship does exist between soul and body which is promoted by the gradual transformation of our bodies into the larger body of Mother Earth, as the Torah prescribes, let's not miss out.

Though I cannot bear to even visualize or imagine such a scenario, much less speak of it openly in this manner, for the purposes of this discussion I'll add that I would want a place to go visit you, to talk to you, and it would hurt me not to have it, and I would be so sad if my children didn't have it. Please do not deprive me of this. It's probably one of the most basic human instincts.

Having said all of the above, I cannot accept anything less than for you and Mommy together to see my children grown, and see me personally into late middle age and beyond, and—perhaps, who knows—even onward and upward into senility. I beseech you please, Daddy, employ that well-known will to live of yours to satisfy my extreme need for your presence.

I apologize more than I can say to be putting up an obstacle for you and to be hindering you in carrying out what you believe. Please forgive me.

Love,

Sarah

His response arrived a few days later, by express mail.

Dear Sarah Kit,

Please rest easy. I'm changing my will and all is well.

Love,

Daddy

IN LATE AUGUST of 1990, three months before my father's unexpected death from a heart attack, my parents and I were searching one Saturday night in Jerusalem for a nice place to eat out. But Shabbos ends late in the summertime, and all the kosher establishments were still closed. In the company of several tired, cranky little grandchildren, we were driving from one place to another, my mother and father getting visibly weary from these nocturnal wanderings around the Holy City, when at last, from the back seat window of their rented car, I spotted what looked like a kosher bagel spot. All of us brightened up, my father found a parking place, and off we set, the children skipping happily along before us.

Upon reaching the restaurant, however, a closer inspection indicated that it wasn't what we were looking for.

"But, Sarah," my father implored, baffled. "It says kosher."

"I'm so sorry, Daddy. It's not kosher. It's kosher-*style*." Back we all piled into the car.

Setting off again, it suddenly dawned on me that the Hilton Hotel had a dairy restaurant, one floor under its lobby, which would certainly be open by now.

A half hour later in the hotel elevator, having knocked in vain on the closed doors of the darkened Kumsit Coffee Shop, we were rising up now through the bowels of the Hilton. I had just noticed my father's ashen face, when our eyes met, and out of the blue, he said, "I'm glad you're leading a religious life."

I felt my mouth fall open. "You are, Daddy?"

"Yes," he said with that small nod of his, of certainty. "It's consistent with my values."

My mother looked over at him, then at me.

That was the end of that, and since this was the last time I saw him, there was no opportunity to discuss the matter again. But years later when my mother and I talked about it, we both thought that Daddy had seen how even his little grandchildren were willing to go through physical and emotional discomfort for the sake of an ideal, and that this wasn't unlike what he had sought to do in his own life.

For me, honoring my parents—an idea which to me as a girl had seemed so quaintly out of date—was the pinpoint through which I had to pass. It sufficed in itself to transform my world, and served from then on as the unmoving center of a benevolent, unspeakably beautiful universe. From darkness to light, that single point was my North Star, and led me all the way home, to G-d.

ONE MORNING about seven years ago, I was hanging laundry out on our porch and my eye was caught by the sight of a little man with a white beard and black hat down below in the yard, coming our way along the sidewalk.

Could it be? I was astonished. I'd always wondered what had happened to him.

But as the man came closer, I saw it wasn't he.

The next day on my way to the neighborhood supermarket, it happened again. Wasn't that he, crossing the grass? I almost ran to see...but stopped. No, it didn't even resemble him.

That afternoon, I was at a bus stop downtown, waiting for the #22. I glanced to the left to see which number was arriving and saw, from the side, a tiny olive-skinned man with a white beard and a black hat.

Just then he turned to look, too.

"Rabbi R.!" I cried. "Is that you?"

He looked perplexed. His face was a thousand years older, and he was frail and bent and as shrunken as a leaf. "Who? You—are?"

"Sarah Cousins!" I exclaimed. "From New York City! How are you?"

"Oh!" *His face, wreathed in wrinkles, smiled.* "You are here? In Israel?"

I nodded happily.

"At garah po?" *[You live here?]*

"Kein!" *[Yes!]*

"At nesuah?" *[You are married?]*

"Kein!"

"Yesh lach yeladim?" *[You have children?]*

"Kein! V'nechadim!" *[And grandchildren!]*

He laughed.

"Rabbi R.—tamid ratziti l'hagid lecha. *[I've always wanted to tell you.]* Todah! *[Thank you!]* Todah rabbah!"

"Ein b'ad mah *[You're welcome]*," *he replied.* "Ah! Otobus sheli! *[This is my bus!]* Shalom!"

And with that he disappeared.

OFF THE FACE OF THE EARTH

Getting settled at my desk before the 8:30 bell a few days into second grade, I was just taking out my pencil box, when from across the room a mild commotion got my attention. Over by the coat rack, standing at the center of an inquisitive, talkative group of my classmates, was a new boy. He was fair, with light-brown hair, and his eyes were cast shyly down. He wore a gray-and-white-striped T-shirt.

As I looked on from where I sat, the floor beneath my feet melted and tilted a little—a not unpleasant sensation—and some sort of sickeningly sweet, electrically charged nimbus of cotton candy took a slow spin inside my mind.

I thought nothing of it, and the moment was already gone. But from that day on, my own light went dim.

I was a darkened moon, pulled out of orbit by an unseen sun.

Second grade passed, third grade, fourth grade.

THE NEW BOY (I used to spell out his name again and again in big capital letters in my blue-lined notebooks, encouraged by the fact that his name and mine started with C, and that when Miss Affleck read the daily roll call, mine never failed to come right after his) was different. He didn't seem to want attention. He didn't show off. But I wasn't the only moon revolving around his inward gaze. Marion liked him, Donna liked him. Linda and Claire and Susan liked him. He had risen effortlessly and naturally to the top without trying, precisely because he wasn't. He was even popular with the boys. They couldn't help liking him, too, and taking his lead.

The boy's all-American family was to my mind like the loving, attractive, normal, happy, successful all-American TV family of *Father Knows Best*, the show that everyone everywhere watched on Sunday nights at seven. He lived in a rambling, green-shuttered, cozy old white Colonial set back from the road—not so far off the road as to appear antisocial or weird, or to reveal *otherness*, the way *mine* did, nor so large or imposing as to diminish anyone's basic sense of self-importance and thereby rouse the sleeping dogs of envy and self-doubt and associated put-downs...*those snobs, who do they think they are?* But it was indeed far enough away from the road—bits of white-and-green happiness peeking through the trees—that you knew this was a nice family that actually had no use for you. Neither your friendship nor your admiration. The one time I was inside their house, when our after-school girls' club met one time at Barbra's house (how unbelievably lucky she was, to live next door to him!), the boy's father was so fatherly, and tall, and smoked a pipe. He did surely know best, towering over all; a benign, silent, watchful presence.

The boy's quiet, unostentatious mother had a lovely, warm smile and wore Bermuda shorts.

His older sister was a china doll, and gave off the same maddeningly aloof serenity as her little brother.

No one else knew—I never mentioned him to anyone—how my worldview and self-image had organized itself around that boy's face. I didn't know it myself.

I just felt bad, and wanted to be like the other girls and live in a house closer to the road, not behind a lot of trees. Some trees were all right, especially if there was space between them, and you could see through to the house—the boy's house—on the other side. But our house was behind a real forest.

That boy's averted face was the outward expression of my heart, and intrinsic to my heart's desire, it seemed, was that my love would remain raggedly unarticulated and suppressed and unrequited.

As fourth grade became fifth and fifth became sixth, and the other kids began holding mirrors to each other, passing from one year to another, one classroom to the next, it was never my face that appeared in his. No answering echo came my way.

I, bobbling around out on the open seas, was alone, a moon, adrift with no sun.

Hi Sarah,

How extraordinary to hear from you after such a long time!

I had spotted his name and address—he was a professor now in North Carolina—on a mailing from my hometown's High School Alumni Association, and had sent him a message identifying myself (a married woman, whose name no longer came right after his in the alphabetized list of classmates!) and asked if he would mind answering a question that dated back to childhood.

> *By all means, ask me whatever questions are on your mind. I hate to think of them knocking around in your head all these years. Perhaps we can clear them up, but I can't promise. Childhood was oh so long ago, and my memories of those years can be rather sketchy. But I'll try.*
>
> *The world we live in now never ceases to amaze me. E-mail certainly has a long reach, across distances and back through time. That's great that you and your husband have a family, and that your children are married with families of their own. For better or for worse, my wife and I chose—or, to be more forthright, I chose unilaterally—not to have children.*
>
> *I hope you and your parents and sisters are all well and happy, too.*

I replied:

> *Thank you so much for your swift response. How happily confusing and strange to hear your adult voice—like our parents!—from a little boy I see as my peer!*
>
> *For an e-mail to have pinpointed your location on the planet, a needle in a haystack, is indeed an incredible phenomenon.*
>
> *To skip over the last four decades and plunge in, the clearest mental image I have of you, from my scanty collection, is from second grade, when a new boy appeared in school a few days late. Unlike all the other noisy boys, he was quiet and thoughtful.*
>
> *The second shot is of you perched casually, Perry Como style, on the wooden fence by my mother's chicken coop, out behind our house on Silvermine Road. We were probably about nine. The Girls Tuesday Club was meeting at my house that week, and just as we had hoped without admitting it to each other—it was a girls' club!—the boys came over. This meant Hank Whittman, Norm Swallow, Peter Hindley, and you.*

I think some of the girls were off picking ears of corn in my moth-er's vegetable garden—she had a policy that anything they picked she would cook—and Norm and Hank were chasing my mother's chickens around the chicken yard. But to my amazement, you and I were having a conversation about what seemed to me very profound and grown-up subjects. It was exciting. I was sitting on the henhouse roof, looking down at you on the fence, and we were talking about what we wanted to be when we grew up. You said you'd really like to be a professional baseball player, but probably wouldn't be able to.

You said that your sister Christine had told you that my sister was "aggressive."

I wasn't sure what that meant about her, and me, and my family. I was obscurely pained and ashamed.

Here is the third picture, and this is the one that I wonder if you can help me with. My guess is that you don't remember the incident. You would have no reason to. Its meaning for me was probably not reflected at all in your fleeting experience of it. So although I ask you about it, I share the following with hesitation, for fear that you'll mistakenly think I hold you responsible for a little boy's throwaway line. To find a lost figure from one's childhood, to get a chance to ask him in real time about an event that took place in a buried city of ancient history, but which for me as a child was a defining mo-ment...this seems like a luxury of the modern era. Just being able to speak to you about it will in itself be the healing, probably.

We were in Mrs. Moore's fourth grade. One early spring day during recess, we were all playing tag out on the playground, and it was my turn to be "It." I had been happily running and running, and everyone was running and running away, when the bell rang for the end of recess. Everyone was running back inside to school when I looked around and spotted one boy—you!—who had found a good spot to evade being tagged, on top of a pile of old snow in the far corner of the playground. In a second you would have made it back inside with all the others. But finding myself alone with you on the playground like this—to my great delight—was too much to ignore. I wasn't eager to let the opportunity just pass, but now that I'd caught you, I didn't know what to do.

I victoriously, gleefully stood my ground, blocking you from stepping out of the corner.

You looked at me, averted your eyes, and then, in a plain, flat tone, declared quietly: "I wish you were off the face of the earth."

Do you by any chance remember this? Or have anything to say as to what feeling on your part prompted it? If not, simply speaking about it—to you—in itself sheds some light on an enduring mystery. What I imagine is that you were frustrated and embarrassed by my having succeeded in cornering you and were justifiably irritated that I was preventing you from getting back to class on time. Maybe we did get in trouble for being late—my memory stops here. But if I were to tell you how I took those words, you'd be surprised.

I took them as an indictment of who I was as a Jewish girl. A classic rejection across the board, and, believe it or not, from that day on I stayed on the fringe in our hometown. I stayed outside of things. As far as I know—this could be my imagination—I don't think I ever dared speak to you again.

If I as a little girl could take the rebuke of a little boy as an indictment of my whole self, then something was already brewing that made such a thing possible. There I was, a Jewish child in a suburban non-Jewish town—just a few short years after the Holocaust—who didn't have the slightest notion what it meant to be Jewish or why her people had been so recently despised and humiliated.

If any of this rings a bell, I'm all ears. If, on the other hand, all of this strikes you as baffling, intrusive, and incomprehensible, so be it, and that, too, would serve as an adequate reply.

Hi Sarah,

First, I would like to ask you to forgive me for saying such a cruel thing to you as a child. I don't recall the incident specifically, but I can suggest some reasons why I might have said such a thing, none of them having to do, in any way or at any time or to any degree, with any genuine animosity toward you on my part. I will respond here as fully as I can to your touching, fascinating, and unsettling message.

You'll be interested to know that yes, you have pulled off a truly astounding feat of memory. I did in fact enter Miss Affleck's second-grade class several days late. My family had just moved from Virginia, and when I started at the elementary school, they put me in with the "second level" second graders. Remember, we were all grouped according to perceived ability in those days, and it feels frightfully politically incorrect to even write it now, but that's just how it was. I guess they saw some spark in me that warranted moving me, after several days, into Miss Affleck's class, in with the top-of-the-line kids. I'm amazed beyond words that you would remember such a thing!

Like you, I'm just going to skip the last four decades and plunge in. When you're reaching back to grade school, after all, the last four decades don't matter much anyway.

I want to assure you once again that the terrible thing I said to you back then bears no relation whatever to the way I actually felt about you when we were children. I have a few hazy memories of you too. I remember being at your house for a party, in fifth grade, I think, for your birthday. I recall one day being at your house with a bunch of kids and stealing eggs from your chickens and throwing them at each other, and leaping into your compost pile and generally causing a good deal of mayhem. Your mother, I believe, was none too pleased with me that day. I wonder if that was the same day we sat on the fence and talked?

I remember your mother, who seemed to me very authoritative, but at the same time open and friendly and diligently nurturing, utterly different from my own unhappy mother. I recall you once telling either a bunch of us kids, or perhaps you told the whole class, about your mother fussing over your father's health, making him take castor oil and eat wheat germ and honey or some such things, and thinking how intriguing and avant-garde that sounded, and, of course, back then it was! I remember very well your house on Silvermine Road, what a huge place it was in my child's eye, with its rolling lawns, its outbuildings to explore, and the big main house shrouded and mysterious behind shrubs and trees. My sister Christine may have thought your sister was "aggressive," but

I know she admired your sisters for their intelligence and talent and spoke well of them.

I'll pause for a digression too. I know that you'll be sorry to hear that my sister Christine, a talented, generous-hearted, and beautiful woman, the senior prom queen of 1962, fell victim to addictive behavior. She died in April of this year, at 58, of lung cancer from thirty-plus years of smoking. She had stopped smoking over the last eight years, but it was too late. I still can't think or write about it without tears.

So back to childhood.

Which brings me to the question of why I would have said something so unkind to you. I honestly do not remember the incident at all, which suggests to me that there could not have been any real animosity behind it, because I do remember the kids I truly disliked and fought with. I can suggest a couple of superficial reasons why I might have said that to you. The first is, as you suggested, that it was just a throwaway line, something uttered on the spur of the moment that seemed clever and dramatic. Or, in light of what I said, I might have been having a "Disney moment," imagining myself to be some sort of wizard with the power to make people vanish into thin air.

But from what you tell me about the circumstances of the incident, I suspect that the truth is deeper and more unpleasant. I grew up in a seriously dysfunctional home, Sarah, and I think you probably felt some of the fallout from that fact. To begin with, both of my parents were alcoholics. My mother, thank G-d, recovered after a couple of years of disastrous drinking that had our household in a shambles during my grade-school years. My father's drinking was bad back then and grew worse as his life went on, and he never recovered. On top of that, my father was an angry and abusive man. He didn't often beat us physically, but his psychological abuse was almost unrelenting. Nothing we did was good enough. We didn't talk right, dress right, shake hands right. We didn't do the dishes right, didn't rake the leaves or mow the lawn right. We were too loud, too quiet, too stupid. We lived with an endless assault of scorn, sarcasm, and humiliation. That kind of thing is unspeakably destructive to a child, who has virtually no resources with which to comprehend or respond to that sort of treatment. I never use my childhood as an excuse for my adult shortcomings, but to this day, every day of my life, I contend with the legacy of those terrible years. And though I felt entirely alone as a child, this was by no means the case. I happened to see a friend from our elementary school last September, and she reeled off name after name of classmates of ours whose parents were alcoholics and subjected their children to mad childhoods. The posh houses and manicured lawns of our hometown hid a submerged world of pain we kids could never have imagined.

In light of what I was living through at home, I feel certain that it touched me in all the raw places in my child's psyche when you cornered me that day on the playground. As a kid, my only real source of coherence and self-worth came from my athletic ability, so the fact that you ran me down and cornered me was no doubt a blow, another humiliation. Also, just the fact of being caught and cornered certainly tapped into all the rage and frustration I felt in my home life. Not until I left home for college did I finally throw off the feeling of being trapped and at the mercy of my father, the torturer, and that feeling was perhaps worse during my grade-school years, when it was all inchoate, when I lacked the conceptual power to understand my predicament in any way. When a child suffers the psychological beatings I took from my father, one of the reactions, aside from the grief and loneliness, is rage, the urge to strike back. But I didn't dare do that, of course, with my father. The only way I could vent my anger toward my father was to imagine him dying horrible deaths, getting run over by a train or in a flaming car crash, and I did that all the time. The only other way to vent my rage was at other people, people who didn't deserve it. So I think when you cornered me like that you metaphorically recreated the conditions of my life that were overwhelming me with hurt and anger, and I lashed out at you. And if we were in danger of returning to class late, as you say, then I'm sure I also felt terrible anxiety over the possibility of displeasing the authority figure of the moment, and that was something I tried for the most part not to do, except with Mrs. Moore, with whom I had quite a contentious relationship. But one of my survival techniques within my family was to stay out *of sight as much as possible and to speak as little as possible, to avoid at all costs anything that might spur my father's wrath. So when you cornered me that day, I'm sure I felt humiliated, angry, and anxious, and that, I feel certain, is what caused me to say something so unkind to you and to sound as if I really meant it, because at that moment I probably did mean it. I wanted to cause hurt, but it had everything to do with other people, and the circumstances in my life, and nothing at all to do with you. I would have said the same thing, without question, to anyone who cornered me.*

Do please forgive me. When I was eight, nine, ten years old, all of this emotional turmoil existed below the level of my conscious life. I couldn't have begun, of course, to understand or articulate it as I do now. So I couldn't possibly have had the self-control to reign in the dark urges that made me say something so hurtful.

Your contacting me about this old wound actually clears up what was for me a mystery in my own mind concerning you, and that is why we stopped talking to each other after grade school. After sixth grade we lost the cozy unity of the grade-school classroom, so some drifting apart was inevitable, I suppose, but I remember in high school you and I looking each other in the eyes but for some reason being unable to even say hello to each other. It wasn't hostility between us, just strangeness, awkwardness. It's a shame, because although I was pretty much stuck in my high school jock life—another source of frustration and entrapment—my secret inclinations were literary, and that's the way I thought of you. I had no idea the roots of our estrangement went back to one unfortunate day on a grade-school playground.

I'm not sure what else to say…We can certainly laugh and lament over what time has done to us. I'm not exactly the spry high-school quarterback I once was, and you no doubt have a gray hair or two in that ponytail, but age is no crime. I formally and abjectly retract the terrible words I said to you all those years ago. It was my father I wanted off the face of the earth, my father I was speaking to that day, not you. It will always grieve me, however, to think that I said something so unkind to you and that troubled you so deeply and for so long.

THAT WAS THE END of the correspondence, and my year's subscription to the Alumni Newsletter lapsed soon thereafter. But had I cared to write again, I would have reassured him that on the contrary, those words uttered on a playground one afternoon in the 1960s, words he regrets yet cannot recall or retract, and which may or may not have had anything to do with me, were what started me off on my long, long road, one that eventually took me as far away as possible from my hometown. For what I had gathered from those words was that I was Jewish and wasn't wanted there. The world as I knew it was no place for me.

My sister once told me that if a sailboat sets out from a certain shore, a difference at the outset of just one degree will determine whether the boat ends up in the Far East or the Far West...or, I might add, the Middle East.

In just such a manner did the invisible turbulence in a little boy's life set me out homesick across the sea in search of a mirror, an echo, and a place I belonged, until, at last, I found myself, in Jerusalem's embrace.

RUTH OF YERUSHALAYIM

The voice on the phone sounded neutral. Whether she was just indifferent to the prospect of being interviewed or distinctly unenthusiastic, I couldn't tell. "Would you rather not do this?" I asked.

"No, I'm willing," she said. "But just don't make me out to be a *tzaddekes*. Because I'm not." She gave a mild laugh. "And don't use my real name."

I asked if I could at least use her real first name.

"All right, you can say Ruth. Just not the family name. And as long as you don't mind if my mentally ill husband comes home while we're talking. And my special needs daughter will be home, too, because of Lag Ba'omer."

A FEW DAYS LATER, I locate the rundown building in a narrow back street of one of Jerusalem's oldest religious neighborhoods, the scent of the charred remains of bonfires from the night before intermingling with the barely discernible fragrance of springtime's blossoming trees. I climb up to the fifth-floor apartment.

As Ruth goes into her kitchen to make coffee, I survey her bookcases. One side of the dining room is almost entirely covered floor-to-ceiling with Hebrew *sefarim*, the other with books in English. Taking a quick survey of the titles, I suspect that there is no significant volume put out by an English-language Orthodox publisher over the last thirty years that is not on those shelves.

"Would you like some of this?" she asks, emerging from the kitchen with a carton of some sort of flavored milk designed especially for coffee. "It's sort of like cream, but not too bad with the calories."

I say I'll give it a try, and we take our seats at the table. Unprompted, she begins:

"FIRST I'LL GIVE YOU some background. My parents were from very strong Protestant families. My mother's grandmother was actually Amish Mennonite. My father's grandfather was a Protestant minister, and my mother's brother was a Protestant minister. That brother—when he was a child—supported the family during the Depression by being a boy preacher. However, both my mother and my father completely left religious belief. My father became a scientist and a professor of chemistry. The house I grew up in was completely geared toward science and culture. We were inundated with history and literature and the arts. But nothing religious.

"But during the summer we used to go to the Rocky Mountains in Colorado. We had a tent, and we'd go hiking. At the age of eight, I climbed Long's Peak, and the view from the summit of Long's is..." Ruth pauses to find words. "Phenomenal. Very...majestic. It evokes a lot of awe. When you're standing there, you look out and can see a couple of states. And as you walk along, the Rocky Mountains themselves are tremendously beautiful. The waterfalls. Different plants. Boulders. Rock formations. The smell of the birch trees...I don't know how to...It's a tremendous...Would you like to see some pictures, to give you an idea? They're from a trip I took with my daughter to see my parents five years ago."

Ruth goes over to a third bookcase and returns with a photo album. Against a backdrop of distant mountains, flowers, rock and sky, the carefully handwritten captions identify Ruth, looking about twenty pounds heavier than she is now, and a grinning girl apparently with Down's syndrome, about twelve. Alongside them stand a tall, slightly smiling man and two little boys, whom Ruth identifies as her older brother and his sons. Ruth's vigorous-looking mother and less energetic-looking father, who appear to be in their late seventies or early eighties, sit in front, together on a bench. Her parents' dignified demeanor and weathered faces—straightforward, open, honest, intelligent—instantly remind me of my own parents, of blessed memory: devoutly secular American Jews, intellectual, liberal, ethical, kind. The famous line that my mother told me when I was a child, attributed to Abraham Lincoln, comes to mind: that from the time he turns forty, a man is responsible for his face.

"So both your parents are alive?"

"Just my mother. My father committed suicide three years ago." Ruth looks me astutely in the eye, letting a few moments go by as I process this. "He was a philosopher-scientist. He regarded suicide—*Hashem yishmor*—as the considerate, reasonable, rational thing to do. He didn't want to be a burden. My mother knew that that's how he'd always felt and asked him never to do it. So one day when he'd gotten very ill and very weak, he asked her if she wanted to go shopping and when she came back, he was gone.

"My mother is an amazing lady. She understands people tremendously well. She wanted to go to college to be a doctor, but it was during World War II, and in the wake of the Depression, and her parents wouldn't hear of such a thing. They simply didn't believe in education for women. So she dropped out of high school and worked as a lab technician—in those days you didn't need a degree for that. She's amazing.

"My older brother is a mathematical genius. Literally. Just to give you an idea: when Southern Bell has a breakdown, he's one of the people they call in to fix it. And when Microsoft devised a program for banks, he was the one they called on, to determine if it could be broken into. One indication of my mother's wisdom as a parent was that she never gave me the feeling I was any less because I wasn't as brilliant as my brother."

At this point, some sounds, which at first I ignore—for some reason they don't register as a person's voice—reach us from elsewhere in the small apartment. Only when Ruth gets up and walks down the hallway toward the continuing noise, responding firmly in Hebrew in a steady tone, do I realize that the gruff grunting is someone saying things that I can't catch. Ruth continues answering in low, level tones, whereupon suddenly the girl in the photo album—older now than she was back then in the Rocky Mountains—bursts out from a doorway, stamping her feet in protest and yelling something in an aggrieved, childishly strident whine of anger and complaint. Mother and daughter continue their back-and-forth in the hallway, the child alternately indignant and begging. Their negotiations, I find out later, are about the lunch menu.

Suddenly, from where she's standing down the hall, the girl catches sight of me at the dining room table and falls silent, staring with head tipped to one side and mouth fallen open.

I say shalom.

She ducks out of sight, and Ruth takes a seat again at the dining room table.

"That's Malky," says Ruth with a slight smile. "My youngest. She's a typical teenager. Like a lot of teenagers, she's inclined to argue with her mother.

"*Baruch Hashem*, I have eight kids. My three oldest are very *frum*, my next one is *datiah*, in a very modern offshoot of Breslov, and I have three kids who went off the *derech*. Two are boys, and they're both in the army, and the other is my older daughter. She went off the *derech* starting around ninth grade, but now she's *shomer Shabbos* again. Step-by-step, she's coming back. "Malky—" Ruth smiles ruefully "—is *frum*. *Baruch Hashem*, all my kids get along. They all make the effort to accommodate one another.

"When my daughter was just starting to get wishy-washy about her Yiddishkeit, I asked my mother, 'How do you deal with a child who's going in a completely different direction from how you raised him?'"

Ruth gives a laugh at the irony of having asked her mother that question. "So my mother said, 'You'd be surprised—when the little birds fall out of the nest, they don't fall that far away.' And I see today that that's true. I see how much my thought processes and the way I behave with my children are influenced by the way I was raised. As a tiny example, it drives me absolutely crazy when I see kids from the neighborhood throwing trash outside in the yards and in the street. And the garbage bin is ten steps away! It's a big *chillul Hashem*. Because when we were children and the family was on a car trip together, and we'd stop to eat lunch in a public park, when we were finished, we'd all go around picking up other people's trash. Each one of us would pick up at least ten items of trash so we could leave it cleaner than the way we found it."

"So what happened to move you away from your parents' worldview?"

"Somehow, as a child, I came to a realization that there is a G-d. It wasn't exactly the *Avraham Avinu* concept, that there must be a Creator of all this. It was more just a feeling of awe that nature led me to; it was an innate feeling that there is a G-d. It turned out that my mother's grandfather was probably Jewish, though not religious. So it could be that I have a little *neshamah Yehudi*—something in there that allowed me to realize that there is a G-d. In any case, it's written that anyone who eventually converts is born with a Jewish *neshamah*.

"My first stop in my search for G-d was the local Baptist church. I walked there every Sunday all by myself and attended services."

"How old were you?"

"That started when I was in fourth grade. But after about two years, I decided it didn't make sense."

"What didn't make sense to you?"

"There were a few things that disturbed me. One, that someone as good as my mother would be consigned to hell, with no credit for good deeds, because she didn't believe in Yushka. The emphasis on belief instead of doing. The idea, as I understood it, was that belief gave you a free pass to Heaven. Another was that the people in the church were anti-black. They didn't mind foreign exchange students who were black, but they didn't like American blacks. In our family, I was raised to believe that every human being has infinite value. When I was a child we went once to Florida to do some scuba diving off the coral reef. It was 1964, just before the breakout of the civil rights movement. When we reached the South, the first thing we saw was the segregation: they had three different restrooms: for women, men, and 'colored.' My parents' reaction, obviously, was that this was horrendous. We went to a drugstore where they had two soda fountains, one counter for 'whites' and one for 'coloreds.' My parents sat us all down at the 'colored' soda fountain. The poor waitress was flustered as could be. But my mother made an effort to calm her down and made it clear there was no way we would sit at a whites-only counter.

"After I left the Baptist church, in sixth or seventh grade, I started reading extensively about different religions, and over time, I had problems with all of them. Sure, the Trinity was a stretch, but in general I didn't have a problem with Christianity's miracles per se. If they said Yushka walked on water, that was OK with me. What I did have a problem with was the notion that you only go to Heaven if you believe in JC.

"Then, with Buddhism, it was the idolatry that repulsed me, and the emphasis on meditation. My parents were very geared toward helping other people, and meditation was not going to feed your hungry neighbor.

"Then came Islam. I read a great deal, but the second I came across a philosophical debate as to whether a woman has the soul of a person or a dog, that was the end of that. So much for Islam.

"As for Judaism, it didn't even occur to me to look into it. As far as I knew, it was just what came before Christianity. It had nothing to do with today, and there were certainly no Jews around to tell me anything to the contrary.

"The whole process of looking into other religions took me about three years. I didn't find what I was looking for anywhere, so I just kind of developed my own way of looking at the world. But I was conscious of missing a framework.

"In ninth grade, I joined the school book club—I was already a reading addict—and the school librarian who was running the club, whom I happened to know very well, once had us read a book on theology. She didn't conduct a discussion about the book itself. She just asked each of us in the group to speak about our own personal philosophy of life. When I told the group about mine—that I believed there is a G-d, that He expects us to do good deeds, and that we're accountable for bad deeds—she said, 'If I didn't know better, I'd say you were Jewish. That's a Jewish philosophy.'

"That comment changed my life. Suddenly I understood that I wasn't the only sensible person in the world, that there were other people out there with the same basic worldview that I had. Because up to that point, I felt very detached from the world. On one hand I was very much a part of the world—I did all the things that children like doing, playing and having fun—but inside myself I felt very different from everyone else. So that's when I started reading about Judaism, and I was amazed. At first, I didn't consider Orthodoxy a possibility because I'd read a novel that gave the impression that Orthodox Jews don't allow black people to convert. But I read about Judaism all through high school—I was in high school for three years, not four; I finished high school early—and continued reading about it throughout my first year of college. At that point I decided to transfer to nursing school, and decided to undergo a Reform conversion. So my choice of nursing schools—in Peoria, Illinois—was largely determined by which one was located close to a Jewish community.

"The first year of nursing school, I had a Reform conversion. The Reform rabbi was very liberal, of course, but he was also pro-traditional. He would tell his congregants not to throw away everything in their heritage, that they should learn about different aspects of the religion and try them out. So I took his advice, and slowly began taking on more and more mitzvos. I started dressing *tzniyusly*, and eating kosher. But a year later they replaced him. Within a few weeks, I saw that the new rabbi's services were just badly whitewashed Protestant services. Meanwhile, I had decided to start keeping Shabbos, and one day I said to myself, 'Wait a minute, I'm doing something here that doesn't make sense intellectually. I'm acting like an Orthodox Jew, but according to Orthodox Jewry I'm not even Jewish. If I'm going to do this because the Torah is true, then I have to do it 100 percent. If it's not true, and I don't become Jewish, then as a non-Jew, should I be doing all this?'

"At that point—it was the end of nursing school—I studied and got an Orthodox conversion. And the next year I came here to Israel. I had three basic reasons for coming to Israel. One, I wanted to see the Kotel. Two, I—"

I'm busily jotting things down and don't notice that Malky has entered the dining room, looking up just as she throws herself exuberantly across

Ruth's lap. Ruth holds her in her arms for several minutes, like a baby. They are discussing how many vegetarian schnitzels Malky can have for lunch. About five minutes go by as the solemn dialogue continues, punctuated by occasional outbursts of loud protest from Malky.

Malky gets up and goes into the kitchen, and Ruth follows. While waiting, I turn around in my chair and entertain myself by looking curiously at all the English-language books, secretly hoping to find some of mine, when all at once Malky is now throwing her arms around *my* neck. She is bestowing upon me a long, long hug, like the one she gave her mother, and I'm so touched and honored that I get a little misty-eyed. She likes me? It feels delicious. I try to return the warmth. I don't want her to let go. But she does, standing abruptly and returning to the kitchen.

When Ruth comes back and sits down, I tell her with a certain sort of pride what just happened: "She hugged me."

Ruth regards me with a look at once benevolent and shrewd. "You're a stranger," she says. "For Malky, giving strangers hugs is a very dangerous behavior."

So I gather from this that such expressions of affection on Malky's part are not uncommon, and cannot necessarily be taken personally, or even celebrated.

"AS I WAS SAYING," says Ruth, picking up where she left off. "I came to Israel for three reasons. One, I wanted to see the Kotel. Two, I wanted to learn the language so I could *daven* in Hebrew. And three, I wanted to find a good *shidduch*.

"I arrived two weeks before the Yom Kippur War. If you remember, in those days the basic outlook in the Jewish world was that our problems with Arabs were over because of Israel's tremendous victory in the Six Day War. I can't remember who it was—I or my mother—who brought up the subject of how I'd get in touch with her if there was an outbreak of hostilities, but neither of us took the question seriously because everyone knew for sure that that wasn't going to happen. My mother dismissed the question breezily by saying, 'No news is good news,' and off I went.

"I immediately enrolled as a student at Neve Yerushalayim and got a job at Ezrat Nashim Hospital in Jerusalem as both a psychiatric and a geriatric nurse.

"I met my husband in 1976, through a *shadchan* who came highly recommended. He was mentally healthy when I met him, and as far as the spiritual connection was concerned, the match wasn't at all off the mark. My husband is a *baal teshuvah* from a very rich family. He has the soul of a poet, but his family wanted him to become an engineer. Eventually, he found his way to Yiddishkeit and found his niche there. It was a big sacrifice. If he had done what his family wanted him to do, he would have been in line to head the family's company. He could have had a very comfortable life financially. As a child, and then later when he became observant, my husband was always given the message by his family that he wasn't good enough. Lots of people deal with feelings of inadequacy and it doesn't lead to mental illness, so I can't say 'this caused that,' but one thing's for sure, that his underlying feeling of never being good enough broke him. It all comes back to this: accept your child the way he is.

"Like every parent who has a child who goes off the *derech*, I've done a lot of thinking on the subject. A lot of young people feel they need to change everyone around them, but as you get older, you realize that the only person you can change is yourself. Once, when I was younger, I decided to prove to my mother that *Hashem* exists. My mother wrote back and said, 'Dear, let's just drop religion, all right?' So ever since, that's how we've gotten along."

"But, Ruth, you said that the librarian in ninth grade made one comment that changed your life."

"We can have an influence on other people, but the only person any of us can control is ourselves, and even that is easier said than done. Sometimes I've been asked how I get along so well with my kids who aren't *frum*, and I answer that my job is to be a mother. I'm not *Hakadosh Baruch Hu*'s policeman. If I did all I could so that my children would grow up to be normal, happy, functioning people, and nonetheless this happened due to external circumstances beyond my control, there is always a chance that they'll come back."

"Do you think that having found your own way to Yiddishkeit enables you to relate to them better, and to help them, more than if you were *frum* from birth?"

"Not necessarily. In my case, I was coming from a nonreligious background and discovered the religion with a lot of joy. My kids were running away from religion, or—to be more precise—religious society. It's a very different experience. It involves very different emotions."

I ask how she reconciles herself to anti-black feelings among religious Jews, given her strong feelings as a child about anti-black discrimination.

"Such people have either had bad experiences with black people, or they're picking up on the prejudices that are prevalent in society at large. There has definitely been *siyata d'Shmaya* in my life. The kind of thing that troubled me as a child, I didn't encounter in the *frum* world until I was an adult, and I didn't encounter the phenomenon of insincere religious Jews who violate the Torah until I had the adult intelligence to handle it. For example, my daughter—the one who went off the *derech*—has always had a lot more difficulty than I do dealing with people who are two-faced. I experienced that phenomenon in secular society; I know that every society has a certain number of people who don't practice what they preach, so it doesn't throw me.

"As far as my childhood difficulties with Christianity, there was a lot of *siyata d'Shmaya* there, too. I'm sure there are Christians who would say you *are* accountable for bad deeds, but that's not what I was being taught as a child, and it was my limited childhood understanding that eventually induced me to find Yiddishkeit. The halachic concepts of Judaism that I would have had trouble with as a child didn't come to my attention until I was ready. I met the right people at the right time. Three or four decades ago, I'd feel hurt if I could tell someone was looking down on me because of my background, but that kind of thing doesn't have that effect on me at all anymore. If there are people in my neighborhood who look down on me, I know it's because they can't grasp or understand what's beyond their own personal experience. The important people in the community don't look at me with a label; they see me as a person.

"Judaism cannot force you to become a good person. It can only point you in the right direction. If someone who is *frum* does something dishonest, or anything else, *Hashem yishmor*, that violates halachah or the central ethical underpinnings of Torah, then they weren't brought up with true Jewish values. A lot of Jews are brought up in *frum* culture without much thought. They do things because 'this is the way my family does things.' So it's a lot easier for the negative things from the outside world to filter in.

"The one thing that *was* difficult for me as a convert came up when my children entered *shidduchim*. It hurt me that even though they were very *frum*, they couldn't marry into rabbinical families, but I came to understand that as much as I raised them in a *frum* setting, there *is* a bit of exposure. They're not exactly like kids whose parents are FFB. We saw such *siyata d'Shmaya*. The families that theoretically could have declined a *shidduch* because of my husband's breakdown went ahead with it anyway, and each one of my kids, in turn, married someone who is so well-suited to his or her personality.

"I'd say the most difficult example of halachah presenting me with a problem is associated with taking a non-Jew to the hospital on Shabbos. If I had read about that when I was a teenager, that would have been the end of the story. Even now, I don't know what I would do in that situation. If my mother needed to go to the hospital on Shabbos, would I pass the test? Sometimes I can understand something intellectually, but emotionally I'm not there yet.

"I have lots of *aveiros*. Things I'm working on. I'm not 100 percent. Things from the society I grew up in were ingrained in my system. *Shemiras halashon*—I'm not where I should be. I dress a bit too modern sometimes. I yell at my kids. I lose my temper at times. But I don't think this makes me a terrible person. I just have to be honest with myself, and being honest with myself is an uphill battle.

"My younger kids started going off the *derech* not long after their father had his first psychotic break and started behaving very inappropriately in public, which of course caused them a lot of shame in front of the community. Somehow, we were all handling it all right, though. In my daughter's case, she was a very *frum* girl up until eighth grade, when something else happened at the same time. Just at that juncture, at the end of eighth grade, she found herself in the large group of girls who hadn't gotten accepted into any of the Bais Yaakov high schools. The principal told us that the policy was that girls who had older sisters had to be given precedence over the others. All those girls were in limbo for several months, feeling insecure. And embarrassed. We waited all summer. It was excruciating. But my daughter handled that, too, pretty well. Eventually, the night before the first day of school—I don't know why they couldn't have done this a little earlier—the teachers and administrators got together in a meeting to divide up all the girls who didn't have a place, and she ended up in the high school that she wanted, after all.

"The first day of classes, the teacher was reading the roll call and when she got to the name of my daughter, she said, 'All's well that ends well.' That remark let on to all the other girls that my daughter was one of those who hadn't been accepted, and that she'd only gotten in at the last minute. My daughter had kept it a secret from her classmates.

"That teacher is considered an excellent *mechaneches*, and to tell you the truth, she really is. But with that one statement, she unintentionally destroyed my daughter's *emunas chachamim*. It's like when you're making a piece of pottery. You have to be so careful of every small gesture. It takes a lot of skill. You can fashion a pot very quickly on the wheel, but you can destroy the clay in a split-second if you press on a weak spot in the wrong way.

"There are a lot of *bachurim* in this community and in other *frum* communities who want to make more money than they grew up with in the *chareidi* world. If my sons had been given the opportunity to have an academic education within a *frum misgeret*, without being labeled *sug-bet* (second-best) because they don't want to become *kollel* men, then I believe that they wouldn't have decided to go into the army. Not every boy who doesn't want to learn is going off the *derech*. If you put him in with the kids who are going off, he'll be influenced by them. If the only training available in the *frum* world to such boys is along the lines of bookbinding, they're going to say, '*Bookbinder*? Give me an English class!' Too many kids are getting lost. I'm looking around me at the system we have in place, and for too many kids, it's just not working.

"When Malka was born, I accepted her for what she was, and I learned from that to accept all my children for what they were. It's a process, learning to accept the fact that your children are individuals, that they're not here to boost your self-esteem, and to really appreciate that each one of them has his or her unique positive attributes. It may sound strange, but I never stopped being proud of my non-*frum* or more modern children. They're all *menschlich*.

"When my daughter was a teenager, and a lot more off the *derech* than she is now, she told me that when she would get married, she was going to take advantage of all the available testing during pregnancy because she didn't want to have a special-needs child. So when she did get married and got pregnant, I purposely didn't question her if she was doing any testing. I felt it was not my place to butt in. However, when we went for the birth and she was in labor, one of the doctors on duty saw on her chart that she had a special-needs sister, and said something about it. She looked him in the eye and said, 'I want you to know that my sister is one of the best things in my life. Thank G-d that no one ever convinced my mother to do testing.'

"Sometimes I feel as if I've been through a whirlwind, but I have learned to take care of myself."

I ask what that involves.

"To take a mundane example, it means staying on a diet. To succeed at it, I have to be honest with myself. Let's say I want a piece of cake, and I say to myself, 'I'll eat this and won't have supper.' But if I know that the real truth is that I'm going to end up eating supper anyway, so I'm lying to myself. Then, of course, you feel life is unfair—here I am starving myself, and the diet's not working! How come?

"Taking care of myself means allowing myself the luxury of a ceramics class once a week because I need it for my emotional well-being. I have something to look forward to every week. I know women who go hiking every two weeks or go swimming every week. But you don't have to spend money. You can go for a walk in the nearest park. Or take an hour and a half one morning to read a novel.

"A friend of mine had a child who died young, not long before Malky was born. Throughout the pregnancy, I had been *davening* very hard to have another girl, and after she was born, I took the baby with me to a *bris* one morning. A lot of people at the *bris* were commending me for how upbeat and positive I was, and in the midst of the crowd I caught sight of this friend. I went over to her and said, 'Sometimes I feel like screaming: This isn't the baby I dreamed of! This is not the girl I *davened* for!'

"My friend answered me like this: Having *emunah* doesn't mean that no matter what happens, my life is hunky-dory. *L'kabel yissurim b'ahavah* doesn't mean, 'This is great, thank you, G-d.' It's being willing to put one foot in front of the other and keep going.

"May I ask what your hardest test has been?"

"Having a husband with a major mental illness is the hardest *nisayon* I have to deal with. It's sort of like being a widow, but he's…still there. The person I married disappeared. However, today there are a lot of things available to treat mental illness. If the spouse can get good advice and is persistent in pursuing treatment, there's a lot that can be done to help the situation. When all is said and done, just as I have to accept my kids for what they are, I also have to accept that my husband is not exactly the same person I married, which I think is true for a lot of people. I read a story in one of the magazines a while back, about a woman whose husband stopped learning and she went into a deep depression, and I thought to myself: people change, people react to what goes on in their lives. That doesn't mean if a husband is abusive, or there's some other situation that makes divorce advisable, that one shouldn't avail oneself of that halachic option, but it's not something to do casually. A person is not a coat."

I ask Ruth if she ever asks *Hashem* why—after everything she did to become a Jew—He's giving her such big blows.

"Look, for anyone who has a big *nisayon*—and most people do have a major *nisayon* at least once in their life—the important thing is not to be upset if you don't have the *emunah* to accept it with open arms. You're allowed to be a person; you're allowed to be upset. You're allowed to have sorrow. Keep on living life the best you can and doing mitzvos the best you can and eventually you learn to grow with the *nisayon*. Maybe there are *baalei emunah* whose belief and trust is so great that the experience of their *nisayon* doesn't follow this pattern—but for most of us, there's a period of grieving, a feeling of *why me?* That's part of the normal reaction. Eventually, hopefully, one works through this. With the passing of time, people usually see the positive things that were gained from the experience.

"There's no guarantee in life, and *Hakadosh Baruch Hu* is running the show. It's sort of like having a role in a play. Let's say you have the starring role, you're playing the part of the heroine. On opening night, the director informs you that you're going to be playing some minor character, or you're going to be the villain—a role you really don't want to play. You may initially feel upset and angry that you're not playing the character you wanted, but if you totally trust that the director knows what he's doing, that he has your interests at heart, that he's not out to get you, you'll come to accept the change.

"Sometimes *Hakadosh Baruch Hu* takes you and throws you into the deep end of the swimming pool, and you have a choice, to sink and drown, or to swim. I choose to swim."

As I gather up my stuff and get ready to leave, Ruth brings me a bottle of Mei Eden water to take along on the bus.

Once again, it takes me a few moments—when Malky raises her voice in protest—to understand that she's saying the bottle belongs to *her*. "*Zeh sheli!*" she cries. "*Zeh sheli!*"

"*Hi tzrichah mayim*, Malky," says her mother quietly. *She needs water.* "Can you give it to her?"

Malky cocks her head to one side, contrite, appears to see the justice here, and with a thoughtful silence, conveys her assent.

THE MUSICIAN'S WIFE

"**I** was around twelve. In sixth grade."

I had just asked Adina Black when and how she and her husband, Nissim Black, had begun their journey to Judaism. Seated across from me at her dining room table in Jerusalem, she was being climbed repeatedly, like a tree, by her baby boy, around ten months old. The Blacks' three-year-old girl was staring at me, the visitor, and their eldest child, a girl around ten, was being tutored in the next room by a young, *frum* married woman from the Sanhedria HaMurchevet neighborhood. Adina's two other children, two little boys, weren't home yet from *cheder*.

Upon stepping into their apartment, I'd recognized the particular trademarks of Pesach cleaning, and said something to that effect. Adina had smiled a very wide, very gentle smile, with the softness that would serve as the persistent undercurrent of our conversation.

"I was reading a lot on my own," Adina recounted, "and on the day this happened, the day I'm talking about, I was sitting on the school bus in Seattle when a Muslim girl who went to my elementary school came over to me, and out of the blue she said to me, 'You know, G-d is One. You Christians believe G-d is three.' I told her no, that's not true, what does she mean by that? How could she put Him in a box and say He's One?

"The Muslim girl said, 'You know, three. Father, son, holy ghost. That's three. It doesn't make sense. How do you have three gods?' And to myself I was thinking, *It is kind of true.* After she said that, that's when I started reading the *Tanach* by myself. But I couldn't find CGC in it anywhere, so I—"

"What's CGC?"

"Oh, that's the sect my family belonged to. Cogec." She waves it off dismissively with one hand. "Christianity has a lot of different sects. So I asked my stepfather, 'Where does it say that G-d is three?' And he said, 'When there's something you don't understand, you just believe.' That's the answer you'd always be given: You have to believe. You just have to have faith. And so I thought, *OK*. But then, when I started high school, in ninth grade I was learning about the Sabbath, that the Sabbath is supposed to be the day of rest, when a—"

"Who were you learning with?"

"No, I was just learning by myself. A very close friend of mine in CGC had left Cogec and had gone to the Seventh Day Adventists. I was like, *Really!!? Can I go there, too?* And I did. I told my family that I'd decided to move to Seventh Day Adventists. The main thing is that the Sabbath is moved from Sunday to Saturday. You can do whatever you want, except that you're not supposed to go shopping or drive anywhere or watch TV, but if you do, OK."

Adina continues: "My sister is ten months younger than I am. We're similar to each other, and have always been very close, but we're definitely very different from each other. My sister was one of the popular ones in high school. I was the quiet one no one knew. The introvert. I hardly spoke to anyone. People didn't know we were sisters."

The image that comes to mind for me, from my suburban, non-Jewish Connecticut high school in the late 1960s, is the school population of perhaps ten black students among the whites, each of whom stood out in any crowd. "Really? They didn't know you were sisters? How many black students were there?"

"No, it was an all-black school, my high school in Seattle." Adina picks up her thread: "I met my husband when he was fifteen and I was seventeen. He was one of the popular ones. He invited me to his sixteenth birthday party, but I told him I didn't go to parties. Parties weren't forbidden by my church, but I'd been brought up in a religious Christian family. I knew the environment at the party was not my lifestyle.

"I think my life...I'd had my own questions and my own journey. Long before I met my husband." Adina looks off to the side for a few moments. "My husband grew up completely differently. And he was on *his* journey.

"We graduated high school and got married, and were married a few years—we hadn't yet had our first child—but the process had been going on for quite a while for both of us, separately and together.

"We were new parents when my husband's mother was *niftar*." Again, she pauses. "It was a tremendous blow when she died, a terrible, terrible loss, and in that same period, we both lost our jobs. At such a time, when the difficulties, the blows, are overwhelming, my husband naturally started to question life. At such times in life, you have no choice but to look up.

"I was busy being a new mommy, I was so in love with my little girl. I remember thinking, *What is he doing? He needs to be looking for a job instead of sitting and reading books all day!* But that's what he was doing during this difficult time, he was in the living room reading, from morning till night, and I was in the other room crying, thinking to myself, *He has to go out and get a job!* He was reading all these books, from early morning to night. Then, one day, he said, 'I have to tell you something.'

"It made me nervous, the way he said, 'I have something to tell you. I need to talk to you.' So I took a seat on one side of the room, and he was on the other, and he told me, very respectfully and gently: 'I don't want to celebrate pagan holidays.'

"I'd never heard the word 'pagan' before. I just sat there and felt totally confused. I had already left the Seventh Day Adventists, and during that long break, my questions and doubts hadn't left me. Life was very rough. I sat there across from him feeling it was all just much too much for me. I just didn't know. And I was thinking, *How am I going to tell my family?* Because if you question it, you're just told to have faith. Now my husband was saying to me that the whole foundation of Christianity is intertwined with paganism, which holds that there's more than one god.

"That's when our process really began seriously. I decided to learn with him."

I ask if they'd had a teacher.

"No. It was me and my husband. And I decided I was not going to involve my family. Our first Pesach...Oh, my!" Adina tips back her head with a soft roll of laughter. "It was so difficult to clean! We thought we were the only people on earth who knew what we knew. We thought, *Who else is keeping this? Who's doing this aside from the two of us?* We were alone."

"You mean you didn't know about Jews?" I ask Adina incredulously.

She shakes her head, no.

"You never *met* Jews?"

"If I did, I didn't know."

"Didn't you know that Yushka was a Jew?"

"No, I didn't know...they never told me that. So I didn't know. I know it sounds so strange. It's so weird to look back." A pause, and then, quietly, "We tried our best."

"You discovered the Jewish G-d alone, Adina?"

"Yes. We were completely alone."

"You were like Avraham and Sarah. It's unusual. It amazes me."

She falls into a pensive silence before continuing:

"After being alone for a long time, my husband heard somehow about Chabad.org., and he started learning online. But we were stuck. And the reason we were stuck was fear. About JC. I remember a conversation around that time that I had with my husband, when I told him how scared I was. I said, 'I can't take this anymore. I don't believe in the whole JC thing.' I thought I was going to go to hell for not believing in JC. The fear had been so deeply instilled in me as a child. It was during that period that I decided to tell my sister what was going on with us."

"Even though you were so close to her, you hadn't told her yet?"

"Right. She's my best friend. And I'm hers. But I hadn't told her what was happening with us. So one day, I called her up and said, 'I have something important to tell you.'

"'OK,' she said, 'so tell me. Whatever it is, if it's such a big deal, tell me now.'"

"I told her I couldn't tell her over the phone. So she came over to where we were living—"

"You were still in Seattle, both of you?"

"Yes. And my sister said, 'OK, so what is it?'

"That's when we had our first long talk about paganism, and that's when my sister told me that her fear was overwhelming, too, like mine. But she'd never told me, or anyone, all her life. She'd always been scared to say her questions and doubts out loud. And suddenly, she fell to the floor."

"What do you mean?"

"Literally. She fell down. To the floor."

"WHAT DID YOU MEAN," I ask again, looking at my notes more than a month later, "by '*my sister fell down.*'"

"She fell down," says Adina. "She was shocked."

Pesach has come and gone. Again, I'm sitting opposite Adina at their dining room table. And again, climbing her like a tree, is their baby boy. Walking through their front door earlier, for a second I wasn't sure it was the right apartment—this one was so spacious and expansive, with its large windows running wall-to-wall on opposite sides, opening wide the whole living, dining, and kitchen area to breezy sunshine.

Then it dawned on me: when I was here the first time, Adina had been turning the house inside-out for Pesach cleaning.

Adina has been in and out of hospital a few times during this interval, for issues related to her current pregnancy. She's also been involved, with her husband, in a search for an Orthodox community with a *chareidi* school to their liking that would accept their eldest child. *Baruch Hashem*, Adina tells me happily, they have found what they sought. A contract for an apartment in Beit Shemesh had been signed a few days before, and G-d willing, their children will all be installed in their new home by the time schools open in Elul.

For now, however—since the girls' school for grades *aleph* to *hei* that the Blacks had wanted for her had not accepted their eldest daughter, now age ten—she was in the kitchen, learning with her tutor.

"OK, I'M NOT JEWISH. So what am I? If this is the truth, then why was I born outside of it—outside of what's real?"

Adina is describing her thoughts and feelings during the period that she and her husband were studying together, before their conversion. I interrupt her to claim that there are parallels between her experience and mine. We were *both* born outside the truth, she in the Christian world, and I in the secular world: she as a black American daughter born to a deeply religious family, from which she had to separate painfully when she became a *giyores* and made aliyah; and I, as an American Jewish daughter in a quietly anti-Semitic, gentile town, the only Jewish child—with a Jewish name, after my grandmother—in school, given no formal Jewish education but born to deeply idealistic, humanitarian Jewish parents with deeply held Jewish values...a family from which I, too, had to separate painfully when I became a *baalas teshuvah* and made aliyah.

"But you were born with the essence," counters Adina. "You were right there. That's a lot. I didn't have that connection. I don't want this to sound harsh...but...when a person converts, you're no longer connected to the non-Jewish roots. You take on so much, and leave so much. You don't want to offend your family. Your mother. Your father. Yet you want *emes*."

Again I interrupt with claims of similarity, insofar as I, too, experienced that separation.

"But as a Jew, your lifestyle, your life, everything, is different," Adina protests. "A Jew who's born Jewish, you can still connect to your Jewish roots. For me, the place I love going when I have to go back home is Chevron. That's where I connect to *my* Jewish roots. Because of *Avraham Avinu*. Whenever I'm greatly discouraged…because not everyone is always so nice…whether it's because they know I'm a *ger*, or because we look different, because they assume whatever negative things they assume about us because we're black…I strengthen myself with the knowledge that such things are not a true representation of *Hashem*. I have been spit upon by Jews who were dressed religiously, and my children and I have been taunted with the word *kushi*. I feel that *Hashem* isn't pleased with that behavior. I go to Chevron and I *daven*, 'Help me, *Hashem*, how You helped *Avraham Avinu!*' I remind myself that not everyone accepted *Avraham Avinu*. I encourage myself by thinking, *Avraham did what I had to do.* It takes boldness and courage. It takes will and desire.

"Something I learned when my husband and I read *The Garden of Emuna* [by Rabbi Arush] at the very beginning of our journey, before converting, was that every smile or warm greeting that a person gives someone else, and every frown, is from *Hashem*. And that every smile that *I* give to someone, and every frown I give, *that's* from *Hashem*.

"So if someone calls another person a name or rejects him, *gam zu l'tovah.*

"In the process of converting, my sister and I were told by Rabbi Arush, 'Don't confuse Jews with the Torah. If Jews are not behaving the right way, if you see someone with *peyos* or with a long skirt, and they're not behaving correctly, don't get their *middos* mixed up with Torah. Everyone has a *yetzer hara*. And unfortunately, some people are not aware.

"There are things that could make a new convert ask, *Who is Hashem? Why did I do this? How did I do this?*

"It's why I like to keep my eyes on *Hashem*…why I hold on to *Hashem*…because the halachah of the Torah is *emes*. I tell my kids: Not everyone dresses the same, not everyone eats the same *hechsher*. Don't expect them to look like you or think like you. That doesn't mean we're not going to love the other Jew. You have to make it your business to love every Jew, *no matter what*. I'm talking specifically about Jews, rather than speaking more generally about 'human beings,' because that's what we are: Jews. We are people who are naturally set apart. When it comes to people who are seemingly not religious, you see it.

"There's always something special about the Jewish People.

"What was it that Avraham did that was different from anything before him? He brought in *Hashem*. Connecting with *Hashem* is our purpose here. It's in a person's relationship with *Hashem* that he finds meaning in life.

"I like telling my children the famous story about Avraham's father, who was an idol-maker. One day his father told Avraham to guard the idols, and Avraham destroyed them instead, all except one. And in that idol's hand Avraham placed a big stick. When his father came back and was so distraught to find the idols destroyed, Avraham blamed it on the idol with the stick. 'But he's not alive!' cried Avraham's father. 'He's not real!'

"Back when my husband first spoke to me about paganism, I was unaware. I had no idea what paganism was. I remember how with our families we had to *ease* our way out, very gently. Xmas was one of the first things, and after Xmas, Easter. I remember how my sister and I were told by a relative during that period that she and I were responsible for tearing the family apart.

"It was a tough time. I thank G-d it's over, and that we are where we are. Our children have never been exposed to the non-Jewish holidays or lifestyle. From the day my daughter was born, we have not observed any part of it, *baruch Hashem*." Adina smiles her soft smile.

I ASK HOW her daughter is doing.

There's a long silence. And then:

"It's hurtful. I tell my daughter, 'Be happy, *Hashem* created the world for you. The trees, all of nature, etc., etc. It doesn't matter what other people may say and what other people may think. What matters is that *Hashem* loves you so much that He created the world for you.'

"The truth is, throughout this whole process of her not being accepted, I discovered that there are many kids who are not being accepted in schools. In my daughter's case, it could be her skin color. Or that she's a *ger*.

"In the case of other children who aren't accepted, maybe the father wears a blue shirt, or he works instead of learns. It could be that one parent is white and the other black. For whatever reason, the school administration decides: *This is not the kind of child we want in our school.*"

I'm sitting at the table listening to Adina, thinking: their daughter is such a young, innocent child, and so shy. And *tzanua*, like her mother.

Adina is saying, "I believe it's the school's own reputation that is being considered, more than the child. The school is truly more important to them, though they would find that too hard to say. And think about it. The school thinks they're rejecting one child. But they're affecting an unknown number of children in the next generation, and the generations that follow.

"My daughter has asked me, at times—at times when she's in tears—'Why aren't I in school?' She doesn't understand.

"You have to know, throughout this whole journey, I've found close friends I'm still in touch with. Friends…who've lost sleep on our account. I wasn't alone."

I ask Adina if she has seen the video of the *Gadol Hador*, Rav Aharon Leib Shteinman, *zt"l*, in which two *chareidi* fathers are hoping that the *rav* will reverse his own earlier *p'sak halachah*, in which the *rav* had supported a certain couple's desire to register their children in a particular school. The two fathers in the video, on the other hand, are seeking the *rav's* suppport for the school's rejection of the two children in question, maintaining that the applicants were not the right "fit" for the school, and they ask rhetorically if it's the school's responsibility to place the children. Is the *rav* truly in favor, they ask, of forcing the school to grant admission?

"Do I have a choice?" responds Rav Shteinman, his voice rising. "Where do you want them to go? To the moon?!"

The two fathers chuckle amiably, and Rav Shteinman grants them a very faint, very sad-looking smile. The conversation goes on and on.

One of the fathers declares, "But he [the father who is insisting on applying to this particular school] is *meshuga!*"

"**You** want that school, too," counters Rav Shteinman. "Are **you** *meshuga*?"

At last Rav Shteinman pounds with his fist three times on his desk, his voice rising with each bang of his fist: "*Gaivah!*

"*Gaivah!*

"*Gaivah!*"

Adina says no, she has not seen that video. The Black family doesn't have Internet in their home. They decided years ago to protect their children almost completely from exposure to, and knowledge of, the digital world, including awareness of their own father's celebrity.

Is their eldest daughter proud of their father? I ask. My son-in-law told me once that Nissim Black can't walk through Geulah or even Meah Shearim or any other neighborhood in Israel without being besieged by people who want to take selfies with him. He's famous. And that Nissim is always patient, and stops for people with utmost kindness.

"You can ask her yourself," Adina replies. The tutor has just left. And the daughter—whom you, the reader, may have noticed remains unnamed here, in honor of her privacy—is cooking something in the kitchen. Her mother calls her over and encourages me to ask my question again.

"Do you feel proud of your father? When you're in the street and people crowd around him and want to take pictures with him?"

She gives a shy little shrug of one shoulder. "I don't know."

I wait a moment. She's thinking.

And at last she says, just above a whisper, "He's my father."

I'VE STAYED LONGER than the anticipated hour, but before leaving I ask Adina if there's anything else she'd like to say. She considers this, then says:

"My goal is to please *Hashem*, that's what matters.

"There are neighbors who are not so nice. I want to take the good, and teach my children to take the good." Adina is smiling. "To leave the bad and take the good.

I point out that it sounds like the halachah of *borer*, and she turns her head toward the kitchen, gesturing to the row of windows that look out into other windows, all the shadowy reflections reflecting reflections within reflections.

"I have a neighbor," says Adina. "She is a blessing. I've learned so much from her, and she doesn't know it. We don't speak the same language. She speaks Hebrew, I speak English. So that's it—we say hello to each other. But she has done so much for me. She doesn't know it, but she has. When we meet up with each other anywhere, she always asks with such a beautiful smile, '*Mah shlomech?* How are you? *Shalom! Boker tov!* Hello!'

"I have been learning from that smile.

"You know, I always wondered, *How can I get everything done?* There is so much to do all week, and then on Thursday, and Erev Shabbos. On Motzaei Shabbos I used to be so tired, I'd just leave everything for Sunday and go to sleep after putting the children to bed.

"Then I started to notice my neighbor through the windows on Motzaei Shabbos, staying up late, cleaning up the house all by herself, and smiling to herself as she worked! That's when I saw how it's possible. It was a light-bulb moment: *I love a clean home. So I'm going to do that, too.* So I did. I started doing what she does, cleaning up on Motzaei Shabbos. And now, when the children wake up every Sunday morning, the whole house is clean and ready for everyone, for the new week.

"My neighbor is beautiful, inside and out. She has done so much for me, without knowing it. Her children are also very sweet and loving people.

"The goal is to live a life that pleases *Hashem*. If we focus on our own *avodah*, we won't be as concerned if our neighbor does something wrong. And we won't be interested in putting other people down.

"I want my children to know that they will encounter hardship in life. In every person's life, there are certain things along the way that stick out more than others. I think of them as peekaboo moments. Those moments teach you something you shouldn't forget.

"I don't want to ever lose the love, the sensitivity, the desire, the will...the passion to serve *Hashem*. And that's what I want to give over to my children. Because I want each of them to have a close relationship with Him. That's the purpose of life."

THINGS THAT STAYED

Every once in a while during my four years of high school, something they were teaching in English class would get my attention. And although as a teenager I would have found this hard to believe, whatever made enough of an impression to penetrate the dreamy ozone layer that protected me from the outer world during adolescence would remain with me for the rest of my life; thoughts and ideas that were buried alive in my brain.

I can count on two hands those rare things that struck a chord, and like a tuning fork, would go on reverberating through the decades their low, nearly inaudible hum. Among these were two poems by Robert Frost. The first (whose title I don't recall, but I think it began with "R") told of a man on his front porch, looking down at the sea.

> Summer was past and day was past/Somber clouds in the west were massed.
> What would it take my standing there for/Looking down hill to a frothy shore?
> Leaves got up in a coil and hissed/Blindly struck at my knee and missed.
> Something told me my secret must be known...Word had somehow
>   gotten abroad.
> Word I was in my life alone/Word I had no one left but G-d.

As you might know, that's not an entirely accurate quote. I could get up out of my chair right now and look in the bookcase for my old, long-unopened copy of Frost, or—if that's more physical exercise than I care to indulge in at the moment—could Google "Summer was past and day was past." But that would short-circuit the slow, pleasurably frustrating, nostalgic process of feeling my way along the large, echoing seashell of imperfect memory, in search of the missing words.

The other Frost poem began approximately as follows:

> Tree at my window, window tree/My sash is lowered when night comes on
> But let there never be curtain drawn/Between you and me.
> Vague dream-head lifted up out of the ground/And thing next most
>   diffuse to sound,
> Not all your light tongues talking aloud/Could be profound.
> But tree, I've seen you taken and tossed/And if you have seen me while I slept
> You've seen me taken, and swept/And all but lost.

In the forty years since I first read those lines, in the various homes where I have lived, there has not been a tree out a window that didn't acquire more beauty in my eyes, and that I didn't love more, on account of that poem.

Then there was a poem by H.D. (my ninth-grade English teacher told us that the poet's real name was Hilda Doolittle), which I've tried so many times to find again, without success, that I wonder if I really read it. One day, years later in Los Angeles, at my mother's bedside, the poem's lines came to mind, springing up unbidden and familiar, and helped me to navigate the incomprehensible event I was then witnessing, when with my own eyes I saw my mother traveling, in a fraction of a second, from life to death.

> Like a light out of our hearts
> Like a bird out of our hands
> You are gone.

Then there was:

> In the middle of my life
> I found myself in a dark wood.

It's understandable that these opening lines of Dante's "Inferno" would have struck a chord for a girl who felt as if she inhabited a dark, inscrutable world, but "the middle of my life"? How unimaginably far off "the middle of my life" then seemed! Middle age was as much a fairy tale as *Jack and the Beanstalk*, as inconceivable as nuclear war, as surreal as the idea of some future time called "the twenty-first century."

Which brings me to *lacrimae rerum*, the one and only detail I retained from Mr. St. Clair's second-year Latin class (for which he was kind enough to give me a C instead of an F). *Lacrimae rerum* means "the tears of things," and it opened a window of understanding for me in a world where I felt like the only teenager around who wasn't cheering along with the cheerleaders. (The cheerleaders' hardships would only become known to me in conversations at a high school reunion forty years later.) *Lacrimae rerum* served as a two-word acknowledgment, a validation, of the darkness where I wandered: a wandering, wondering Jew.

I thought poetry would save me, and it did, back then. It intimated and confirmed my inborn instinct, natural to all human beings, that there's another, enduring reality more real than the one we see with our eyes. Poetry served as a life jacket that kept me afloat until my real ship came in a few years later, to rescue me from a godless world.

GROWING WITH
MY GRANDCHILDREN

O ne summer night in Jerusalem, the parenting teacher Miriam Levi
advised the young mothers in her "Discipline with Love" class to
start keeping daily journals. The journals would serve as a record, she said,
of our progress and improvement (*or lack thereof,* I thought) while taking
the course.

The next morning after the kids left for school, I located a pen and an old
spiral notebook, got myself a cup of coffee, and cleared off a place at the
kitchen table.

On the first line, at the top of the page, I wrote "June 22, 1986."

I recall those moments: ignoring the sink full of breakfast dishes and the
pile of dirty laundry, gazing out the window at the unpopulated hills of
Ramot and wondering what to write, unaware that this would be a turning
point in my life. My inner ear knew the tone I wanted: the wryly ironic
voice of the put-upon mommy, exhausted but loving, profoundly serious
about child-raising yet cutely self-deprecating. I imagined how the women
in the class would laugh. They'd identify.

But...what was there to say? Nothing special was going on. Dr. Levi's ads
had appealed to me—I knew honing my disciplinary skills was important,
that's why I'd signed up—but I was a passionately devoted mother already.

Finally, for starters, I settled on the bedtime hour—probably as enter-
taining a subject as any—and set about recounting our typical marathon
from the night before.

I can remember what happened: how putting the familiar scene into
words brought back the details, and how as more details resurfaced, the

more I recalled; how as the dialogue filled out and my view expanded, I caught sight of myself through my children's eyes, and the story unfolding surprisingly on the page before me, in my own handwriting, began making me uneasy.

The lighthearted writing exercise, designed to amuse, was morphing into...something else.

How was I talking to my children? It frightened me that if not for putting pen to paper, I wouldn't have given yesterday's bedtime a second thought. Suddenly I was struck by something Miriam Levi had said in the workshop: *A mother's ordinary impatience and routine words of anger, arising from simple low frustration tolerance, can make her child feel "low."*

So that's how my diary-keeping began, and it did in fact serve as my witness, not only for the duration of the workshop but for the three years that followed. All the little victories and secret failures, the endless highs and lows of child-raising, which normally would have been forgotten by the time I dropped into bed each night, were now being set down in black and white. It was like having another mother right there in the house with me, looking over my shoulder. A judgmental and demanding critic—after all, they were her children, too—yet an understanding listener, as well. And someone who, by the time my diary came to a close, had grown into the trustworthy advisor I'd always wanted.

As Miriam Levi anticipated, the obligation to truthfully report on my own behavior had brought about changes in the reality I was describing.

Thirty-three years have passed since my last entry in that journal, when our eldest was eight. The future—which back then seemed impossibly far-off—is now. The children are grown. The children have children.

THE CHALLENGES THAT CONFRONT me now are so different from what they were back then. Then, there was always too little of two things: sleep and time. These days, there's plenty of both. Back then, life kept me on my toes. Now, it often finds me on a chair. Then, motherhood pushed me relentlessly to go beyond my nature, my physical limits, my ego; small people were always breaking through my borders, and I could find my identity in their absolute need of me. Spiritually speaking, motherhood was an involuntary self-development program that came with a built-in motivational coach—the famous maternal instinct—urging me to work on my bad habits and negative traits, for my children's sake. I had to be present nonstop, physically and emotionally, and there was no such thing as escape.

Being a good grandmother, on the other hand—so different from being a mother!—is, above all, about simply spending time.

Now there's escape, and relaxation, and slipping mindlessly downhill. Nowadays I have to consciously impose on myself that which motherhood once provided spontaneously: a demanding daily structure, as if I myself were a dawdling child in need of discipline with love.

At this stage, and age, the greatest danger is wasting time, failing to properly treasure time, of which less and less remains. When we're young, our growth comes about by way of everything we increasingly acquire on the way up, step-by-step from babyhood on: new skills, new physical and mental capabilities, more and more as years go by. We reach the mountain-top, spend whatever amount of time we're granted up there, then set off on what our physical selves experience as a descent. Now our growth comes about in precisely the opposite fashion. As our skills, capabilities, and talents...our energy, vigor, and sometimes even our infinitely precious, hard-won intellectual understanding...fall by the wayside, one after the other, we have to get to know and accept the physically limited human beings we're becoming. But the more of our powers we have to leave behind, the larger our spiritual selves can become. When we're young, we grow by way of what we gain; when we're old, by what we lose.

Preserving daily events with words, day after day, in all their apparent incompleteness and incoherence, is conducive to observing fragments of life that would otherwise fly past unnoticed. To look over your own shoulder, pen in hand, heightens your awareness of time. To write about them is to actualize for yourself the Torah principle that all events are significant, and meaningful—if not yet in your own eyes, then in G-d's.

There is no moment in anyone's life when "nothing special's going on."

THE STORY OF A STORY

O nce upon a time in the 1990s, I brought a *she'eilah* to Rabbi Nachman Bulman in his Maalot Dafna home. "Do you think," I asked apprehensively, placing shyly before him a small pile of typewritten pages, "that it would be all right to publish this?"

Rabbi Bulman sat down to read, I sat down to worry, and as the minutes ticked by, Rebbetzin Shaindel Bulman filled and refilled our teacups, replenishing the cookies as I finished them off.

It was the Rebbetzin who had suggested that her husband could advise me on a writing-related matter, not only in his capacity as a renowned Talmudic scholar and prolific author, but as an erudite connoisseur of English literature. I'd been working, on and off for years, on an autobiographical story: writing and rewriting, revising and polishing, and sharing it, as I went along, with the various individuals represented therein, to get each person's ongoing approval and go-ahead. Those twenty or thirty pages were the nucleus around which the rest of my life circled, and I felt, without realizing it, as if succeeding in getting it published would secure my place in the shifting sands of time, forever...as if, in a way, I would never die.

A *baalas teshuvah* for two decades, I still felt secretly like a misfit in Orthodox society. My first book—the diary I had kept as a mother of young children—had been published a few years previously by an Orthodox publisher but had been rejected by the company's usual distributor. The latter didn't wish to take on a book that was likely to incur the *frum* public's opprobrium, and possibly rabbinical censure: the Orthodox world wasn't ready, in the distributor's opinion, for such a personal first-person account, with its descriptions of a *chareidi* mother's parenting failures, and her struggle with doubts and insufficient *emunah*, as evidenced, for example, by her fear of having children "too close together, one after the other."

I took secret, fervent pride, that afternoon, in the fact that the Rebbetzin—who was the real McCoy, the genuine article, a true-blue, dyed-in-the-wool, genuine FFB with *yichus* and reputation in spades—had recently joined my first writing group.

The unpublished story I'd brought here for inspection was for sure—as the saying goes—"too *frum* for the *frei* and too *frei* for the *frum*." I wasn't hopeful.

RABBI BULMAN GLANCED at the clock. Almost an hour had passed.

He took off his spectacles, rubbed his eyes, and set down the stack of pages upon the dining room table. "Mrs. Shapiro," he intoned, turning to face me.

Within me I cringed.

"Not only would it be all *right* for you to publish it..." The earth paused on its axis. "...You have a *responsibility* to publish it."

I didn't dare believe what I'd heard. *OK, what's the catch?* "Rabbi Bulman," I said, "what do you mean?"

"It's a responsibility. What the *frum* world needs is its own genuine literature."

I was incredulous.

I was thrilled.

Suddenly, I could be transparent. *To be me was good.* "Rabbi Bulman..." A long-suppressed question had popped up abruptly from the depths, unbidden: "I don't know where I belong in the *frum* world."

Without hesitation, then came the words that would illumine for me the path of my life, from that moment on:

"You belong with your typewriter."

A decade went by. One day, having completed the autobiographical story, and having received two rejection letters (one of which explained that "the story's religious content won't resonate with our audience"), a letter of acceptance arrived, from a big American magazine! My heart soared, I was on top of the world. It even said, unbelievably, that payment would be such-and-such an amount per word!

Proudly, with exultation, I delivered the news to all those who were portrayed in the story, and to several other individuals whose respect I hungered for; to these, I affected a more casual air.

Late that night, the phone rang. The person on the other end was someone whom I love, and she sounded distraught. "Sarah, I'm sorry, but I can't give permission to publish that story."

A rush of bitter anger had surged up in an instant, like a rocket, from those aforementioned depths. "Why didn't you tell me this before? I asked you before, and you always said yes."

"I know, but I just didn't realize how I'd feel, until today, when you said it's going to be published. I'm a very private person. You're a writer, so I know it's different for you, but for me, I'd be so embarrassed."

I couldn't call Rabbi Bulman about these changed circumstances. He had died. I called Rabbi Zelig Pliskin, author of *Guard Your Tongue*, the authoritative English-language volume about *shemiras halashon*. Rabbi Pliskin listened carefully to what had happened, the whole long *megillah*. He empathized totally with my dismay, my disappointment, my devastation, and said I had to withdraw the manuscript.

What?

There's no choice, said Rabbi Pliskin.

But...

You can't embarrass someone in public.

But she's the only one. No one else is emba—

You have no choice.

But Rabbi Pliskin...

You have no choice.

BACK THEN, WHEN ALL of this took place, I experienced giving up that story as a sacrifice, a *kapparah*. In fact, however, as I eventually started noticing that I was still alive (albeit with less *gaivah* than would have otherwise been mine), I stopped bemoaning the fact that that particular piece of genuine literature would have to enjoy a peaceful afterlife in my file cabinet. As a result, there is—in a small corner of my *neshamah*, no matter what else happens—a bright little spot of happiness that doesn't get extinguished by other mistakes.

As the saying goes, you can't go wrong by doing right. The halachah of *shemiras halashon* protected me from hurting someone I love with the written word, an irrevocable injury that once inflicted, can't—unlike a manuscript—be withdrawn.

In one of his long-ago Thursday night talks in Flatbush, Rabbi Avigdor Miller spoke of the responsibility we each have to write down the events of our lives, so as not to forget *Hashem*'s myriad kindnesses; to keep a written record for ourselves of the unique stations each one of us, like our forebears, passes through on our journey through the *midbar*.

Those twenty or thirty autobiographical pages, that took so many years to compose, were eventually thrown out, to make room in my filing cabinet for other things. For it was the act of writing, and then of tearing them up, that had preserved, for me alone, the nucleus around which all the rest of my life could circle.

THE ALPHABET OF HAPPINESS

The story of my life
Syllable by syllable
From the hospital:
At first I said *Oy vey* I'm going to die!
Then
Oy
I'm going to live

Marcie Alter

The first time I stepped foot into Marcie's world, it was like finding myself in the classic nightmare of paralysis: the dreamer needs urgently to escape but suddenly can't move and can't make a sound.

It was a friend of my daughter who had suggested the visit—she thought this was someone I'd like to know, which turned out to be an understatement—but *bikur cholim* in a Catholic hospice...it wasn't in my comfort zone. (Walking by sometimes on my way to the Kotel, I'd been surprised to see *frum* women going in through the cathedral-like entrance, and wondered whom they could possibly be visiting. Little did I know that half the patients in there are Jewish.)

By the time I finally passed under that archway myself, months had gone by.

A nun directed me to Room 25. Averting my eyes from the curled-up human form on the bed to my right—an ancient-looking woman of indeterminate age, her dark hole of a mouth fallen open—I pulled up a chair by the bed in the opposite corner, alongside another visitor. Emuna Witt, a well-known disciple of Rabbi Shlomo Carlebach, was reading aloud the morning *berachos*, to which the young woman who lay next to her, flat on her back, attached to various tubes and medical paraphernalia, was silently giving slight nods to signal amen.

So this was Marcie Alter. She greeted me with her eyes.

A bunch of stuffed animals lay in a heap at the foot of her bed. Taped up all around the wall were drawings and greetings from friends and family, handwritten quotations from Torah, and photographs of smiling faces.

Little by little in the coming weeks, by pointing to letters of the alphabet, Marcie would answer my questions about the events that had brought her here. A single mother and graphic artist in her thirties, she had made aliyah in 2003. In 2006, she was left paralyzed from the neck down after failed surgery for a brain aneurysm. Although her body is inert and immobile, she is fully conscious and "herself," mentally and emotionally. She retains slight spastic-looking movement in her forearms and four of her fingers, and can shake and nod her head. Aside from this (and I explicitly mention the following because even in her presence, it takes visitors a while to grasp the extent of her disability) she is unable to eat, drink, speak, move her legs or feet, or use her hands. For example, she can't hold a book or turn a page, or use a writing utensil. If she has an itch, she can't scratch it (nor tell anyone else to do so). If, when being pushed in her wheelchair, one of her feet happens to fall out of position and drag on the ground as the chair moves forward, she can't lift it. When her scarf slips down over her eyes, she can't adjust it. She breathes through a surgically created hole in her throat; when the opening gets clogged, she must wait for someone to clear away the mucous. Since her vocal chords and facial muscles are included in the general paralysis, she can't cry, or laugh.

Her lips sometimes press together and lengthen slightly; those who know her recognize that at these moments, she's smiling.

It must have been about twenty years ago that *The Jerusalem Post* carried a report on survivors of an earthquake in Armenia. Pinned under the ruins of his house in total darkness, inaudible to rescuers, one man couldn't move, if I recall correctly, for ten days. A shattered water pipe happened to be leaking drops of water onto his face, some of which he was able to catch by leaving his mouth open, which saved his life. I remember how trying momentarily to imagine myself in such a situation almost made me want to scream, while here before me was a fully sentient person who for four years had been silent, pinned down inside the ruins of her body.

Later that morning, Emuna introduced me to the handmade alphabet board that Marcie uses to converse. As someone holds the rectangular piece of cardboard firmly before her, she spells out words by pointing in her distinctively shaky manner to the letters, one by one. The ABCs are written out in capitals, with black magic marker, and below them appear the numbers from zero to ten. Below that are the words MOM, BEN, BROTHER, THE, AND, END (for end of word), and THANK YOU.

Two of the photos on the wall caught my attention—one of a curly-haired, laughing young man, and the other, of a woman in her twenties, in a striped maternity dress, gazing clear-eyed and steadfast into the camera. "Is that your son?" I asked her. Marcie nodded, indicated that she wanted the alphabet board, and pointed to "BEN." "And that one? In the striped dress...? Is that...?"

She nodded emphatically.

"You?"

Her eyes smiled.

To sit there next to Marcie was to suddenly confront my own life's fabulous embarrassment of riches, and grand panoply of complaints, and to feel obscenely undeserving of my own good fortune.

A FEW MONTHS WENT BY, and it was the fourth night of Chanukah. For various reasons I was home alone, and the loneliness of lighting the candles by myself was creeping up on me. I prepared the menorah lackadaisically, catching sight of my dark reflection in the glass of the window as the four flames flickered. In all the happy-looking windows of the building across from me, rows of little yellow lights were burning.

When the candles went out after half an hour, my heart was cast abruptly adrift. What should I do with the long winter evening ahead of me, out on that frightening, empty sea?

THE LIGHTS ALONG the second-floor hallways of the hospice were already dimmed for the night when I arrived. I'd never been here at night before, and, as usual, tried not to glance intrusively into the rooms as I walked by fast on my way to Marcie's room.

At the door, I was unsure if she was still awake. It was only 8:00, but here, too, the overhead lights had been turned off. I took a few steps inside. In the semi-darkness she lifted a forearm and waved it jerkily up and down.

I sat down by the bed and told her how I was doing—not great—and then, as usual when telling her about any of my own difficulties in life, felt ridiculously, reprehensibly petty and spoiled. "Marcie, you know, sometimes when I'm walking down the street I think to myself, what would Marcie feel if she were doing this, and for a few moments, I exult in being able to walk, and talk, and move. I exult intensely. But, of course, my appreciation doesn't last long, and soon I'm taking it all for granted again. I know that shouldn't surprise me, but I keep expecting that having seen some of what you go through every hour—because it's so much more difficult, and qualitatively different from anything in my own life—that it will change my perspective once and for all and I'll just be grateful from then on. But that's not what happens. I still suffer over whatever I suffer. Even though I realize it's so slight in the grand scheme of things."

She gestured toward the alphabet board, and I held it for her as she spelled out: *everyone has his pekele*

"Don't you feel annoyed at people, that they don't appreciate what they have?"

She shook her head, no. *Me too*

I didn't understand.

Wish I appreciated more

"You mean before you got ill?"

She nodded.

"How do you get through the day, Marcie. You must go through a lot of—you know that phrase?—'long dark night of the soul.' Right?"

A wry expression in her eyes said, "You got it." She pointed again to the letters. *Used to pray to die in my sleep*

"You used to? You mean you don't anymore?"

She shook her head no.

"What changed?"

She rolled her eyes upward and lifted a forearm, as if to say, who knows? Then she spelled: *Today one of my lows a new nurse*

"She didn't know how to do things?"

It hurt I was angry

"Marcie, I just can't imagine such a thing. And things like that must happen all the time. When I first met you, I thought you must be different from other people, and that accounted for your ability to bear it."

She narrowed her eyes in question, not sure what I was getting at.

"Now I know you're just like all of us. So what I want to know is, really, how you manage."

I try not to think about what I am missing

These words struck me as if she'd just tossed an enormous key my way. All I had to do now, supposedly, was turn the key. But where was the lock, or even the door? "You don't think about what you're missing...that's amazing. That's what people can't *stop* thinking about. But you're missing...everything, at least the way most of us would see it. So what do you think about? A stupid question, I know, but really, what do you think about?"

She jerkily lifted a forearm, pointing upward.

"*Hashem?*"

She nodded.

"You know, my son-in-law told me that when you visit someone in a hospital, the halachah is not to stand higher than the person's head, because the Shechinah (Divine Presence) is over the bed of a sick person."

I feel it

"You do, Marcie, really?"

I don't feel alone

On the table at the foot of Marcie's bed, there was a menorah, unlit. "Marcie, shall I light the Chanukah lights?"

She nodded, so I got a match from the nurses' office. For a while we watched the candles together, and in some inner corner of my mind, a shy little thought flickered: *This is happiness.*

AVNER SAVORAY, AN ELECTRICAL ENGINEER, married Lea Dalia Adler in 1963. "In 1997," Avner told me recently on the phone from his home in Herzliya, "Dalia experienced her first symptoms. We were in a professor's office when she received her diagnosis—Lou Gehrig's disease. We were sitting side by side, and we turned and looked into each other's eyes. And in unison we both said, 'Life must go on.'"

"In unison?" I asked.

"In unison. It was our spontaneous reaction. And believe me, life went on. We traveled around the world...to New England, Norway, South Africa, Alaska. In spite of the fact that she was in a wheelchair, she enjoyed it. We both did. She was brave. She accepted it.

"When a person becomes PALS—paralyzed with ALS—he cannot move, he cannot do anything except for look and listen. The brain, though, continues to work as before, even better."

I asked in what way it works better.

Avner replied: "In general, whenever a person loses one of his abilities or senses, the other abilities and senses become better. So with ALS, when all of a person's physical abilities are lost, the afflicted person—remember, he is all the time looking and listening—often becomes much sharper mentally. This is what happened to my wife. But such people cannot communicate by talking, and we have to give them all the benefits of technology to continue with their lives. One of the main tools for this is what is called a 'head mouse,' a device that enables a person to operate the computer cursor by moving the head.

"ALS is a progressive disease. When Dalia got to the point of no longer being able to talk, the head mouse had not yet been invented. And by the time it was invented, she could no longer move her head. So we communicated only with her eyes. I would show her the *aleph-beis*, pointing to the letters one by one. When I reached the letter she wanted, she would blink her eyes. Believe me, it took us ages to complete one sentence. For five years we had such conversations, and believe me, they were long conversations, many of them in the middle of the night.

"I installed a TV camera and a transmitter in front of her bed, to monitor her face in every room of the house, even the bathroom. With a small TV receiver, I could see her from wherever I was, if her facial expression changed, or if she moved her eyes.

"I lived with her like this for eight years. I didn't send her to any hospital, of course. All the treatment was done at home.

"My wife became ill when she was fifty-three years old, and she passed away when she was sixty-two. She passed away in her own bed. Soon afterward I decided to continue to support all the ALS people in Israel."

"You make no profit from your work with patients…"

"Of course not, I do it for my wife, in memory of her. I feel good to be able to help people in this situation. It is my occupational therapy. There are other people, like Marcie, who are in this condition because of an accident, or some medical mishap. Such people can continue using the head mouse all their lives. I don't have numbers, but many of them are Israeli soldiers, young and old, who have been paralyzed in combat. So I import the devices and provide them to all those who need it. From 2 a.m. to 4 a.m., I am sleeping; the rest of the time they can reach me. They cannot just be presented with the equipment, of course. I train the person in its use and give him the technical and operational support. In the United

States, the brand name of the head mouse is 'SmartNav.' It's a wonderful invention.

"There are about five hundred PALS throughout Israel. The number remains more or less stable because as we lose a certain number, just about the same number of people are entering the disease. The most common form of the disease is known as 'sporadic ALS.' It may affect anyone at any time."

I asked Avner if the disease ran in Dalia's family.

"No, thank G-d."

"When you say, 'thank G-d,' do you—"

"No, no, that is just an expression. It means nothing. I am not religious at all. Is Marcie Alter religious?"

"Yes."

"And you?"

"Yes."

"Well, I have seen through the years that there are two ways of looking at it, when a person falls ill. He can say, 'G-d help me now to accept it,' or 'For G-d's sake, why did He do this?' I never asked Dalia about G-d, but I know what she would say. I do not want to offend you. But if you wish to know, when I was at the cemetery before she was brought to her grave, I said that I opened an account with G-d. He didn't have to take her. What for? She was so good, really a good person.

"We loved each other very much. We lived together for forty-two years. I miss her."

MY DAUGHTER, a special education principal, told Yedidya Levine, one of her colleagues, that a mute and paralyzed woman in the French Hospital didn't have a computer communication device. Yedidya consulted Debbie Ben-Tal, a speech therapist at Yad Sarah, who came to the hospice to do an evaluation of Marcie's case, then consulted Avner Savoray, who traveled from Herzliya to deliver the head mouse and connect it to a laptop, which had been donated by Rebbetzin Devorah Green of the Old City.

Avner spent an inordinate number of hours at Marcie's bedside, assessing her situation and testing the device, then returned to Herzliya to create and refine a program designed uniquely for her. He then traveled back to Jerusalem to teach her how to use it.

Rebbetzin Tziporah Heller and Ruth Shlossman, among others, raised funds to buy the head mouse, pay for the speech therapists' evaluations, and pay for the creation and installation by Yossi Blum, a computer expert, of a supplementary program known as a "grid."

After much practice and a great deal of trial and error (her professional background in computer graphics serves her well), Marcie has become proficient in using the head mouse. While she still uses the alphabet board for conversation, she can now write, as well, by "clicking on" the alphabet on the computer screen. A little round silver sticker, stuck onto her forehead above the bridge of her nose, activates the cursor as she moves her head from side to side. She writes while in her usual position, lying flat on her back, head slightly raised on the pillow.

Marcie is now in touch with her family and friends by e-mail, and she is also writing about her life, past and present:

BETTER THAN GOOD FRUIT ANYWHERE ELSE, BY MARCIE ALTER

I first heard it somewhere at the age of twenty-eight, the line people say in twelve-step programs. The saying goes: "Even my worst days clean and sober were better than my best days using drugs and drinking." I filed the saying away because it was a good and powerful saying, but didn't suspect that one day those words would resonate with me personally, echoing in a very different context.

The summer of my sixteenth birthday, my mom sent me on a tour of Israel with the Jewish Community Center, among kids my own age and background. That meant mostly Reform or unaffiliated with a smattering of Conservative kids, the forerunner of the Birthright trips of today. I remember standing at the Kotel and looking up to the clear blue sky and knowing that G-d exists. I knew with complete faith that G-d was watching over me. From that moment on, I never had a doubt. I maybe didn't do what I was supposed to do, or say, but from that moment on, I believed in the G-d of my fathers.

When I finally made aliyah at the age of thirty-eight, the question was not, "Why did you make aliyah?" but rather, "What took you so long?" I finally understood on a gut level that Israel was qualitatively different. What had taken me so long was that I had forgotten about the dream. And I didn't want to take Ben away from his grandparents. So I waited until he could decide for himself.

I was religiously observant and living on a kibbutz when I noticed how much sweeter the fruit tasted than in America. In America the fruit often looked pretty, but it tasted like Styrofoam compared to the sweet and juicy fruit that was served daily from the cool, air-conditioned dining room of Sde Eliyahu, a religious kibbutz. The kibbutz suited me just fine. I was finally getting it right. Mostly the little things made a big difference: be on time, never say no, get to know my adoptive family, and try to speak the language. When I looked around to make friends, I found kibbutzniks.

After being a single mom in America for eighteen years and hence on duty twenty-four hours a day (my son was now in yeshiva in America), kibbutz life with three hot meals per day, air-conditioning, and no bills was like a walk in the park. I was delighted by everything. Lunch was the best; a fellow ulpanist had aptly said, "It's all about the lunch." And that delicious fruit...grapes the size of plums...melon that melted in the mouth...even the bad fruit was good.

I had left my aging mother in America, knowing that my brother would provide good care, and having discussed the subject with him. Nevertheless, I was drawn to the elderly. I had a secret hope that one day my mom would want to travel to Israel, and would resettle on a kibbutz with me.

I told the powers that be that I wanted to work with the kesh-ishim, the elderly, not the zekeinim, the old. My first assignment was as the nighttime aide for an elderly woman who had suffered a stroke. Before bed she often had a snack of pomegranate. It was my job and pleasure to separate the juicy red seeds from the bitter white rind. She then ate the seeds with a spoon, and spit out the tough, internal part, swallowing the juice. Later, I was trimming the vineyards when my Ethiopian coworker took some pomegran-ates from the next field and simply bit in, spitting out the hard parts. I tried, and found it cool and refreshing, in the hot sun. The seemingly bad fruit tasted sweet and good.

When the ulpan ended, I looked for a job on the other religious kibbutzim with a letter of praise from the manager, but no one wanted a single woman, almost forty. So I found an apartment in downtown Jerusalem and took a job as a sales agent in a large telecommunications company—definitely like eating bad fruit. I had worked in America for ten years in graphic design, and never in my most desperate hour would I have considered phone sales. For the privilege of living in Israel I was willing to put up with a bad job.

After a year in the city, I spent three months in the West Bank village of Bat Ayin, learning Torah and drinking goat's milk with chocolate. I arrived there in late spring, just in time to see the purple almond blossoms on the trees in full bloom on the next hilltop.

One day I got a call from Esther, the manager of the Bayit Hakeshatot. There was an elderly woman on the kibbutz named Shulamit in need of full-time care. She was suffering from mild Alzheimer's disease and was in need of a helping hand. Just like that, I had a job and a place to live.

For the following year, it was my privilege to be Shulamit's metapelet. For her eighty-sixth birthday, one of her granddaughters organized everyone to buy trees from the Jewish Agency—and Shulamit had eight-six descendants, though she had lost track of them all. I asked who was who, for both of us. Shulamit was kind and generous, as well as smart, and she became a beloved friend; she would patiently answer me when I asked the same questions about Hebrew again and again. She accepted me like family.

Once a month, the little Yekke shul had a Carlebach Shabbos, and everyone would join in together singing the rhythmic tunes that reminded me of the American Indians.

Then my world fell apart.

I HAD LAST LIVED in my own home just before making aliyah to Israel. It was a very small house—just big enough for me and my son, one cat, and one dog. I had worked hard, and with family help, qualified for the mortgage. But I recall one evening when my son and I had just moved in, that I was standing on the front porch thinking that we were not quite home yet, that planting trees was futile. In my heart, I knew that the house was a temporary investment, that Israel was my home.

My mother's parents had always been a good team. Poppa Kleber made the money, and Nana Kleber distributed it to charity. Dorthea Kleber presided over the sisterhood of her synagogue and helped bring the famous stained-glass windows of Marc Chagall to the Hadassah Hospital of Ein Kerem. I wonder if my grandmother ever imagined that one day, I would seek out the brightly colored synagogue windows as a patient in that hospital.

MY FIRST SYMPTOMS APPEARED almost three years to the day of my aliyah. My regular doctor said it was nothing but a muscle spasm in my back and possible depression. So then I found a chiropractor.

I told him my symptoms. They were: numbness and tingling on my left side, extreme fatigue, and difficulty swallowing. The chiropractor said it was a problem for a neurologist, but when he could find no one to see me the same day, he instructed me to go back to my doctor for an immediate referral.

That evening I treated myself to a steak dinner, which I had trouble swallowing. The next morning, I set out from my friend Devorah's Jerusalem apartment to the same doctor I had visited the day before, confident of a quick resolution and a quick return to work. Yet I knew in my gut that something out of the ordinary was going on. I did not have a vitamin B deficiency, as a doctor in Beit She'an had told me. Nor was there anything wrong with my back. And I was definitely not depressed; in fact, things were going well. I loved my job. I loved my elderly charge as if she were my grandmother. I was earning a decent wage, with all my living expenses taken care of by the kibbutz. I was a little sad about having recently sold my little house in America, but I had money in the bank, and I was paying back my debts. Above all, I was at ease about my son; he was on the derech, and I was proud of him. He had elected not to make aliyah with me and was a boarding student at a small yeshiva in Baltimore. He was also there to cushion the blow to my mother for my absence. Having hugely underestimated my role, I was relieved by his success. Soon, he would have more need of those qualities.

I told my regular doctor what the chiropractor had said. He hemmed and hawed, but I was prepared. After a sharp discussion about loyalty to the insurance provider versus loyalty to the patient, I got a referral to Hadassah Hospital, and there began my whole new way of life.

They told me I had a brain hemorrhage, a cluster of veins that was bleeding into the brain. The doctor called it a cavernous angioma, and on the MRI it looked like a balloon, right in the middle of my brain stem. The doctors were less than forthcoming. I just wanted them to fix me so I could go back to my nice, quiet kibbutz.

Hashem had other plans.

THE IMPLICATIONS THAT my brain was bleeding sunk in slowly. I had always taken my good health for granted, as I had my parents' love. I'd never had any health problems that losing twenty pounds wouldn't cure...except for a bad cigarette habit of about half a pack. In those early days at Ein Kerem, I often limped to the outside smoking area. When that became too difficult, I decided to quit smoking. Why not? I had once quit for five years.

The doctors had adopted a wait-and-see posture but I felt I was getting a little worse every day and pushed them to operate right away. I bought a plane ticket for Ben, got the name of a brain surgeon just one floor up, and hired someone named Karen to keep me company. They transferred me to the neurosurgery ward. My speech had become garbled, as if I had a mouthful of marbles.

The first brain operation was a complete success. Kibbutz people were there when I woke up. And so was Ben. All the bad symptoms had disappeared. I could walk and talk normally, and eat and drink. We laughed at nothing and ate Chinese takeout food. The next day Ben and I walked together to the mall across the street and ate ice cream. The vendor said we were boring because we only ordered chocolate and vanilla. I said happily that brain surgery entitled me to be as boring as I pleased, and a look from Ben said that he agreed. We lingered at the bookstore and then at the health-food store, where I confidently bought goat's milk yogurt and maple syrup.

Ben went back to the US.

After two days, my symptoms started coming back. They began feeding me through a tube in my nose. It hurt, and I pushed to get a stomach tube. I was finding it hard to speak. I went to rehab at Hadassah Mount Scopus for three days. Now there were more symptoms. A CAT scan showed bleeding from the surgery.

On Shabbos, I went down on the Shabbos elevator. The beautiful Chagall windows in the little synagogue were dark overhead. Every inch of the walls is covered with names of donors, engraved testimony from all around the globe that a hospital in Jerusalem is everyone's business. I looked in vain for my grandmother's name, but I felt a sense of unity and gratitude, nevertheless.

The special Shabbos meal was home-cooked and free to all. I saw a little child hooked up to an IV bag, and his dazed young parents. But that wasn't why I choked on my food or why I needed to sit as the Shabbos elevator made its inexorable way, floor by floor, back up to the seventh floor. The doctor had told me that all of the cavernous angioma had been removed, but when a camera was inserted up my femoral vein to my brain, it showed the same cluster. My symptoms had all returned and my brain was still bleeding.

I think I had forgotten G-d. I still prayed daily, but I trusted that I would walk away from the wreck. Until that night, I had trusted that the doctors would simply fix me. Now I began to pray for my life, just that I would live. I felt very close to death, and I was afraid. The doctor scheduled me for a second operation that Sunday.

My second operation was the end of eating regular food. Even though I now had a tube in my stomach, I could still walk to the bathroom by myself, and still thought I would recover quickly. After three days, on Tishah B'Av, I was returned to Ein Kerem. It was the last day I walked. A camera was inserted again in my right femoral artery and up to my brain stem in search of something. The fact that they didn't find whatever they were looking for was declared good news by the doctors. But to me it was bad news because it meant no new repairs. The doctors decided against more surgery unless something catastrophic happened, and as if on cue, I stopped breathing and lost consciousness. They decided on one more surgery.

I awoke from the third surgery packed in ice because I had a high fever. Somewhere along the way, I got a hole in my throat so I could *breathe without a respirator. Ben was back, and my friend Miriam from Pittsburgh had come, which was a great comfort.*

I was transferred to Mount Scopus for rehabilitation. Things get fuzzy from this point. Days and nights ran together, and my injured brain started to deliver nightmarish hallucinations. One of the most persistent was that the hospital could fly. The hospital took off for New York, mortar and bricks, taking patients, doctors, and distinguished guests. I imagined that my father was driving in the old wood-paneled station wagon to come to my rescue. In my lucid moments, I realized that my father of blessed memory had died ten years earlier, and I knew I was having delusions. I was being turned into a robot through my IV lines, the ward was a boat on fire, the male nurse whose nameplate said "Jihad" (not my imagination) was a covert enemy in charge of the hospital. The woman next to me had resumed breathing, which meant that she needed to be rescued. I was in a suitcase that might or might not float. The most frightening was that Ben was in mortal danger. I panicked whenever he didn't answer his phone. The hallucinations often involved my death. I didn't talk much about them because I knew how far-out they sounded, and I didn't want to go to the psychiatric ward. But at the same time, I was convinced of the reality of these strange imaginings. I was terrified.

I had heard of the term, ICU psychosis, and I guessed that it applied to me. In order to calm myself, I thought of how much my parents loved me, and that Hashem, Who can do anything, surely loved me that much. It was around this time that with the help of the kibbutz rabbi and his wife, I changed my name to Emuna Netziah bas Yehudit.

I was on a respirator and I realized that this was serious. Catastrophic. No way out.

AFTER FOUR BRAIN OPERATIONS, *it began to dawn on me that I might be stuck with this level of disability, that there was nothing else to be done. I cursed the resiliency of my body. Ben read to me from Job until I realized that Job was righteous, but I was not. I related to the line from Job that spoke of "those who wait for death and it does not come."*

I spent one year in two rehabs but never regained my functions. I couldn't walk or talk, or use my hands. I couldn't swallow or breathe without a hole in my throat. Nor did a scratch on my right cornea heal. Like eating very bad fruit, indeed.

I felt trapped in this body. People came to visit, both friends and friends of friends, sometimes from far away, making my sickness a little easier to bear, and I begged Hashem to look at their kindness and get nachas from His children. They said prayers, or learned Torah, or played guitar and sang, or told me about their lives and shared their loved ones with me. Even when I was less than polite, they understood. When someone treated me unkindly, I prayed for Hashem to pay attention. I still think this way. But I have become far more accepting, and I no longer wish for death, only that my condition shouldn't get worse, and that Mashiach should come quickly.

The best thing is that I hear Torah, and the message is that Hashem loves me, and my trials are really for my benefit. The same as when I was healthy. And it could always be worse. I'm not on a respirator anymore. I lived my first forty years the way I wanted. And I had three good years in Eretz Yisrael. Hashem must really want me to write. It is all I can do.

I landed in the French Hospital, just outside the Old City. It is truly a special place. Many of the aides come from Europe, particularly Germany, to volunteer. They cheerfully change dirty diapers, wash or shower patients, and answer about a million requests a day. Anything they get by way of compensation is intangible. A smile or a thank you goes a long way. But many of the patients in the fifty-bed hospital are nonresponsive. Even though it is a Christian hospital and administered by nuns, there is a supervising rabbi from the Old City so the Jewish patients have kosher meals.

Yes, there have been some pretty bad days here, but the bad fruit in Israel tastes better than good fruit anywhere else.

AT 8 P.M. on the last Thursday of every month, holidays permitting, Rabbi Zelig Pliskin leads the Happiness Club. Attended by people across the religious spectrum, and held free of charge in Jerusalem's OU Israel Center, the hour is a free-wheeling exploration of the subject, with verbal exercises designed to condition our minds, whenever possible, to choose light over darkness.

As someone who rather likes exploring the meaning of life's darkness, I first attended warily, hoping that whatever was being celebrated on those Thursday nights wasn't equivalent to some sort of ban on tears. The answer came after the class had gone on a few months, when Rabbi Pliskin remarked that really, he would have preferred the name "Joy Club." The word "happiness," he said, sounds more global, and some people find it intimidating, as if it's being demanded of them. "Joy," on the other hand, is associated with a more fleeting experience, a state of mind that can be momentarily accessed by all of us at almost any time, under virtually any conditions. "It's impossible to be happy all the time," Rabbi Pliskin said. "Life on the planet has all kinds of difficulties, and humanity undergoes suffering, and virtually every person experiences sadness and strife. Someone recently complained to me about something he'd read in one of my books, that you have to work at being happy. He didn't like that. But it's the reality. Nonetheless, all of us can access joyful moments, no matter what else is going on in our lives. It's something you can train yourself to do increasingly, until it becomes habitual. All happiness is in the mind, and wherever you go, your amazing brain goes with you. Let's say it together: 'Wherever I go, my amazing brain goes with me.'"

The room resounds with fifty voices, some less tentative than others: "WHEREVER I GO, MY AMAZING BRAIN GOES WITH ME."

"Thank G-d, I can breathe!"

"THANK G-D, I CAN BREATHE!"

"Thank G-d, I'm alive!"

"THANK G-D, I'M ALIVE!"

Rabbi Pliskin has described to us his Happiness Club with the three-year-olds in his niece's *gan*, where he stops by sometimes while walking to his office. "If you get a three-year-old chanting, 'A, joy! B, joy! C, joy!' he doesn't think to himself, 'Now, wait a minute. Maybe Mommy won't give me my favorite lunch when I get home today. I can't be happy now.' A three-year-old is in the present; we all have an inner three-year-old."

Rabbi Pliskin has frequently encouraged us to start other happiness clubs, so I finally put up a sign for one in my neighborhood. But he visits Marcie from time to time, and when I told him about it, he suggested we meet instead at the hospice, with her. "Mentally and emotionally," he said, "Marcie is in a better place than many of us."

—Original Message—
From: Marcie Alter [mailto:marciealter@gmail.com]
Sent: Thursday, October 14, 2010 4:53 PM
To: emuna witt; Jackie Beecham; Orap Kalfa; R. Ilana Loeb; Sara Yoheved Rigler; Sarah Shapiro; Ruth Shlossman; Star Miller; Chaya Malka Abramson; Zehava Rochwerger;
Subject: Dear Happy Heads,

Dear Happy Heads,
We will meet on Yom Rishon at one oclock. Allthe ones are in honor of *Hashem*. Have a good Shabbos.
Love marcie emuna

IT'S SUNDAY AT 1 P.M. We used to meet on Mondays at 4 p.m, but Marcie asked if we could change the time, to remind us that everything comes from *Hashem*. This week, we're talking about things we've done recently that have made us happy.

Orap says that she succeeded in raising enough money to buy good boots for every soldier in her brother's IDF unit. Sara says it has made her happy to be helping an organization that raises funds for needy families. Marcie uses the alphabet board to say: *The nurse hurt me and I wasn't mad at her.*

Ruth relates the amazing happiness she feels at having donated one of her kidneys to someone she doesn't know, who would have died without the transplant. I talk about how happy I was every time I opened the refrigerator on Shabbos, because I'd cleaned it on Friday. Zehava says that Marcie makes people happy by the way she receives what people want to give her, without bitterness. Marcie says that through a window, she saw in the distance an Israeli flag, and felt victorious. Chaya Malka says that she was understanding of her teenage daughter. Star describes her fear the last few days about certain symptoms, and how she has tried to preserve her equanimity, and to trust that whatever is happening to her is for her good.

I try to remember the poem by Emily Dickinson that goes something like this:

> To make a prairie
> It takes one clover, and a bee, and reverie.
> Reverie alone will do
> If bees are few.

I tell them how that poem has always helped me to feel all right about just having the potted plants that fit into our small *mirpeset* (porch), instead of the acres of woods I grew up with in Connecticut.

We talk about which *middah* (character trait) in ourselves is the biggest stumbling block to our happiness. Marcie says that for her, it's anger. For me, it's jealousy. Two others say it's their judgmental inclinations, another that it's her sense of inferiority. Ruth says, "What gets in my way of happiness is fear of unpleasant surprises. Also having to leave Israel for work every few months makes me very unhappy."

Star says, "I stress on all the little details of life. They come to me in the middle of the night and keep me company for hours!"

Marcie spells out: *Maybe we can find some kernel of goodness hiding inside.*

–Original Message–
From: Marcie Alter [mailto:marciealter@gmail.com]
Sent: Sunday, December 05, 2010 11:55 AM
To: emuna witt; Jackie Beecham; Orap Kalfa; R. Ilana Loeb; Sara Yoheved Rigler; Sarah Shapiro; Ruth Shlossman; Star Miller; Chaya Malka Abramson; Zehava Rochwerger;
Subject: dear group, reminder that

dear group, reminder that we meet today at one. If everyone brings asmall snack, we canhave a chanukah party! Jackie will bring drinks.

IT'S BEEN A YEAR since Marcie and I watched the candles together on the fourth night. She's in her wheelchair this afternoon, and today it's just me, Marcie, Jackie, and Shelley. Shelley, who lives down the hall, had a brain tumor some years ago. Though she is physically capable of speaking, she can't find the words.

Jackie has brought drinks, as Marcie suggested, and while passing around a container of chocolate Chanukah *gelt* that Marcie has on her bedside table for guests, Jackie asks, "Marcie, doesn't it bother you to see us eating? I know you want us to, but…"

Marcie squints and looks up at the ceiling, presses her lips together, nods. Her eyes are saying both yes and no. On the alphabet board, she spells out: *I miss food.*

We talk about the foods we love. (Wherever you go, your amazing brain goes with you.) I talk about the Snickers and Milky Ways of my childhood.

Marcie spells out: *ice cream*. Jackie talks about a meal she once had as a child in a restaurant in Switzerland some forty years ago, during a trip to Europe with her parents. The creamy textures and tastes of the various cheeses that the waiter brought to them that day at lunch have lingered on in her mind all her life, an elusive ambrosia.

Marcie asks if someone can read something out loud. I leaf through the old notebook in my purse and find notes from a class given by Rebbetzin Tziporah Heller, dated August 22, 2010.

> *The darkness is real, but there are openings to get out of this darkness. There are many doors. If you are a person of truth, you can find the opening. The highest level is when a person is always thinking of Hashem. You have to bring light to a dark place, but that doesn't mean you have to pretend there is no dark place. Hashem is the light of truth that penetrates the darkness. Some people have light of truth within them, and they can light up what's around them.*

We get up, pull shut the door to be as mindful of *kol ishah* as possible, and all join hands and sing: "You Are My Sunshine, My Only Sunshine." Marcie nods. Shelley looks on.

Before we leave, Marcie spells out *1 minute at 4*, a reminder (I always forget) about the one minute every day at 4 p.m. that we're all supposed to spend being happy. Later that afternoon, the ping of the computer announces an incoming e-mail:

—Original Message—
From: Marcie Alter [mailto:marciealter@gmail.com]
Sent: Sunday, December 05, 2010 17:01 PM
To: emuna witt; Jackie Beecham; Orap Kalfa; R. Ilana Loeb; Sara Yoheved Rigler; Sarah Shapiro; Ruth Shlossman; Star Miller; Chaya Malka Abramson; Zehava Rochwerger; Chaya Malka & Simcha Abramson;
Subject: Did you

Did you do yourhapp y homework? Iamhappy! Yay!
Get happy! LoveMarcie

A WRITER'S INTERNET TALE

A big writer's block showed up one day, settling down in front of my laptop.

Generally speaking, I try to ignore this phenomenon. My philosophy is: *don't say its name.* Preserve its status as a figment of the imagination. Look the other way and it will drift off to sea.

But months went by. It wasn't drifting off.

Since I'd grown accustomed over the years to the glow of the computer screen, I continued showing up at "work" each morning at my desk, exercising my civic duty to keep track of current events online. There were a lot of words all over the place: attacks and counterattacks, prophecies and predictions, polls and twitters and twitters and blogs, bulletins and headlines, breaking news and shaking news, commentary and updates and op-eds. I didn't need to find my own thoughts. There was such a tsunami all the time of entertainment, with other people's words and opinions and ideas.

Falling silent scares anyone who depends on writing to convince himself, or herself, that of course she (or he) exists and has significance—real significance, not only the delusional kind. And given the fact that vast regions of many writers' left brains have been known to turn out the lights and shut down (sometimes remaining vacant for decades, even as their right brains keep stringing sentences together for who knows what purpose), what would I do with myself—not to mention who would I be, and why, and for whom—if I never wrote again?

In the past, I'd been comforted by the reply of the prolific artist Käthe Kollwitz, who upon being asked if she ever had intervals in which she was unable to draw, reportedly declared: "Of course, I do. Doesn't the land have to lie fallow sometimes?"

My own land was lying fallow for I don't know how long. Past became present and the present streamed by, and my brain became formatted for computer compatibility. It seemed to me that my mind's neural pathways had merged on the molecular level with those of the Internet.

"Only connect!" That was the ancient twentieth century's rallying cry, the twenty-first century's passive surfing was quenching that inborn thirst for connection with my fellow man (and with many famous celebrities) minus all the fuss and bother of relating to other people, with their human nature.

I felt lost, almost as if—shall I say its name?—I was *addicted.* And with fear and surprise, I realized I was. Not so much to the news itself, as I was to the medium. The flicker, the flash, the zip, the zoom, the interactive this and interactive that, and the cursor flying 'round the screen, anywhere on earth I wished, at the whim of my touchpad. Above all, to what was I addicted? To not thinking. To letting the bright computer screen do my thinking.

My symptoms had me in their grip no less than those of any other addiction, and were accompanied by the classic set of behaviors, such as startling from embarrassment when family members found me online, and sleepwalking toward the computer in the middle of the night.

Withdrawal was slow and laborious. I had to *daven* in the morning before checking my e-mail. Every time my thoughts ran into a silence, I had to resist the urge to fill it with sound and movement from the computer screen.

As the echoes died down, and piles of garbage were carted out (though some of it remained in my brain for eternal recycling), I felt empty. Without minute-by-minute updates, I was a lonely soul adrift in space, thrown back onto my inner void...

WHEREUPON MY SOUL STIRRED, and opened her eyes.

One by one, like mute little lambs coming back home, words and thoughts appeared, and some of them I recognized. They were mine!

And here—as if to prove it—they are. In this sentence.

I still must refrain from Internet's magnetism...must avert my eyes from the flashes of light, must resist the thrill of global flight...the fast, easy sense of connection...and remember how to walk the old-fashioned way, by putting one foot in front of the other, and to think thoughts, and to write them down. If not, my mind will be lost to me again.

Which just goes to show ...

...that if you, too, have become addicted to the screen, you, too, can reclaim your mind, and discover your thoughts, and recover your words, and do whatever you're supposed to do with your life.

AN AUDIENCE OF ONE

A few days before this interview took place, its two participants—interviewer and interviewee—agreed that the better part of wisdom would probably be to cancel. For in response to an e-mail from me asking if there were aspects of his life and work on which he would particularly like to focus during our upcoming discussion, Rabbi David Refson, much to my chagrin, had replied:

> I have zero interest or even willingness to talk about *any* aspect of my work and life. My teacher, Reb Elya Lopian, *zt"l*, taught us that the *kavod* from any publicity that we seek out is taken from our reward in *Olam Haba*. At my advanced age, a self-serving "advertorial" about myself is the last thing my *neshamah* needs!

To which I replied:

> I find it hard to imagine a conversation about Neve and its history without involving the topic of your life and work.

At this moment, even now, I still don't know exactly how that preliminary stumbling block was removed from our path. All I can say is that the impasse, and its resolution, served perfectly to introduce me to the director of Neve Yerushalayim, the Orthodox world's preeminent Torah institution for *baalos teshuvah*, where from one generation to the next, for the past fifty years, assimilated Jewish women from around the globe have been seeking, and discovering, their spiritual inheritance.

AT TWO MINUTES AFTER the hour, in strode a tall Rabbi David Refson for our 9 a.m. appointment, declining my offers of refreshment as I showed him to his seat. "Sorry to be late," he said. "I don't like being late. I met someone I know outside. A grandson of Ronnie Greenwald, *z"l.*"

"Was that a neighbor of ours?"

"You don't know who Ronnie Greenwald was?"

"No."

"*Really*? He was a hero. Well. For another time."

"Rabbi Refson," I begin hesitantly, "I hope it's all right with you if we start off the interview with questions about your life."

"Absolutely!" He dismisses my question with a casual wave of the hand—blowing off our previous exchange as he would a puff of smoke. "I'm happy to discuss anything you wish. Full speed ahead. As the *Baal haTanya* instructed, 'Always transcend the obstacle.'"

"Thank you. So to begin, I'd like to ask if you ever anticipated when you were growing up that one day, you'd spearhead what would initially be a revolutionary concept in *frum* society: an institution to provide adult Torah education for assimilated Jewish women."

"Well. The short answer? No. I did not. The long answer...I grew up in a religious environment, in England, in a town called Sunderland. All my Jewish friends and I went to non-Jewish schools, and Hebrew school in the afternoon. I didn't learn a thing in Hebrew school. Really, nothing at all. In retrospect, I would say that this was a function of my resentment about having to spend my evenings studying, while my non-Jewish schoolmates were out enjoying themselves.

"My father was a man of wealth, an entrepreneur. He did very well. And he expected me to take over the business.

"In 1963, I went to Israel as a member of Bnei Akiva, a very Zionist youth group. I had been in yeshiva unsuccessfully. Yeshiva was clearly not my career path. But my father told me before I left, 'When you go to Israel, I want you to visit Rav Elya Lopian.' They knew each other. Now, Rav Elya's story is very interesting. In Europe before the war, he had been the head of the Kelm Yeshiva, the center of the Mussar movement. In any case, Reb Elya asked me why I was not in yeshiva. I don't remember exactly how I responded, but whatever I said was clearly unsatisfactory. He said, 'We do not normally take people of your standard to our yeshiva, but I feel so indebted to your father that I feel I must make an exception. It is not proper that the son of my friend Avrohom Abba Refson should be an *am ha'aretz.'* He then proceeded to book a call (that was how long-distance calls were made in those days!) to ask the Rosh Yeshiva, Reb Elya Mishkovsky, to make an exception in my case. I couldn't hear the response of the Rosh Yeshiva, but it was clear to me that there was no great enthusiasm on his part. And all of this was going on without once asking me for a reaction!"

"Rabbi Refson, you were saying, about Rav Lopian, that his story was very interesting…"

"Yes, well, you see, in Kelm, Rav Elya had been at the height of his fame and fortune, a star of the Mussar movement. What happened was that in 1929, long before the Nazis came to power, he got a distinct feeling that he had to leave Eastern Europe. And that is what he did. People thought he had lost his mind, absolutely. He emigrated to England.

"In England, nobody was interested in *mussar*. They were interested in making money, in climbing out of poverty. Reb Elya had a terrible time there. And so, years later, when my father came to visit me in Israel, Rav Elya told him very sadly that in England, he had had twenty-five *bitterer yohren* [bitter years].

"Rav Elya had nine children. And the good side of it, of course, was that all except for one son, who had stayed in Telz, all his children and descendants escaped the Holocaust. So after the Second World War, it was Rav Elya's sons and sons-in-law who became the great *roshei yeshiva* of the '60s, '70s, and '80s. He himself didn't have *talmidim* from his years in England, but his sons and sons-in-law all became famous.

"It was miraculous." Rabbi Refson gives one slow, wondering shake of the head. "To leave Kelm at the height of his fame and fortune…at the height of his profession…Think of it…Chazal say that you can't sit at two tables. Rav Elya said, in the name of Rabbeinu Yonah, that you have a choice: reward here or reward in the next world. If people give you recognition of their own accord, then you're not responsible. But if you decide you *want* fame and recognition, and you *seek* recognition, and you *want kavod*, then it comes off your *cheshbon* in the next world."

I ask Rabbi Refson how one can reconcile that reality with what is written, that the only *yetzer hara* that increases with the years, as a person ages, is the desire for honor.

"Yes. A person who lacks identity," Rabbi Refson replies, "takes his identity from what people say about him. I believe the explanation is that people have an enormous fear of dying and being forgotten. And therefore, they reassure themselves that they are respected, because they want to believe that that respect will transcend their passing. Every American president in our time has been obsessed with his legacy—how will he be remembered? Obsessed with what his rank will be. Will he be remembered as a great president or an average president? All of them, they all have libraries built to house their documents and papers. And who goes to study the papers? No one! You know, I'll tell you a sto—no. Never mind."

"No, please, tell me! What story? Anything you don't want me to include, you can tell me and I'll delete it."

"Well..." Rabbi Refson ponders a moment. "All right. I had a business partner back in the 1970s, a son-in-law of David Rockefeller. Paul Growald, a Jew, who married Rockefeller's daughter, Eileen Rockefeller, after she converted. I was in Manhattan for Neve business one day in the early '70s, and Paul said to me, 'Let's take out my in-laws to dinner.' I was uninterested in this, so then he said, 'Let's go over to their townhouse for drinks.' And that's what we did.

"As David Rockefeller drank—it's what all of them did, after a day of work they'd go out for drinks. They'd drink before dinner and after dinner. And during dinner." Rabbi Refson chuckles. "So as he drank, David Rockefeller became more and more talkative. And he told me a story about his grandfather, John D. Rockefeller. They all called him John D. So David told me that when John D. was getting up there in years, he grew increasingly upset that everybody in America knew him as a robber baron. He was said to have enriched himself at the expense of the impoverished masses. John D. was very upset about this, that this was going to be his legacy. He said to himself, now how can I change this? So he came up with an idea! Rockefeller University! But after the university was built, John D. realized that it hadn't helped him at all! Now people were saying, 'Who's *behind* Rockefeller U? The Robber Baron!'"

Rabbi Refson pauses here to smile wryly. "The point being: you can't escape your legacy. Oh, and David Rockefeller also said to me, after he'd had a few more, 'Rabbi, if you ever decide to cross the line, I can get you the job as the priest of St. Thomas.' That was the local Episcopal Church."

"What?! He was joking, of course."

Rabbi Refson tips back his head with a happy laugh. "Oh, no. He wasn't joking, he was drunk. Rockefeller was a big donor to the Church. He said to me, 'We need someone like you in the Church.' So his wife, who was sitting there in their living room with us, said to him, 'Dear, even you can't do that. You can't offer a Jew the job as the priest.' And he retorted, 'Oh, yes I can. In that church, I get what I want.' You see, he was drunk, and he owned the Chase Manhattan Bank." Rabbi Refson laughs again, heartily, and changes the subject. "I gave someone an interview once, which he promised he won't publish 'til after I die. It was sort of like a postmortem clause. I told him that I was prepared to be candid with him provided that whatever I did not wish to be published while I was still alive, he could print after I die."

"Why didn't you want it published?"

"Too much about me."

I ask Rabbi Refson if he can reconcile that with Rabbi Avigdor Miller's statement that every person is obligated—that it's a non-optional *mitzvas asei*—to remember, to keep a record, to write down everything that has happened to him in his life, all the stations he has passed through person- ally along his own forty years in the desert. For otherwise he will forget all the kindnesses *Hashem* has done for him.

"That's for the person himself, it's not for others. It's for ourselves that we mustn't forget."

"Why not tell others?" I ask. "People can inspire each other. And educate each other. We learn from other people's life experiences."

"True. But if my purpose is sharing in order to impress you, then that's wrong."

I ask how a person can escape the desire to impress.

"By playing to an audience of One."

"You mean *Hashem*."

"Yes. If the purpose is to show other people a superior mode of behavior, well, that's fine. For example, people often think that certain things are impossible to achieve. By sharing the stories of *gedolim*, people realize they can go a lot higher. The Gemara tells such stories in order to show to what heights a person can aspire."

"So, Rabbi Refson, what about a person telling his own stories?"

"If he's doing it to benefit others, that's good."

"And what if he's doing it to benefit himself, as well as others? I'm thinking of something else I heard on a tape by Rabbi Miller: that if you do something good for yourself, you're helping a fellow Jew."

"Well, because it can become addictive. Once you see how people are im- pressed by you, it can take over your life. You do things to impress people. It's two different things: talking about one's life in order to impress, or, on the other hand, doing exactly the same thing in order to inspire."

"And if inspiring others impresses them?"

"That's perfectly all right. If my intention is to inspire, and people are impressed, that's not my fault. It's fine. Let's say a person thinks he cannot study more than four hours a day. I used to think that; then I found out that it's not true. I have students who will tell me that they can't do it, and I say, I used to think that about myself, then I discovered that it's an artificial limitation. The same goes for doing *chessed*. And even for the amount of sleep that we think we really require. Have you ever heard someone say, 'If I don't get enough sleep, I'm a zombie!' Then we hear how little sleep the *gedolim* have, and ask ourselves whether we really require eight hours' sleep. After all, when we are really enjoying ourselves, we make do with far less. Reb Elya taught us that this is one meaning of the dictum of Chazal, that jealousy of scholars promotes wisdom."

I ask Rabbi Refson if the question of doing something good for other people's approval or doing it for purer motives—for *Hashem*'s approval—is especially an issue for those who have grown up under the influence of British culture, because of the English emphasis on doing what's proper.

"Proper," he retorts, "is a *goyishe* concept.

"My late father, *zt"l*, was exceptionally successful in this world. And I noticed that he was careful to talk to my brother and me about both his successes and his failures. He spoke to us about where he had gone wrong. He would tell us that he did such and such and it didn't work out, and he would tell us why."

"You mean in his business ventures?"

"Doesn't matter whether he was talking about business or other matters. What I'm saying he was trying to do was to inspire us not to be afraid of failure. Afterward, I found out that many fathers only tell their children about their successes. The result being that the children develop an exaggerated fear of failure. They think, *My father never failed, so I can't fail*. So if there is a chance of failing, the children won't—they can't—do things. They have a terrible fear of failing.

"My late father, when I was born, was over forty. My mother, too. I have one sibling, who was born a year after me. I was therefore brought up by mature parents. They weren't learning parenthood on the job."

"Wouldn't you say that when it comes to parenting, learning on the job is inevitable?"

"Yes. True."

"And arriving at age forty doesn't necessarily mean that a person is mature."

"Right again. But one's chances of being mature are better at forty than at twenty."

"I'm sure you're not recommending postponement of marriage and parenting till age forty, are you?"

"No, certainly not. They would make a problem for me if they heard me saying that in Meah Shearim! I'm simply pointing out the advantages of having mature parents. There are many benefits. My parents brought to their parenting a certain maturity. On the other hand, because my father's father and my father's grandfather all died very young, he didn't want to leave orphans."

"Did your father die young?"

"Yes." Rabbi Refson sits and thinks for a few long moments before continuing. "You know, we always imagine that other parents are like our own parents, and then we find out when we talk to our friends that some of the building blocks of personality were missing. That they were teaching the wrong things."

"Was your father religiously observant?"

"Oh, yes. Yes, absolutely. But there was no Jewish school for the children of observant families—the Jewish population was too small for that—so like all the Orthodox parents at that time and place, there was no recourse for them other than to send their children to a non-Jewish school, and to Hebrew school in the afternoons.

"In the gentiles' school, there were only four Jews in my grade, all four of whom were at the top of the class. Now, some of the Jewish parents told their children that they were innately superior, but *my* father told me that I was a big fish in a small pond. He saw the danger in allowing class rank to become the governing factor in a child's self-esteem, in deciding how clever he is. This served me well when I went to yeshiva and discovered that in the yeshiva environment, I was regarded as thoroughly mediocre!"

"So, Rabbi Refson...it sounds as if your father indoctrinated you quite well."

"It wasn't indoctrination. It was education. Absolutely. Education is not indoctrination. My late father taught his two sons very well. One of the things he told my brother and me was that there are two groups in life that are condemned to misery: one is the group of bright people who think they are brilliant, and the other is brilliant people who think they are geniuses. He explained that both kinds are miserable because when they don't achieve what they imagine they're supposed to achieve, they come to the conclusion that there is a conspiracy in the world, of the mediocre against the outstanding. They tell themselves false stories—which they themselves come to believe—about why they haven't achieved what they expected to achieve. Their expectations outstrip reality. It is a dangerous place to be."

"What you're saying, Rabbi Refson, reminds me of a line attributed to the writer Kurt Vonnegut, that educators teach children how to succeed, but what they should really be teaching them is how to fail, because that's usually what happens."

"Well, that's not quite what I'm talking about. What actually happens is that *before* we *succeed*, we fail. And if one is not careful, the failure can cause a sense of hopelessness. Rav Yitzchok Hutner used to say, you can afford to lose battles, but you cannot afford to lose the war. Failure is what happens along the way. And after each failure, you're more capable. As King Solomon teaches, 'The righteous fall seven times and get up.'"

"Can you share a time that you failed?"

"Oh!" Rabbi Refson gives that dismissive wave of his hand, as if brushing off a fly. "There are too many of them to remember. Many of my brilliant ideas turned out to be failures. Too many failed seminaries and programs to even recall."

"Schools besides for Neve?"

"Oh, yes."

"So how did Neve get off the ground?"

"Back in the 1960s, I put an ad in *The Jerusalem Post*, 'Jerusalem Yeshiva Courses for Adults,' and to my surprise, the great majority of respondents were women. I was so surprised. I'd been expecting male respondents. Most of the women who responded were in their late twenties and early thirties, and I was twenty-four. Some of them were ten years older than I! So I went to Rav Shlomo Wolbe, and he told me to open a women's seminary. He said, 'It's fine, just don't let them know your age.' He also revealed to me that after the Second World War, he had opened a *baal teshuvah* seminary for women in Sweden.

"In any case, that's how Neve began. I left 'Jerusalem Yeshiva Courses,' and Rabbi Baruch Horowitz morphed it, so to speak, into Dvar Yerushalyim, which exists to this day. And with Rabbi Chalkovsky, a master educator, and Rachel Levy, who was one of the original students at Gateshead Seminary, we started Neve Yerushalayim. Rachel Levy, too, was a highly experienced educator. She was *niftarah* about twenty years ago.

"What did I learn from this experience? I learned that you need mature people to serve as teachers. So then I requested Rabbi Eliyahu Munk to come join us. Rabbi Munk was the eponymous rabbi of the famed synagogue of the German kehillah in London. He was a pillar of Torah and a pillar of common sense. And he came. He taught every single day at Neve for eleven years, up until the day he died. He was our advisor. He had seen everything in life. When he came to us, he was already past the age of seventy-three.

"Rabbi Munk once listened in to my counseling of a Neve woman and afterward said to me, 'You immediately responded by considering what could be done. In my experience, you must first consider if *anything* should be done, because doing *nothing* is often the best option. Only if you conclude that *something must be done* should you then consider *what to do*.'

"This advice has saved me on countless occasions.

"We also used to go every week to Be'er Yaakov, to ask Rav Wolbe our questions."

"What kind of questions? Can you give some examples?"

Rabbi Refson laughs. "You know, I don't have any sisters. Only one brother. So one of my questions was, what do you do when a woman cries? And what was Rav Wolbe's answer? 'You have a box of tissues on the table!' Another question that we asked Rav Wolbe: 'What *mefarshim* should we use when we teach *Chumash*?' And Rav Wolbe told us to search for those that inspire, that bear a contemporary message.

"We learned something extremely important from Rav Wolbe, which he said that he himself had learned as an educator in Sweden. He said that most of the young women in the seminary that he started after the war had come from religious homes, but they had no education; they had arrived in seminary after being in Nazi concentration camps for five or six years. So what was the process by which they became religious? Once you know the process, said Rav Wolbe, then you know what to teach, and how to teach it.'

"What stands in the way of becoming religious? It is not a lack of knowledge. That's not how it works. It's not a lack of knowledge that stands in the way. It's a lack of inspiration, and a lack of feeling comfortable with being religious. You have no idea how important—you would never imagine how important it is—how the people around you influence you, how they react to you. What will your parents say? What will your friends say? *Will I lose my friends? Will I lose my parents?* Rabbi Noach Weinberg believed that you could prove to people that Judaism is right. That Judaism is truth. That G-d created the world, that He gave the Torah at Sinai. And that once you prove that, the person gets up and shouts, 'Eureka!'

"I disagreed with Rav Weinberg.

"For the last twenty or thirty years, philosophy has been a dying subject. Two hundred years ago, Rebbe Nachman said the only place one could find people who were philosophically inclined was in France, and even today, turn on a television in France and you'll see philosophers talking. But in our society, nowadays, people don't make decisions in life on a philosophical basis. When people profess philosophical doubts, it is simply a way of avoiding religious obligations. As soon as someone 'proves' to me that G-d exists, that He gave the Torah at Sinai, and where G-d was during the Holocaust, etc., after getting answers to that, I will suddenly give up everything and go to live in Meah Shearim? In my experience, it's not like that, certainly not for women, and not for men, either. In fifty years, not one woman has ever told me she prefers scuba diving or shopping to sitting in *shul*. It is always framed, instead, in terms of belief. Yet the truth is that we're in a generation in which people fire off the arrow, then draw the circle.

"Chazal made an identical statement two thousand years ago. Jews have never worshipped idols except as a way to do whatever their hearts desired.

"You have to teach students enough so that it speaks to them. Women know what they want out of life. Women want a life with meaning and purpose. They want children. A family. They want an honest, sincere, appreciative husband. And they have to be shown that the way to acquire this happiness is by marrying someone who has an obligation to act this way.

"A few weeks ago, a donor came to Neve—an observant person, the son of a well-known rabbi—and he was looking to see what Neve is all about. We introduced him to six students. One was a stockbroker. One was a dentist. Another was an accountant. One's in PR. Six successful women. They told him their stories. He listened and listened, and finally he couldn't help himself and he said, 'Why did you become religious? You had it all.' So one of the women said to him, 'Don't you understand the difference between success and fulfillment?' But he didn't give up. He said to them, 'So was it trauma that brought you to religion?'

"The women were looking around at each other, with an expression on their faces that was like, *What's with this guy?*

"So one of them said, 'I failed driver's ed twice.'"

"She was joking?"

"Of course she was. Her point was that trauma was not what brought her to Neve. Trauma is very rare now as a path to becoming religious. Rav Wolbe wrote a *sefer* after the Six Day War, and in it he made two points: Miracles rarely produce lasting *baalei teshuvah*; they didn't make people religious at *Har Sinai*, and they don't make people religious today. Miracles don't work. And traumas don't work."

"The students you chose to bring to the donor, Rabbi Refson, they were all professionals, right?"

"Yes. That's the kind of student we get at Neve nowadays. And the average age of the Neve student today is postgraduate. The majority have been to college. And they have professional qualifications. They've done what was expected of them in their secular culture, and it didn't bring them fulfillment."

"Rabbi Refson, when I was becoming observant in the 1970s, philosophical questions *did* play a huge part in my process. It did for everyone I knew back then. Maybe in part because of the Holocaust—it was so close behind us. So Rabbi Weinberg's approach, Rebbetzin Weinberg's approach, was just right for us. What I needed, I think, was to realize that my fellow human beings can't know the answers to the kinds of questions I was asking, but that being a committed, believing Jew isn't a matter of having answers to philosophical questions. Being able to keep posing the questions, though, to express them to a knowledgeable, trustworthy person—who wouldn't condemn you for asking—that was essential."

"Yes, you're right. The process of becoming religious changes with every generation. I see it at Neve. Every five or six years, there's a massive change in the Neve population. When you run a school like Neve, you come to realize that the process of becoming *frum* is within each person. You can give the necessary information. You can provide certain inspiration. But essentially what you have to do is avoid ruining that feeling inside them. You can't exhibit prejudice. You can't be a racist. And even if you are a racist, you can't afford to let them know it. All you have to do is not say the wrong thing." He pauses before continuing. "Playing to an audience of One is the prerequisite."

I ask what his involvement at the yeshiva consists of nowadays.

"Well, I'm still traveling five months a year to do Neve fundraising, and when I'm back home in Jerusalem, I teach at the school twelve hours a week. There are various schools on the Neve campus now that share the classrooms and the facilities. I oversee these various schools, and meet regularly with the heads of each one. There are three separate schools for women from religious families, programs for Israeli-born students, and for students from other countries, from non-English-speaking backgrounds. There's a high school for American *olim*, and a mental health facility for *chareidim*—the largest one in Israel. There's a post–master's degree training program in Clinical Psychology, and other degree programs. The cultural integration of the diverse student populations enriches the educational experience in myriad ways, for everyone."

"My *mechuteniste*, Batya Barak, was one of your earliest students, Rabbi Refson, in the 1970s. She's told me how after she got married, she used to bring her young family to you and your wife quite often for Shabbos. My daughter-in-law was just a toddler then, but she remembers it."

Rabbi Refson nods, remembering.

"How many graduates have there been altogether, through the years?"

"Approximately thirty-five thousand."

"Rabbi Refson, do you have more Reb Elya stories?"

"Oh, yes. Many."

"Can you share one now?"

His gaze turns toward the window, where summer leaves are turning to fall.

A few long moments pass.

"All right. Another Rav Elya story.

"I was once with my teacher at a wedding, and he called me over and said, 'You speak English, David. Go over to that fellow over there and tell him to come to yeshiva.' I looked and saw that Rav Elya was pointing to a young man with a long ponytail. This was the hippie era, you know. And I said under my breath, '*Rebbi*, he doesn't look like yeshiva material. And anyway, you can't just go over to someone and suggest that he turn his life around.'

"Now, this was, of course, some twenty years before Rabbi Meir Schuster did exactly that, with such massive success. At the Kotel. So Rav Elya said to me, 'Just do what I say.' When I again objected, this time with: '*Rebbi*, please, I'm *British*. I need an introduction to him,' my teacher became very agitated, and he said, 'Tell me, if that fellow's pants were on fire, would you wait for an introduction? I am *telling* you, *the whole person is on fire*. Go and speak to him.'

"So I did. And while the young man was very pleasant to me, he declined my suggestion, and I returned to Reb Elya to report back. My teacher must have identified a certain 'I told you so' triumphalism in my response, whereupon he quoted Reb Chaim Volozhiner—the founder of the Volozhin Yeshiva—who said, 'We are not obligated to succeed, merely to try our best.' And then Reb Elya said, 'In the next world, David, people will blame us for not doing our best to persuade them to have been better Jews. To escape this accusation, we are *obligated* to present to them the option of Torah.'

"Now, I am not suggesting that my teacher was a prophet, but he was teaching me a lesson, and it became the cornerstone of my life and career."

Rabbi Refson glances at his watch. "Oh!" He practically leaps to his feet. "I'm late! Please excuse me, I must go." He expresses a courteous thank you, bids me and my family a very good Shabbos, and with that, larger than life, he's on his way.

THE TAMTZIS

I first met Sudy Rosengarten around 1981, on our muddy, rock-strewn settlement in the Judean Desert. She'd come all the way out from Bnei Brak as
the guest of her cousin, who lived a few caravans away from ours.

The diminutive woman from Bnei Brak looked like a typical Chassidic
housewife, modest and plainly dressed, which in my eyes made her all the more
remarkable. For—my neighbor divulged—her cousin had a book contract and
a ten-thousand-dollar advance from Bantam Books, one of America's biggest
general-market publishers. Her husband and young children were making do
without her for three days so she could have some uninterrupted writing time as
the deadline loomed.

Her glamorous predicament filled me with longing, for I, too, wanted to write,
desperately. But for mothers on the yishuv, life was about sponja and mud and
dinner and bedtime. All I had to show for my literary leanings was a shelf full
of diaries, a few unfinished aerograms addressed to my parents, and a small
collection of rejection letters from various magazines.

Years passed.

In 1991, I was just setting out on a search for Orthodox women writers, and
the first person who came to mind was Sudy Rosengarten.

I tracked down her number—she was still in Bnei Brak—and at the sound of
that frank, direct, down-to-earth voice, almost felt as if this were an old friend
on the phone, though we'd hardly exchanged two words a decade before. Would
she permit me to use an excerpt, I inquired, from that book she'd written, for an
anthology I was compiling of Orthodox women's writing?

"Oy, you mean my novel?" said Sudy. "That book was never published."

"You're kidding!"

"No, the publisher said it was too Jewish. Too religious."

"So why didn't you publish it in the frum world?!"

"Ach..." There was a sigh. "Have you heard that expression, 'Too frei for the frum and too frum for the frei'? The frum publisher I went to—they said the novel was too secular."

"But there are a lot of other publishers. Why don't you—"

"Look, I gave up on all that a long time ago. And you know, gam zu l'tovah. That novel's stashed away in a drawer somewhere. I don't think I could find it even if I wanted to."

Two decades went by.

One sunny autumn afternoon in my Jerusalem living room, Sudy Rosengarten, now a great-grandmother, spoke about her life as a writer. Her most recent book, An American Saga, follows An Onion for the Doctor, a collection of stories, and Worlds Apart, a memoir about the beginnings of the Bais Yaakov movement in the United States.

Rabbi Nachman Bulman once said: "What the frum world needs is its own genuine literature." Sudy Rosengarten is one of the writers who's been giving it to us.

SS: *You've written a lot of stories based on your life, Sudy, but in "real life" you've always been a very private person. Why did you agree to this interview?*

SR: Because my husband said I should. My first reaction was, "Oh, no." But when I told him about it, he said, "Why not?"

It's true, I prefer being behind the scenes, at home, away from the public eye. That's how we were brought up. Then my writing goes and puts me out there.

SS: *So why put yourself out there?*

SR: Look, many *frum* Jews think about themselves that they're not nice people, because they're not the way they want to be. We want to be the best people we can be, then we look in the mirror and see an individual with deficiencies. I want to show people that the deficiencies are universal. We have our ups and downs, and we aren't terrible people because of it. When we fall, we don't stay down, we can get up and try again. We want to pass our tests with honors, but to be a human being is to have faults and not always live up to expectations, our own and other people's. The *yetzer hara* doesn't make us bad, it makes us human. We all go through *nisyonos*. We have to try very hard to pass through these tests, but we're not going to be holy, holy,

holy all the time. *Hashem* created us with *nisyonos* and the *yetzer hara*. He created the world in such a way that there would be so many things working against us.

But He is rooting for us to pass. When we don't pass with flying colors, there's a universal feeling that it's the end. But it's not. It's the beginning. That's our opportunity to grow. We can try to see what was lacking, what we have to work on.

This is the main thing that gets me writing, to touch on things that people find hard to talk about. A lot of people don't understand why I try to understand my feelings, why I dig to see what I'm thinking and feeling. I think people are afraid of seeing what's in there.

SS: *Can you give an example of something you've written about that you yourself found hard to talk about?*

SR: When I was a young woman taking care of my old, sick, unhappy father-in-law, I had a lot of responsibility. There was a lot of work. I looked at some of my relatives I thought were having it easier in life, and I resented them. I didn't want to feel that way. But I did. So I felt guilty. Years later, I understood that in that kind of situation, there's bound to be resentment. It's very common. It's normal. I didn't understand that we're people, not angels.

SS: *Which world are you referring to?*

SR: My world. The Chassidic world. That's the only world I know. I can only talk about what I'm familiar with. The problem was that I often touched on things that in our world were taboo. Certain areas were hushed up.

SS: *Such as?*

SR: Things having to do with marriage, with relationships. I wrote about these things because they bothered me very much and I thought it would help a lot of other people, too, who I knew felt the same way. By the standards of the Chassidic world, the novel brought some hidden things out in the open. But when I handed it in to the secular publisher, for them it was as if I'd done nothing. In their world, everything is so open, so blatant, it leaves nothing to the imagination. They told me to "flesh it out more," and I couldn't.

SS: *So then what happened?*

SR: That was the end.

SS: *Of what?*

SR: I stopped writing.

SS: *How long did that last?*

SR: A long time. The thing that really made me stop was a *pasuk* in *Tehillim*. One day during that whole episode with the publisher, I was reading *Tehillim*, and all of a sudden I was struck by the line that goes, "Don't find fault with my *tzaddikim*. Don't touch my anointed ones, and don't speak badly of my *nevi'im*." I thought to myself, I better back out. This isn't for me to talk about. Whatever questions I have shouldn't be made public. Let me just shut up.

Eventually, what actually happened was that the *rabbanim* themselves realized that things were not all as they should be. To a very large extent, they themselves corrected the situation. It's different today from what it was back then.

SS: *How so?*

SR: I'm not the one to explain this kind of thing, the changes that have taken place in Chassidic society.

SS: *Can you speak about the changes in your own life, in relation to writing?*

SR: In 1969, when I was coming over on the boat from America, I met the wife of the Orthodox author Meyer Levin. I showed her some of my stories, and she later introduced me to the editor of *Hadassah Magazine*. *Hadassah*—whose readership for the most part is secular Jewish, and Reform or Conservative—eventually published a few of my stories about the Chassidic world.

You know, there's a big magnet pulling people who are far away from the *frum* world. Some of them have nice memories, some have bitter ones, but there's often something—a grandfather with a beard, a holiday, a family custom—that they remember, and they yearn for something. Even the ones who are so assimilated they don't have any such memories, there's still something pulling them, in spite of themselves. They're curious. They want to know about Orthodox Jews, for better or worse.

Meyer Levin's wife and I stayed in contact through the years, and she always told me I should write a book. But aside from *Hadassah*, and a few little things I wrote for the magazine *Yiddishe Heim*, I never had a market that I was aware of. The stories you took for the first

Our Lives Anthology were the first things I had published in a book in the *frum* world. Lots of people gave me advice about my writing through the years, how to negotiate my way between the two worlds. When people helped me, I gained a lot—but I was also not gaining. I had to let my way of expressing myself find its own way. I found that I had to write not the way other people do it but the way I do it. When I stopped having people help me, it went better. I couldn't work within other people's frame, I had to let it come out. Finally, I came out with my first book, *A World Apart*.

Nowadays, I let the stories come out, and then, if I'm too open, my editors take care of it. Sometimes it makes me very unhappy after some piece of my writing is published and I see what's been taken out. But I let them do it, I go along with it. I think they're better at this than I am, at knowing what should and shouldn't be said.

SS: *In your stories about growing up in Williamsburg, you've described how the Jewish immigrants of that era were engaged in a constant struggle to survive in America. There couldn't have been much encouragement to become a writer, or was there?*

SR: It could just be in the genes. My mother was always writing, sending postcards every Rosh Hashanah. Wishing everyone in her family a healthy year full of blessings. And my sister was a good writer.

SS: *But was there something that prompted you to develop your writing further?*

SR: To answer this, I'll take a few steps back.

Jews usually came over from Europe either because of the draft system or because of poverty. You've probably heard that in Europe, it was common for *frum* people to put pots full of water on top of the *blech* Friday afternoon, so if neighbors came by, they wouldn't see there was no food for Shabbos. The poverty was very bad. People were ashamed. My father was born in 1909, and like everyone else, he'd heard that in America he'd be able to take care of his family. As it turned out, not only was there no money, there was also no Yiddishkeit. The children of those religious immigrants—my generation—grew up between World War I and World War II, when America was a Jewish desert. The future of any community is in the children's schooling, but there were no yeshivas and no such thing as Bais Yaakov. No Jewish education at all.

To be a Shabbos observer was almost impossible because there was a six-day work week, and Sunday was the day of rest. If the boss realized that a worker had left early on Friday—and in winter that would mean having to leave very early Friday afternoon—then when he came back to work Monday morning, he'd be out of a job. For fathers, it was a very difficult test. A lot of these men tried to do their own thing—to collect rags and sell them in bulk, and traveling salesmen used to collect bottles and bottle different products. They'd think up all kinds of things to sell.

For children, America was dazzling. By American law, kids had to stay in school till age sixteen. But the *yetzer hara* became very active, telling children to go peek. Parents had no money for recreation, so if kids wanted pocket money to go to the movies, to go to Coney Island with all its shiny scenery, they couldn't go out to work unless they went out to work on Shabbos. So they did.

People eventually started taking it for granted that they would lose their children. They just threw up their hands and said, "What can we do?" They tried to deal with it, but what *could* they do? You might ask why their fathers weren't teaching them, but the fathers were not available. The fathers were struggling in the sweatshops with every ounce of their strength, eighteen hours a day. When Shabbos came, they didn't have the energy to start fighting with the kids to sit down and learn. They were utterly drained and exhausted. And seeing the dazzle and sparkle of secular society, the children weren't interested.

The parents were very unhappy about it, so they would find someone who didn't have any *parnasah* and hire him to teach their children. But what happened was that the kids would be sitting till 3 p.m. in public school (the way they did things in those days, kids had to sit with hands folded, or the teacher would come by and smack their hands with a ruler), then they'd have another hour with a *rebbi* their parents hired privately, someone with no pedagogical training. The boys would hear the non-Jewish kids outside on the street playing games, screaming, having a ball, while they had to sit there in *shul* learning *aleph-beis* and how to *daven*. They hated it.

The father's responsibility to give over the Torah, and Torah values—the tradition that had endured from *Har Sinai*, father to child—it stopped right there, in early twentieth-century America. There was no future. The situation didn't look good for Klal Yisrael.

But *Hashem* never leaves us forever. *Hashem* has promised us. So in every generation there are some special people. Even when things look so bad, you find special individuals who feel responsibility for the survival of Klal Yisrael.

For the next part of the story, we're going to take a big jump, to about 1939 or 1940. Yeshiva Torah Vodaath had started in Williamsburg. Boys were beginning to learn. But for girls there was still nothing.

America—then as now—was a Protestant country, and public schools followed the American curriculum. My sister and I—she's a year and a half older—were in public school. Most of the children and teachers in that particular school were Jewish, but in school we did what the *goyim* did.

It happened that in that particular school, something unusual was going on, an experiment in education. The school wanted to test out some new, advanced educational programs, so I was in a special class. And I loved it. I was happy there. It was challenging, it was interesting. There were all kinds of activities.

One of these activities was the glee club. And in the Xmas season, we'd sing Xmas carols, and made plays about the child in the manger. Then we'd come home and sing the songs. You can imagine what our parents felt when we brought those songs home with us. "*Oy*, what's going on here? What's going to be?"

Now, in those years my father *davened* in the Bostoner Rebbe's *shul* in Williamsburg, and in that *shul*, there were two men, two of the special people I mentioned. One was Reb Moshe Lieber and the other was Reb Gershon Kessler.

These two men decided this could not go on. Here they were, getting reports about atrocities in Europe, while in America the girls from religious families were singing Xmas carols. They figured, what's going to happen to Klal Yisrael? They realized they had to do something because there were no girls for those boys in the yeshiva to marry. The girls hadn't been educated and weren't prepared to lead such a life. So these two men started going house to house, trying to get the parents—people they knew from *shul*, people who were interested in remaining *Yidden*—to convince them to send their daughters to a new religious school.

At the same time another one of these special people—a young man, Avraham Newhouse, who had been a *mechanech* in Europe and had been rescued from the Holocaust—told these two men that he would work with them and help them start a girls' yeshiva.

The parents were not interested, though. And they had their reasons. There had already been several attempts to make a religious school for the girls. One had been called Bais Rochel, the other Bais Leah. They hadn't had the proper teachers or the proper funding, and the schools had closed down. Then, when the girls returned to public school, they'd been demoted to a lower grade so they could catch up. So that was very bad, and the parents were wary. They wanted their kids to have a good education.

Meanwhile, in the advanced program at IGC, at the public school, we were having a ball. I loved learning, and they had put me in the most modern, progressive class. The teaching staff was 99 percent Jewish, and the student body was 99 percent Jewish, but the curriculum and the whole educational system had its foundation in Protestant American culture.

SS: *What's IGC?*

SR: Oh, that's what the school was called. Sometimes we'd try to figure out what the letters stood for, but they never told us. My teacher was Mrs. Fromkies. When Mrs. Fromkies asked me in school one day, "What do you want to be when you grow up?" I said, "A nurse," and she said, "Oh no. From IGC, you girls can go higher. You can be a doctor. You can be a lawyer."

This was our dilemma.

SS: *Mrs. Fromkies wasn't religiously observant?*

SR: I don't know how religious she was, but once a year she used to stand in front of us and talk about Chanukah, and one day she brought a Chanukah menorah to school. All the windows were decorated with pictures of Xmas trees and holly and bells and Santa Claus, and she took the menorah and stuck it in the last windowpane, in the corner. And I was ashamed.

We lived then in a two-room basement apartment. We lived in what was called a railroad flat, which was essentially one long hallway with rooms on either side. On the left of the dining room there was a tiny kitchen. My sister and I slept in the big front room with our grand-mother, then in back was our parents' room.

We were very fortunate. My parents both worked. We had enough to eat. But who knew about fancy furniture or even nice furniture? You needed some chairs, you needed a table and some beds. You took care of the basics.

My sister was the cook. I was the one who cleaned. I remember my mother telling me, "Don't wash the floor! Let people in!" because after I'd do the floor, I didn't want anyone coming into the kitchen until the floor had dried.

My parents taught us that when people came to the door, you had to give *tzedakah*. We were taught by example that that's what money was for. You had to worry for other people.

When guests arrived, they were always taken into the kitchen. One night during the Xmas season when I was about eleven—my sister must have been about twelve and a half—the two rabbis came to our house. We were already in our pajamas, and we had been hearing things from behind the door. My father had been asking a lot of questions, and we were terrified. My mother opened the door and asked us to come in and talk to the rabbis. I remember we had to get dressed fast and make ourselves presentable.

They started out by telling us what was going on in Europe. We had thought the people saying these things were deranged. The whole community couldn't believe that the things we heard were true. All over America, it was kept quiet, because if it had come out into the open in American society, America would have had no choice. We would have had to join forces with the rest of the world against Nazi Germany.

Reb Gershon Kessler was very solemn, very stern. He told us that the only way to save the Jewish nation was to educate the children and to spread *Hashem*'s word among them so that Jews would know *Hashem*'s *ratzon* and make a *kiddush Hashem*.

Reb Moshe Lieber reached us in a different way. He was very soft and gentle. When he spoke to you, his words entered your heart. He looked the way I as a little girl imagined *Hashem* looking. He spoke to our *neshamos*, as if we were adults rather than little girls, and we couldn't help responding in kind. He said, "It's difficult for us to put such a heavy responsibility on young children like you. But we have no choice. Jews can never consider themselves individuals. Each one is responsible for the *klal*." This is the way he presented it, with such a love and gentleness, and he conveyed such understanding of our feelings. He said that he knew we were so happy where we were. He appreciated fully that we weren't looking for anything different or new. He tried to impress us, though, with our responsibility to the whole Klal Yisrael. He said that if we were able to help, we couldn't wiggle out of it, we couldn't escape our responsibility. Our people needed us.

From that time on, we saw everything in terms of this idea, this feeling, that we were not individuals. We would have to build something that would enable Am Yisrael to survive.

So we made the switch, and my mother went out to work to pay for our tuition.

It was a struggle. The new school, called Bais Yaakov, couldn't get decent teachers. They'd hire people who for one reason or another couldn't get jobs in the public school system, and these were often people who had no training. They'd start teaching and quit, because they couldn't discipline us. In the same class there'd be three kids in second grade, four kids in fifth. It was one great big mess. The electricity would shut off. The plumbing was always broken. We'd sit in class during the winter with our gloves on.

Rabbi Newhouse knew how to handle all the problems, though. He would come in and say what a great job we were doing. If we just kept going, he'd tell us, it was going to be the greatest. We believed him. He was very influential.

At that time Rebbetzin Kaplan had a seminary, and every night she used to give a crash course for teachers. She was preparing groups of girls—older girls and young married women. There was one group in east New York, another in Manhattan. What the teachers heard at night they would teach us the next day.

We kids had a lot of questions, and they had a hard time with us. As for me, I had been so happy in the other school, learning all kinds of things. I was very angry. I missed the learning in the other school. I became a terrible troublemaker.

SS: *What kind of trouble?*

SR: Oh, for example, one teacher was always busy with her hair and her primping, so I'd tease her. I put a cup of water on the door to fall on her when she opened the door. Mean things like that. I was just terrible.

Rabbi Newhouse finally called my mother to school, and the three of us sat down in his office to talk. I gave him all my complaints, I was telling him all these stories, that we weren't learning anything secular, but neither were we getting *ruchniyus*. He knew that what I was saying was true, especially about the teachers. Now, that Rabbi Newhouse was a real psychologist. He told me how hard my teachers were working, and that I'd made such and such a teacher cry. So this made me cry. I didn't have a hanky, and he gave me his hanky.

The next thing I knew, he had imported a teacher from *Eretz Yisrael*, Miss Graineman—her married name became Mrs. Wilman—and she knew how to handle us. The really good pedagogy came from *Eretz Yisrael*, and she really gave us Torah and *Nevi'im*. Now we felt we were doing what we were meant to do. My sister got a wonderful teacher, too, Miss Adelman, from Europe, a student of Sarah Schenirer. Things were beginning to move. We were getting what we had been promised.

Rabbi Newhouse always had an eye for the future. He saw what was happening to the boys in yeshiva, that whenever yeshiva wasn't is session, the children would be dazzled again by all the glitter of America. So he opened a summer camp to ensure that the whole atmosphere of Yiddishkeit would not leave us.

When the Lubavitcher Rebbe came in 1942, he started outreach. They found us in the *midbar*, and they started planting on a large scale.

After the death of my mother's mother, my mother's father moved to *Eretz Yisrael*, remarried, and had more children. He used to write letters, telling us all about the Holy Land. He used to give our address to all the *meshulachim* from *Eretz Yisrael* who were coming to raise money for the old Jewish *yishuvim* in Yerushalayim. They knew they could stay with us as long as they needed to. My parents had a high-rise studio couch in the kitchen, for guests, and my mother would also open up a cot at the end of the dining room and put sheets over the chairs so no one would see them when they were sleeping.

My mother hung a key on a nail outside the door. All the *meshula-chim* knew where the key was hidden, and so if they arrived when my mother was at work and we were at school, they'd be able to come in by themselves. Our front door had a window. I knew when I came home from school that if the light was on inside, we had guests.

When it came time for my sister to graduate from Bais Yaakov, Rebbetzin Kaplan told us about Sarah Schenirer's work, and about the Haskalah going on in Europe. She told us how so many Jewish houses were divided, how in almost every *frum* home there was usually at least one member of the family moving away from Yiddishkeit. The Haskalah was having an impression even in yeshivas. It was taking over Europe. Rebbetzin Kaplan was giving another crash program to prepare young women to go overseas, into the little towns in Poland. As soon as there was a group of young women who were strong enough to spread Yiddishkeit, off they would go, across the ocean.

Then Hitler came and all of that was lost.

SS: *You were saying, how you became a writer...*

SR: Well, during that period, when very few Jewish families dared take their girls out of the public schools to put them into the Jewish school, Agudas Israel was very anxious for Bais Yaakov to keep going. They organized a group of women who used to visit us in school and tell us how special we were, and how valuable it was, what we were doing. One day, one of the women announced to the seven girls in my seventh-grade class that we were going to have a writing contest on the subject, "Why I go to Bais Yaakov," and that there was going to be a prize. Our teacher told us on the spot to sit down and write a composition. I remember I was eating a chocolate cupcake and an apple. I was very hungry. Whenever I write I get very hungry.

SS: *You still do today? You get hungry when you write?*

SR: [*She laughs and nods.*] With a passion.

I won the contest and got the prize, a silver necklace. Maybe that was the beginning of my writing. All of a sudden, I didn't have to be a troublemaker anymore. I was getting my attention from writing instead. All of a sudden, I had *hishtadlus*. I used to come home after school and just sit down and write. It was just my own little things, but I thought they were very important. I had a purpose in life now. I'd write until late at night. I remember my mother coming in and putting a sweater over my shoulders because it was cold, and saying, "Sorah, *zisselah*, it's so late, go to sleep," and I'd say, "It's all right,

Mommy, I'm almost finished." And she would let me finish. She didn't force me to go to sleep.

There was something else that happened, too. My sister wrote beautifully, and one time she wrote something very good for another contest and won, but after that she stopped. I think she had a feeling, "It's more important to let Sudy be the one in the family who writes." She didn't want to squash me. Can you imagine that? Standing aside for someone else? I'm not sure I realized it at the time. She was giving me the full space. To this day, anytime an occasion arises in which she has to express herself, she writes just beautifully, but she wanted me to have the full field. That's greatness, in my opinion. She was ready to give away something she might have excelled in so that the other person should have something.

Today, when my books come out, she's the first one to buy a whole bunch of them, and she gives them out.

We are born as takers, and the whole Torah is supposed to change us from takers to givers. This is what my sister was, and is. A giver. It makes me very proud to have her as my sister.

There was also something else that got me to write.

In high school we had a very nice teacher, a non-Jew, and he was a very caring person. He didn't even teach English, he taught us economics, and until they brought him in to teach us in Bais Yaakov, he didn't even know what Jews looked like. But he was so impressed that these young girls were devoting themselves to religion instead of to all the mundane *shtuyot* that the teenagers he taught in the public school were busy with. He so admired the way we dressed modestly, and the things we were interested in. A few of us who liked writing put out a newspaper, and he encouraged me very much in my writing.

He gave us the feeling that writing was worthwhile. We had in mind that there was some purpose to our writing.

It was before the *baal teshuvah* movement, when people were trained in colleges and fulfilled their talents. All those years, everybody knew there was a need for Jewish writing, but there was nothing to read other than what you could find in the public library, and the magazines we used to pick up on the stands, which had stories.

I remember reading and reading and reading. It would be late at night and my father would come into the room, so we'd shut our eyes and all of a sudden, we would be snoring away. These were not the kind of books and magazines that could help us develop spiritually. They certainly didn't add to our *yiras Shamayim*. It was just entertainment. It helped us to relax but didn't help us to grow.

Today the Jewish bookstores are full. Kids have a lot to read. Adults have a lot to read. Sometimes, though, you have such holy, holy books, and we don't feel we can ever get there. They don't talk to us in the same way as stories about normal people who have to pick themselves up.

In 1948, I graduated from high school and wanted to stay with my grandfather and go to seminary in *Eretz Yisrael*.

Then the War of Independence broke out. His children from his second marriage would tell us later how my grandfather died of starvation. People would come around to distribute food, and he refused to eat. He'd say, "I have already lived my life, give it to the young people."

This was the feeling my parents and grandparents raised us with—you live for other people.

SS: *Do you think the same is true today?*

SR: To say that today it is not as strong, you can't say that either, because there is so much *chessed* and *hachnasas orchim*.

But as a child I lived it more. I remember my mother looking to help other people. Today you get involved so much with your own family. Today you don't go out as much, looking to help other people. I'm ashamed how involved I am with just my own family. Our children are all grown with families of their own, *bli ayin hara*, but I'm still so overwhelmed with the needs of my own family.

In our generation, too, there are people who worry for others. But our families are bigger today, much bigger, than those early generations of immigrants in the United States. In those days you found very few large families like you have today.

SS: *Why do you think that is?*

SR: Because of the good *chinuch* that teaches us that it is a blessing to have large families. Bais Yaakov and the yeshiva system turned over Klal Yisrael.

But the thing they had that we're weaker on today—I'm talking about the real, real old-time Jewish people who grew up before the war—was a way of looking at life. The essence of their way was they didn't expect life to be easy.

You know, we're Bobover Chassidim. One time a number of years ago, there was some kind of gathering that was going on—a whole group of families came together for a specific purpose, to accomplish something. The accommodations turned out to be very bad, very uncomfortable. I forget what exactly, but the food, the sleeping arrangements, everything was uncomfortable. I saw someone I knew, one of the women who had come from far away with her family, and I said to her, "It must be hard for you with the children under these circumstances."

She looked at me with an expression on her face of—I don't know how to describe it—a look of surprise, amusement, incredulity. With a little smile, she asked me—she wasn't just saying it, it was a real question she was addressing to me—she said, "Who says that life has to be easy?"

Nowadays, your husband says a word to you that's not good, and it's the end of the world. I look at my in-laws. They didn't know life was supposed to be easy and comfortable. There was no such thing. They knew life was a struggle.

This is it, this is the main thing, what we call in Yiddish, the *tamtzis*. If life gets hard, you accept it *b'ahavah*.

THE LIGHT FROM CYBERLAND

Y ears ago, when my children were children, there was one picture book I especially liked reading aloud: *The Wretched Stone*, by author and illustrator Chris Van Allsburg. In those days—the mid-1990s—my children didn't object to hearing it more frequently than their own favorites, for it was one of the only bedtime stories that didn't put *me* to sleep along with them.

The story is about the crew of a nineteenth-century clipper ship, which in the course of an ocean voyage comes upon an island that doesn't appear on any maps.

The sailors disembark to forage for provisions, and though they find nothing edible, they do discover a strange glowing stone. Curious, they take the luminous object back on board, and for lack of anything better to do with it, store it down below, in the ship's hold.

"The glowing stone," the Library of Congress summary informs us on the copyright page, "has a terrible transforming effect."

And for reasons that will soon become apparent, the book fed my pride. It made me feel like such a good mother.

WE FIRST SEE the smart, skilled, experienced sailors of Van Allsburg's tale as they're hard at work, diligently carrying out their daily maritime duties.

Next, they are pictured up on deck, telling each other stories under the stars, tiny men out in the middle of nowhere, in the vast darkness, sustaining their spirits through the interminable, moonlit nights at sea.

Storytelling up on deck, however, is soon set aside in favor of a new, less demanding source of relaxation. Like moths on a lampshade, the crew is soon spending not only their off-hours but more and more of their on-duty hours, too, seated in front of the glowing stone, inexplicably mesmerized.

The captain, who unlike his crew is not magnetized by the stone's light, tries desperately to get his men back on schedule. But the longer they sit and gaze, contentedly entertained, the harder it gets to pull themselves away. As the vessel, unattended, drifts off-course into increasingly rough seas, the crew—oblivious now to lightning and thunder and other such disturbances—have lost not just their sense of direction but their grasp of what it means *to have a destination*, and of their own role in *getting somewhere*. As wild waves and winds wreck the sails and crack the ship's mast, the lonely, horrified captain—at this point the only one on board to be using the power of speech—inadvertently comes upon a cause for hope: he has noticed that if he reads aloud to his crew, he can sometimes get their attention, awakening in their distracted eyes a vague and distant glimmer of...*something*...almost *human*.

When we last catch sight of the smashed and drifting vessel, we now see a huddled bunch of stooped and silent, hairy and slack-jawed apes in sailor suits, their mouths agape...as if trying their best to remember what they once were.

The captain—eyeglasses perched on his nose—holds a storybook aloft.

MY YOUNG CHILDREN WOULDN'T have understood it—even had I tried to explain—what my knowing little grin was all about. For when their mother was a child herself, growing up in America, she would have no more come home from elementary school without sitting down with a snack for her lineup of favorite programs—among which were "The Mickey Mouse Club," "My Little Margie," "The Millionaire," "Queen for a Day," "I Love Lucy," "I Married Joan," "Father Knows Best," and "Lassie Come Home"—than she as a teenager would have willingly missed "Candid Camera" on Sunday at 10, "Twilight Zone" on Friday nights, or Walter Cronkite's flatly delivered "That's the Way It Is," on the CBS Evening News Roundup, which for several years consisted mostly of that day's warfare in Vietnam.

"What are you doing inside on such a beautiful day!" my mother would exclaim, shutting off the TV with a sweep of her hand. "Use your inner resources!"

Inner resources? I didn't know what, or where, they were, or if I had any, but guiltily assumed I would know it if I did. The words evoked in my child's mind a picture of some kind of vaguely unbuilt house in an uncomfortable stage of construction.

Later, throughout my own child-raising years, an old and dear friend of mine who, like me, was now an idealistic young wife and mother in the Jewish State (as innocent searchers, she and I—from different points along our parallel but separate spiritual paths—had both made aliyah) was hired by the IDF to teach English to Israeli soldiers. She needed time and space every afternoon to grade papers and prepare the next day's lessons, and their TV served as a punctual, reliable babysitter. It kept her two little girls happily preoccupied until dinnertime.

All was well until after a few years, my friend encountered some trouble setting limits on her daughters' hours in front of the set and controlling which programs they watched. With time, as her daughters grew, she started talking about the arguments: Should she let them do their home-work in front of the TV? As a teacher herself, this rankled. Should she let them stay up late sometimes on school nights, for something good such as a historical drama, or an old movie classic? What about on weekends? As a responsible parent, where should she draw the line? When had drawing a line become impossible? How about a comedy sitcom, or a documentary? (*"Oh come on, Mom! It's the educational channel!"*)

Maybe she should redefine sitting in front of the TV as family togetherness?

My friend and her husband both had to get up early for work; they couldn't police the living room until the wee hours of the morning, pa-trolling the programs that came on *after* the classic old movie.

At some point, this dear friend spoke of a deep disappointment: she and her husband had struggled to bring their family here, they'd sacrificed proximity to friends and relatives in order to give their children an authen-tic, natural connection to Judaism and its traditions. They had made their escape from the materialism of contemporary culture in order to live more meaningful Jewish lives.

Then Hollywood's long arm reached out across the planet and was hold-ing her family in its cheaply degrading embrace.

I'd listen empathetically—our friendship is still important to both of us, until today—but inwardly I'd be vigorously patting myself on the back. For in the religiously observant Jewish life that *I'd* chosen, television wasn't on the cultural radar screen. In *my* home, *my* community, *my* society, children weren't infected with the habit-forming, deadening passivity that comes from watching too much TV. I would have no more opened our front door to that whole load of garbage (including the educational channels!) than install a radioactive time bomb on our dining room table.

The fact that I had avoided that whole unnecessary conflict between parent and child, and the whole irrevocable waste of time, and the whole arena of temptation that corrupts childhood ideals and infects children's self-image with Hollywood's standards and stunts their imagination—to have deftly sidestepped the whole battleground and disciplinary struggle, simply by not having a TV in the house—oh, what a major, easily achieved victory!

I read in some science magazine somewhere that the brain waves of children watching television were slower than when they're asleep.

My children had been spared, and I was proud.

SO HOW CAN IT BE that here I am now, in the twenty-first century: a grandmother, who has to daily pry a recalcitrant child away from the glowing screen—the glowing screen with which I'm writing these sentences? How can it be that the enslaved child resisting parental discipline is myself?

I have no patience anymore to write things out by hand, and as for typewriters, there's no such thing anymore. If a word processor without Internet capability were one day in the future to become available (I think that actually, by now, there are such computers), I wouldn't buy one. Why go to the trouble, as I used to, of submitting articles *on paper*, in an envelope, at an ancient post office, where ancient souls wait on ancient lines? Publications everywhere these days use e-mail.

Is Internet-dependence a personal habit I can sidestep?

Oh, come on. Who do you think you are?

Above all, how would I know what's happening in the world? I can't wait anymore for the morning newspaper. Today will be old by the rising of the sun, and the rest of the world will have moved on by.

It's the light that entrances, to which I've grown addicted, and it's exponentially more corrupting than television could ever have dreamed.

Filth at your fingertips and at your command. And time flies by unnoticed.

I've grown accustomed to your face.

It's inexplicably mesmerizing.

OF PARKINSON'S
AND PARKING

WHEN A WRITER'S NOT WRITING

If I had known that someday my feet would stop
I would have run through meadows
fresh morning dew
I would have sat by cool sunny waters
and dipped in my toes
I would have danced and danced in the icy snows
If I had known that my hands would stop
I would have written a thousand poems
until I ran out of words
I would have caressed my children's faces
during all my waking hours
and would have signed my name
over and over and over
Just because I could.
Now I cry a million tears
not for what was, and cannot be
but for everything I could have done
If only I had known

Naomi Lobl

Early one spring evening, having waited longer than usual at the Lobls' front door, I knocked again, tentatively. I knew they'd gotten home from Naomi's checkup, because on my way over there in a taxi, I had called from my cell to make sure. "Did the doctor...may I ask if...what the doctor tol...if the doctor told you something?" I had said on the phone, stumbling over my own confusion as to what I was actually saying, and whether I was being intrusive and should have asked another way, or even better, not asked...and meanwhile chastising myself inwardly: *Of course the doctor told them something, you idiot*, before stepping deeper into my mistake with: "I mean...like a prognosis?"

Naomi Lobl and I first met in 1992, when I needed permission to include one of her poems in an anthology of Jewish women's writings. Over time, we have grown familiar and at ease with each other's weaknesses and strengths, habits—good and otherwise—mannerisms, aspirations, fears, hopes, likes and dislikes; and with each other's personal histories in childhood and adulthood as daughters, sisters, wives, mothers, mothers-in-law, and grandmothers. We also know about each other's medical histories. So I was smart enough to know I'd said something stupid. There is a "prognosis" for Naomi Lobl's advanced case of the progressive disease called Parkinson's only in the sense of the famous "prognosis" for the condition called life, whose cure is contracted inevitably at birth.

There was a two- or three-second silence during which I got the impression—from the deep intake of breath on the other end, and long exhalation—that Naomi was debating with herself how to answer an impossible question truthfully.

"Everything's OK," she replied decisively, with the matter-of-fact tone of a mother who's steering a rowboat through the rapids without any oars, yet who must pause midstream to reassure one of the passengers—a scared, precocious child.

What are we? We recite from the Jewish siddur each morning. *What is our life? What our kindness? What our strength? Men of renown are as if they never existed and men of wisdom as if they were devoid of understanding, and ha'kol hevel...All is vanity and vexation of spirit.*

But everything's OK.

LOOKING OUT AT THE VIEW from the Lobls' *mirpeset*, where the sun was sinking in the sky, I took a seat on one of the plastic porch chairs and pushed my thoughts away, letting them drift off unsupervised.

I'd wait a little before knocking again.

My gaze wandered around absentmindedly. I'd always assumed that the area over there to the west was the Ramot neighborhood, but now realized it must be downtown Jerusalem, near Center One and the Central Bus

Station, because there was the big David's Harp Bridge. (Geography's never been my strong suit.) And that bluish streak of haze in the distance was the Dead Sea. Or…a cloud?

Under ordinary circumstances, the window boxes hanging neatly in a row along the porch railing had fared all right out here on this *mirpeset*, not that I'd ever paid them much attention. I had a dim visual impression, in retrospect, of red geraniums overflowing and thriving, and other assorted flowers whose names I didn't know. Now some were surviving, some were dying, and others were dead—all of which was to be expected, given the reduction in care they'd been getting this year from human hands. During one of our previous interview sessions, Naomi had commented with a small, droll smile: "The weeds are having a garden party."

The dark and wild canopy of velvety leaves overhead, however, had at some point since my last visit burst extravagantly into bloom. Looking up, I saw that those flowering vines weren't attached to an overhead garden trellis, as I'd vaguely supposed. My eyes followed the vines back down now, twining and twirling, to a twisty, skinny little gray tree trunk standing like a sentry near the Lobls' front gate—definitely a Middle Eastern, ancient sort of tree. Never saw one like that around Main Street and Elm, that's for sure. All the densely tangled, exuberant growth, weighted down by the burden of its own beauty, had created a joyfully drooping, top-heavy arch over the walkway—all the delicately frilled, tiny new bugle-shaped blossoms exultantly chaotic and welcoming, as if for a wedding. The tree had probably been spared a pruning by virtue of the laws of *shemittah*; a gardener's shears would have clipped and nipped in the bud such an uninhibited, shameless celebration of *Eretz Yisrael*'s earthly gorgeousness.

I checked my watch.

Just then, over the geraniums, my gaze was caught midair by the sudden darting into my line of vision of a shining, tiny black hummingbird, exquisite and iridescent, glistening violet and emerald green in the sunlight; his perfect, elegant little head held high, unseen wings whirring like a bumblebee's, invisibly holding him in place as if he were standing on air; then he was gone.

In this light, at this hour, and from my elevated lookout in the hilly Ramat Shlomo neighborhood, the ivory-colored landscape on the horizon appeared—thanks to an optical illusion—to be undulating and wobbling in the horizontal sunrays, and to be either very far away or very near, take your pick. Whatever its twenty-first-century urban flaws and political conflicts, whatever was being suffered that day by its thousands of ant-sized human inhabitants, these blemishes were momentarily soothed and smoothed away by some soft celestial eraser, forgiven and forgotten in the silvery mirage created by the sun's low-angled glare. Had I believed my eyes, watching the glowering orange ball of fire picking up girth as it dropped through the deepening blue-violet air, I would have reached out from afar to touch with my hand a pale and twinkling fairy tale kingdom...floating face-up and weightless...aloof...*Yerushalayim sheli.*

HAD SOMEBODY INSIDE the house just said my name? It sounded like it, but that could have been the recurrent tinnitus in my left ear, I wasn't sure.

I got up from the chair and stood before the Lobls' front door with head tipped forward, and hearing nothing, knocked loudly and assertively now, as if I were a real adult (a category that, of course, at my age, applies, and then some) and as if I were in possession of any reasonable adult's natural sense of entitlement. Not someone who, standing outside the home of a close friend—a trusted, beloved friend—is still so thoroughly wired for self-doubt that my knuckles balk at knocking loud enough to be heard. Afraid of making too much noise, afraid of bothering them. Maybe Rabbi Lobl was just then helping Naomi down the stairs, or helping her out of the wheelchair onto the couch.

Born within months of each other a few years after World War II, I in a serenely anti-Semitic, sleek American 1950s suburb and she in a German displaced persons camp—our so-called formative years could hardly have been more different, culturally and religiously. I, the baby of my family, and the lonely, only Jewish girl in school from grades one through twelve, had never heard of Shabbos but had heard of Yom Kippur (I thought it had something to do with kippered herring). And she, Naomi Rivkah Stern: the lonely only child of Orthodox Holocaust survivors Reb Moshe Aryeh and Perl Laya, whose five previous children, ages two to thirteen, had been lost in Auschwitz (three in the gas chambers, two whose fate remained unknown after their selection for the Nazis' "medical experiments" on twins). The Sterns emigrated to Williamsburg, in Brooklyn, where Naomi Rivkah grew up as a Bais Yaakov girl. Her siblings' lives and deaths were kept semi-secret from her by the permanently grieving parents. As Naomi Lobl writes in her memoir, *Out of the Darkness*: "They didn't tell me, but they wanted me to know."

"Something shared has more reality for us than something not shared," I once heard Rebbetzin Tziporah Heller say in a *shiur*, and from our dissimilar Jewish childhoods, the two of us, Naomi and I, emerged with something in common: a deeply embedded, virtually permanent feeling of being excluded from a world we longed to join. Yet this imprinted personality pattern came along (it was a package deal, cure *cum* affliction) with a good antidote for that childhood sadness: each of us had a gift for losing herself, and finding herself, in words, and to a large extent the sense of exclusion and isolation was thereby appeased and even transformed. Whatever troubled us...whatever we wanted from afar and wondered about, abhorred, envied, loved, feared, failed to understand...we had someone with whom to share it—someone with time on her hands, who was never bored by a small person's childish imaginings: *ourselves*.

As is the case for many people drawn to writing, it is the act of *finding the right words* that makes us feel satisfied and at home. Each right word is like a golfer's hole-in-one. The urge to create something that we can look at and say, *this is good*, provides a way to refute some perceived deficiency in ourselves or in the environment, and establishes an identity independent of other people's opinions. It's a way to feel we're not insignificant after all, not empty, not unlovable after all. It's how to know we exist, and have a role to play. We belong somewhere. Writing gives rise spontaneously to a self-respect that otherwise would simply not have been in our repertoire of emotions. It is the writing process, more than the completed piece of writing, that turns pain into gain, and can get around just about any boulder that blocks our way. In the act of describing the impediment accurately and giving it a name, even war can be tamed; even Iran's nuclear bomb can be thereby defused...if only in our thoughts. Writing about sadness can make us happy. Writing about deficiencies turns them into advantages. Many questions never find answers, but to find a word that hits the spot is like quelling a midnight craving. Any sorrow can be turned inside out by becoming something to write about.

STARTING IN THE EARLY 1990s, Naomi Lobl and I used to meet each other occasionally at the coffee shop of Center One for a writing *chavrusa*—not that we called it this at the time; it wasn't a formal arrangement. Having someone to write with kept us rooted to the spot, and we got some good writing done in those days, unable as we were to get up and sweep the coffee shop floor or carry our dishes to the sink. (The author Ernest Hemingway is quoted as having said that the hard part about writing is that first you have to clean the refrigerator.) Rabbi Lobl would give his wife a lift from Ramat Shlomo, I'd take the #3 from Arzei HaBirah. The waitresses knew to bring me a cappuccino; for Naomi, her glass of Sprite; and off we'd go, submerged across the table from each other in our separate worlds, sometimes conferring, joking, confiding, but for the most part satisfied to enjoy in each other's company that which had always been a solitary pursuit. The word *writing* had always served as a synonym for "being alone." And now the aloneness was something shared.

I remember the time I was sitting at the table and looked up from my laptop as Naomi was coming toward me across the Center One coffee shop. She was giving off what seemed (to me, because I was starting to know her pretty well by now) an unhappy air, and was proceeding with slow little steps, eyes focused on the floor as if she were navigating an uneven sidewalk before a crowd of critical spectators. I remember wondering what was wrong with her.

One day—it might have been that same morning—she said there was a story she wanted to write about a conversation she'd had with one her granddaughters. She had the title already, "The Question," and had composed most of the lines in her head. But something was wrong with her hand so it would have to wait.

After what I recall as a few weeks, I remember her telling me on the phone that the hand was still a problem. She had undergone blood tests, but the results were inconclusive. Her married daughters were taking turns coming over to help with the house, and her husband was temporarily taking care of things in the kitchen. I recall her saying that she was feeling obsolete, but it wasn't really so terrible. She couldn't write, she couldn't go to work, she couldn't clean the house. But she said there was an advantage: she had time to think about other things in life.

I said that maybe she could dictate that story about her granddaughter to me over the phone and I'd type it up for her. That piece, which Naomi composed and edited in her head, then set to memory before dictating it to me line by line, was published later in *Out of the Darkness*.

In the seven years that have gone by since this conversation in the coffee shop, Naomi Lobl did not regain the ability to write by hand or to type on a keyboard. So her *modus operandi* as a writer has by necessity changed. She composes, edits, and memorizes what she wants to write from beginning to end, then gives dictation to any friend or relative who is available and so inclined. The problem with such an arrangement, of course, is that people are busy and involved in their own lives, as she herself once was and wishes she could be again. Knowing this, Naomi is loath to impose. So most of her writing does not get written.

For the past few years, I had hoped Naomi Lobl would dictate a piece about her experience of this illness. I was especially interested in her experience as a writer who wasn't writing, and how she handled this, given the fact that for different reasons, under entirely different circumstances, I wasn't writing either. But she had always said that she didn't have anything particularly inspiring or new to say about her situation; it was really her own private matter, and in any case, Parkinson's had been written about by many people, so what was the point of speaking about it publicly?

One day, about seven months ago, to my surprise and delight, Naomi Lobl suddenly told me on the phone that there were a few ideas about Parkinson's, and about illness in general, that she wanted to try to share now.

Hence this interview.

I knocked again, decisively. Knock, *knock!* and sharpened my ears. If they still didn't answer, then I'd call Rabbi Lobl's cell phone, and if he didn't pick up—this is what I was visualizing as I stood there—I'd bang on the door! I'd call Hatzolah! Call an ambulance! Call the police!

"*Sarah.*" It was Naomi's voice—calm, deliberate, low-pitched—heard through the door. "*It's open. Come in.*"

> *...Her interest went beyond that of a small child. It was as though she entered my thoughts. The questions she asked were similar to the questions that I had wanted answered when I was her age. I saw a kindred spirit. At last I began to feel that I had someone to share my burden and pain. The age did not really matter.*
>
> *One Friday night during conversation on this topic, she asked me a question that electrified both of us: "Bubby, did it hurt your sisters and brothers when they died?"*
>
> *This was a place I'd never gone to, in all my years of anguish over the fate of my siblings. I hadn't actually thought about it. I looked into my granddaughter's eyes. I could see the anxiety as she waited for my answer, and I, too, was curious to see what my answer would be.*
>
> *I knew two things. One, that there would be no histrionics, and two, that I would tell her the truth, as I knew it. It took a few*

moments to pull myself together. Then I said, "No, it didn't hurt them. They were told that they were going to take a shower. They didn't know they were going to be killed. But instead of water, gas came out of the faucets and that put them to sleep. A deep, deep sleep until they died. Then they were taken to the crematorium, where they were burned." She asked, horrified, "Did it hurt them when they were burned? Did they feel anything?" I answered, "My sweet child, they had already died."

Her face quieted down. Her breathing became regular. And something happened to me, too. The great pain that had been percolating inside me all the years turned down to a simmer. It didn't really change anything, but sharing it with this little girl, and knowing that she cared so much, and knowing that she understood my pain, and knowing that in a way it was her pain, too, comforted me in a way that nothing else could, all those years.

From "The Question" by Naomi Lobl

THE LEFT SIDE of the Lobls' beige sofa, sticking out, as is its wont, several inches beyond the living room doorframe, always serves as a pleasantly happy harbinger for me of my not-yet-visible friend who can't get up to open the front door for me but who is seated, I know, on the other end of that couch, on the right-hand corner cushion. In my mind's eye, I'm already seeing her before I walk in: she in her black snood, a pile of books at her side and a bunch of *frum* magazines and newspapers, and her cell phone and house phone. Her dark-brown eyes (only recently, after all these years of conversing for the most part by phone, did I discover to my surprise that her eyes are not light blue, as I'd always thought) smile to me as I get settled next to her on the couch, with my pen and my notebook and my laptop, and a printout of what we've done so far.

She asks, "Do you want something? My husband made chicken soup."

"Good, I was hoping."

"OK. He went to *daven*, but he'll be back in a few minutes."

This will be our fifth or sixth interview session in person over the past half-year, along with innumerable phone conversations. Back when we started, I took it for granted that interviewing results in interviews. Nowadays, though, given my own internal speed bumps and stumbling blocks, along with the interviewee's persistent second thoughts, retractions, and oral revisions (upon hearing various portions of what she has said read back to her, she dismisses this and that quote with a disgusted little wave of the hand, followed by, "Please erase that"), my great expectations have been—I won't say smashed. *Lowered.*

Today I'm feeling optimistic. I think the interview's pretty much finished.

Before reading the whole thing aloud to her from the beginning, I need Naomi's clarification of something from one of our phone interviews. "The technical details got garbled," I tell her. "I lost my place a few times when I was typing up my notes. I'll read it aloud now from the start of the passage, so you'll get the context. Here goes. '*I found out after doing a lot of research that there is no known cure for Parkinson's. There were rumors about a drug called Azilect, that it might stop the progress of the disease, but this didn't prove to be the case, so the American FDA never approved it. There is also another option, a surgical procedure to place electrodes on the brain. They knock on the skull bone to locate the exact center of the place where the neurons of the Parkinson's that are giving the signals to the neurotransmitters whose neurons are missing, and then they insert electric wiring from the skull along the neck, which is somehow fastened into place.*'"

Naomi is laughing.

"It's picturesque, I know," I say to her before continuing. "Don't you especially love that part about the skull along the neck which is fastened into place? '*And this is instead of the natural neurotransmitter giving directions to the body—the neurotransmitter that is now unable to function. The brain's neurons have died, and the wiring connects to those neurons that are not functioning, and these send the signal to the synthetic neurotransmitter.*'"

Fingers poised over the keyboard of my laptop, I'm ready for Naomi's clarifications, but she gives that dismissive little wave of her hand that I have come to know too well, and to anticipate. "I want to leave out that passage," she says. "The technical details aren't important. The point I wanted to make was about the hopes that were building up in people for a cure—the new drug and then the new surgery. I recently spoke to someone who had the surgical procedure. I asked him how it had changed his symptoms. He told me that he still has to take medication, but he takes less. Some of his symptoms went away and some stayed the same and one symptom became worse. So it's obviously a last resort. And there are special criteria that restrict eligibility."

"Are you eligible?"

"No, they only take people under the age of sixty. I said I was thirty-nine, but they didn't believe me."

Rabbi Lobl has come back from *davening* and comes into the living room to ask Naomi if we're ready for dinner.

The hard part about interviewing is that first you have to have chicken soup.

SS: *How would you describe Parkinson's?*

NL: You mean mine? Everyone has his own.

SS: *Yours. And everyone's. Both.*

NL: Parkinson's is a very insidious disease. It "creeps along on little cat feet," like the fog in the famous Carl Sandburg poem. In the early stages of my illness, it was impossible to realize the total effect I was going to experience.

Parkinson's comes about when the brain stops producing dopamine, and this depletion of dopamine in the brain affects many facets of a person, including the serotonin level, which in turn causes many other changes. The standard approach today is to treat the symptoms. This unfortunately has many side effects, so the drugs are always chosen by trial and error.

A severe case can take over the whole body, but there are degrees of severity. Some people have it milder than others. Even in supposedly mild cases, however, it changes a person's life totally, and I can say it causes preoccupation twenty-four hours a day.

There is no known cure. Every now and then there are rumors of a breakthrough, but they haven't discovered anything yet. There is one method that is used only in very severe, advanced cases. They perform a brain operation to implant a device that sends out electrical impulses, and that could be very helpful. But this has its own risks, and it is not known if the improvements are permanent. Some people claim that they aren't.

SS: *How long have you had Parkinson's?*

NL: My first symptom appeared in 2008, when I had difficulty with walking. I attributed this, however, to a different long-standing medical condition that I have, and Parkinson's never occurred to me. My walking became increasingly labored, then my right pinky began to tremble. But none of the doctors I went to recognized the symptoms. I continued going to various doctors for two years, taking blood tests and undergoing other medical testing. But nothing showed up.

SS: *How could that be?*

NL: None of the tests are totally reliable for detection of Parkinson's.

SS: *So what happened?*

NL: I eventually understood that I had Parkinson's.

SS: *You mean you realized it on your own? The doctor didn't tell you?*

NL: Not the doctor I had been going to. A neurologist told me.

SS: *What did he say?*

NL: [*She gives a laugh.*] He said I had Parkinson's.

SS: *How did you feel when he told you?*

NL: [*No answer.*]

SS: *Is that a stupid question?*

NL: [*Naomi looks over at me with an indulgent, amused expression.*] That's what we do. We ask people who have just been in a *pigua* [suicide bombing]: *Tell me g'verti, how did you feel when you saw the body parts flying?* And the people say, *Welllllll...*

SS: *So how did you feel? I'm asking.*

NL: When I finally received the verdict? As if I'd been shot out of a cannon.

SS: *Then what?*

NL: I was naive. My symptoms were still relatively mild, and I had no idea what was in store. As time went by, whenever I noticed a new symptom being born, I was shocked, appalled. It was like being turned violently upside down and shaken. I had been informed that this is what would happen, but each time a brand-new symptom appeared, I would automatically expect it to go away after a while. When the symptom stuck around and kept getting worse instead of better, which is not what happens in regular illnesses, I felt desperate and angry at my own body, as if it were betraying me from within. I began to grasp that this was the nature of the beast. No matter what my doctors did, this illness was not going anywhere. No matter how much I wished and prayed that it would go away. Eventually I began to accept it.

SS: *To accept it? Or something else?*

NL: I became more resigned to dealing with it.

In the beginning I used to hide. I didn't go out among people. I saw myself through other people's eyes, and when people see someone who is incapacitated or disfigured, it comes naturally to make assumptions about what kind of person he or she is. We mistakenly equate bodily impairment with mental impairment. I remember feeling that I didn't know who I was anymore.

SS: *I remember that poem you wrote, "Who Am I?" Remember? You dictated it to me on the phone. It's somewhere in my computer. I hope.*

NL: Oh, that. It was a stupid poem.

SS: *It's a wonderful poem, Naomi. I loved it. I hope I can find it. My computer has crashed a few times since then. You were saying...about what happened in the beginning, after the diagnosis?*

NL: Gradually I began to grasp that I would be restricted from now on in what I could do in life, which completely unnerved me. I was so scared of becoming a burden, of being seen by my family as a burden.

In high school I once had a teacher, a non-Jew, who taught English in the General Studies department, and I remember his telling us that his favorite line in all of literature—I don't remember where it comes from—was, "For there is nothing either good or bad but thinking makes it so." The idea is that the reality of a person's life is what he believes it to be, even if it is not true.

When I first got the diagnosis, I decided that I would not take the drugs that are given to treat the symptoms. I read about all the side effects that could be, and I was wary of them. Most neurologists I went to recommended that I take these drugs, but there was one neurologist who felt that I would be better off without them, and that I could "treat" my Parkinson's with a walker, and a wheelchair, whatever...as the need arose. But in the end, I realized that I could not do without medication.

SS: *Does the medication help?*

NL: It helps somewhat. It doesn't help completely. And it has terrible side effects. [*Naomi pauses for several seconds.*] Here I could go on and say, "No one but someone who has Parkinson's can understand it" but that's a stupid thing to say because it's true. I really don't have a problem anymore with people not understanding this illness. I don't even try to explain it. I always tell my children, "Thank G-d that you don't understand it."

SS: *Wouldn't you say that the same thing applies for any illness, and by the same token, any life situation, that misperception is the rule rather than the exception? One person cannot fully understand the other one because of all the infinite number of variables that make any one individual's situation unique.*

NL: Being understood is a special issue with patients whose outward appearance is misleading. On the outside, a Parkinson's patient can look healthy, even very healthy, for years. It's often difficult for an observer to realize how sick and disabled the person really is. By looking at a face, you can't tell how ravaged the person might be inside.

SS: *And yet on the other hand, I think of what you wrote about your little granddaughter when she understood your pain, how deeply you were comforted by her.*

NL: In that instance, I felt comforted not because that young child understood my pain but because she shared it.

SS: *Can you give me an example of the kind of misunderstandings that occur?*

NL: For the last couple of years, I have developed a hearing problem and I use a hearing aid, and so when I go to a *simchah*, I can't always hear what a person is saying when there's music in the background.

SS: *But that doesn't actually have to do with Parkinson's per se, does it?*

NL: It has to do with it insofar as I'm in a wheelchair due to Parkinson's, and when people see someone in a wheelchair, basically immobile, they automatically make certain assumptions. If my answers seem inane, they think that I'm senile, or that I have Alzheimer's. Sometimes when people start talking to me, I'm sitting there trying to make an appropriate response, if I can think of one, and every now and then, they could be asking me where I live, and I might answer, "*Betach*, of course."

[*The two of us, Naomi and I, get a good laugh out of this one. She knows that the same marvelously humbling experience happens to me, too, because of my tinnitus. Welcome, dear reader, to the wide and wonderful world of high-frequency nerve damage!*]

Many people I've known for years speak to me as if I'm totally over the hill and through the woods. For instance, they say very loudly and kindly: "Do you know who I am? *Do. You. Know. Who. I. Am?*"

And then I say, "Of course I know who you are." And they say, "Verrr-y *gooooood!*"

> I look for myself in the mirror and see only what isn't there
> I look for myself in my children as they happily flit by
> I am my father I am my son
> but I am really the only one
> I wasn't there when my thoughts began
> I will not be there when they will end
> But somewhere in me there is a little spark
> that will last until the end of time
> that G-d my Creator put in me
> And this makes me who I am
>
> *Naomi Lobl*

Human beings make mistakes, and that is part of the human experience. When I find myself obsessing over the insignificant mistakes of others—*she did this, and someone didn't do that, and why can't they understand, etc., etc.*—I have to take myself in hand and say, *Look, lady, so-and-so didn't intend to make you feel bad. She just felt awkward and said something stupid!* We all make stupid mistakes—it's one of the realities of life among humans. We say the wrong thing and we do the wrong thing. We hurt people without realizing it.

But I don't hide anymore from the rest of mankind, the way I did in the early years, after the diagnosis. I have Parkinson's, but I am still who I am. I still want to live my life!

This illness is teaching me how fragile is the life of a human being.

I once heard an interpretation given over in the name of Rav Binyomin Eisenberger. In the weekly *parashah* of *Re'eh*, *Hashem* says, "I give you today a blessing or a curse." Rav Eisenberger said that in Hebrew, *ha'yom* can be translated as "today" or "a day." This can be interpreted as meaning: *Every morning I give you a day. A new day. You can make it into a berachah or a kelalah. It is your choice.*

The decision is in the person's own hands.

Sometimes there will come a horrible moment when a person falls so low that he can hardly believe he's there. At such a time, he or she can feel: *I cannot go on. What's the point?* Parkinson's has forced me to look harder for meaning in my life. Why is *Hashem* keeping me here? We all have to find our own meaning, and we have to ask ourselves:

What does my life mean to me? Why was I put here? Why am I on this earth?

SS: *Can you share some of your own answers to that?*

NL: I haven't finalized any of my answers. But I know one thing: that when people are on their death beds, they don't regret not making more money. They don't regret not having more material possessions. And they don't regret not getting enough honor in their community. But they do regret not having spent more time with their families, and not having done more *chessed* and mitzvos. When a life is over, this cannot be rectified.

SS: *How do you handle the low moments?*

NL: Sometimes well. Sometimes not well. Having a totally zany sense of humor comes in handy.

SS: *For example?*

NL: A few years ago, we went to a family bar mitzvah in Bnei Brak. Afterward, when my daughter was trying to help me into the back seat of the car to go home, somehow one of my feet got stuck under the front seat. She tried to get it unstuck, but the foot wouldn't move. She tried, and tried, but it wouldn't budge. And then she couldn't get my other foot inside, because the first foot was in the other foot's way. I was just sitting there watching the proceedings. So she said, "Mommy, *you* try to move it!"

I tried, and I couldn't. The whole situation overwhelmed me. I was overcome by a big wave of despair. I said, "Honey, I have no more ability to move my foot than you do."

I found myself suddenly at a crossroads. Two long roads stretched ahead of me into the future. If I stayed where I was and cried, I knew I could go on crying for the rest of my life. And no one would want to listen to me. I had to quickly choose a direction and keep going.

I looked at my daughter and she looked at me, and she smiled, and then, at the same instant, we both burst out laughing. That was it. Once we started, we couldn't stop. We were laughing so hard, the tears started streaming down our faces. We would try to catch our breath, but all one of us had to do was look over at the other one and we'd start off all over again. Passersby were stopping to see what was so funny—some of them couldn't tell if we were laughing or crying—but all they saw was one woman half-in and half-out of a taxi, with an empty wheelchair waiting in the wings, and another, younger, obviously healthier-looking woman at her side. We had to admit, we understood anyone who didn't agree with us that this was the funniest thing in the world. Even we ourselves didn't understand. One woman who was standing there looking at the two of us, said to us very sweetly, "*Ani yecholah la'azor?*" [May I help you?] Poor woman, that was the best thing she could have said, and we burst out laughing all over again.

SS: *Another example?*

NL: One Shabbos I got up to go into the bathroom in the middle of the night and lost my balance. I fell over into the shower, which had water in it. Only my feet were sticking out. I couldn't get up. I called my husband, who is a very deep sleeper. It took a while until he realized from his sleep what I was saying, that I was in the bathroom, on the floor. At this point my nightgown and robe were already soaking wet. He came into the bathroom and said, "Where are you? I don't see you in here." I said, "I'm right here. In the bathroom." And he said, "No, you're not." After going back and forth like this a few times, I finally managed somehow to convince him. He looked down and saw my feet and agreed that I was in the bathroom.

Getting me up required some major maneuvering.

On Sunday morning, I called a friend of mine to tell her the whole story and I was just about to start crying about that moment when I had to convince my husband that I was in the bathroom, but all of a sudden the scene struck me as more absurd than tragic, and I chuckled. So my friend laughed, too. And I laughed. And she laughed. It was so funny. It was wonderful.

I HAVE COME TO DREAD phone calls from Naomi the morning after she dictates a piece of writing. The opener I especially don't want to hear goes something like this: "You know, Sarah, I've been thinking about something, and there's something I want to tell you. You know what I said yesterday, about [such and such]? Please take it out."

Her reasons vary:

I was thinking about what I said yesterday about [such and such] and it's as if I'm giving a sermon. It's been said before, a lot better, by a lot of other people. Please delete it.

Sarah, hi. Can you talk? I've been thinking about what I was saying yesterday, and it's such a cliché.

Please take out the part about...

People don't need to hear from me about...

I've been thinking about something and want to ask why you put my poem in there. It's such a stupid poem.

Sarah, hi, can you talk? [So-and-so] just called me and told me there's a true story in one of the frum magazines by a woman writer with Parkinson's. I don't think people need two articles about a woman writer with Parkinson's.

Sarah, hi, you know that article I told you about? My daughter went back and got that issue and she said it's very interesting. Can you please cancel my interview?

"Hi, Sarah. I've been thinking about it and I have to tell you something. You know what I said yesterday about how Parkinson's is teaching me not to worry about insignificant little things?"

"Yeah...so? What's wrong with it?"

"It's not true."

"What's not true?"

"What I said. I don't understand how I could have said it. I worry about stupid little things all the time. I don't know what I was thinking. So take it out. Please."

"Naomi, we used to talk about things like that long before you had Parkinson's. Remember? I remember talking with you about this—that when one of us hadn't lived up to one of our ideals, that didn't mean the ideal was false, or that we were false. Or hypocritical, etc., etc. Come on. I'm not saying anything you don't know. People don't move to some higher level and stay put there like rocks on the side of the road."

She gives one of her soft, amused, nearly inaudible chuckles on the other end of the line, and I'm encouraged. Maybe I'll be able to keep that paragraph. "Naomi, come on, please think about it."

"I thought about it."

"So look. Think about it: Is it true or is it not true? Does having Parkinson's help you to discriminate between significant things and insignificant things?"

"Yes. I said it, and it's true, and we've said it many times and other people have said it a million times. It's a cliché, Whether or not I said it isn't the question. I know I did. It's getting dangerous to talk to you. I feel like I'm being bugged by the Mossad. That's not what I'm objecting to. It's the whole interview that's making me uncomfortable. It's blowing me up into some kind of *tzaddekes*. I've been thinking about it and there's no such thing."

"No such thing as a *tzaddekes*?"

"No. As something small and insignificant."

"Oh, so what you're saying is that everything's significant. No such thing as small stuff."

"Right."

"Oh, so if that's what you're saying, I agree with you completely. There's no such thing as insignificant, so what has that got to do with what we're talking about?"

"What are we talking about?"

"That everything's significant. So we agree!"

"No we don't." She laughs. I laugh. "How did that happen?" says Naomi.

SS: *Why did you always say no before, about writing about your illness for public perusal?*

NL: I had a conflict in me—to keep quiet, to keep the illness a secret, or to reveal it.

SS: *What would be the advantage of keeping it a secret?*

NL: A lot of people don't like to talk about their illnesses, and don't want people to know.

SS: *So something changed?*

NL: Yes.

SS: *What changed?*

NL: I decided that I should try to help remove the stigma.

SS: *The stigma of Parkinson's?*

NL: The stigma attached to being ordinary. Most people have it in them to be heroic, but most of the time we are ordinary people. When a person is limited by a progressive illness such as MS or lupus, *lo aleinu*, with little hope of getting better, he or she shouldn't have to demonstrate to anyone that they are noble, or holy. They should be able to feel confident of having their family's respect, and their own self-respect, without keeping up an image of being heroic and optimistic and spiritually strong.

SS: *Are you saying it's heroic to not try to impress people as heroic?*

NL: No. I'm saying that a person who's ill is probably going to feel overwhelmed in the beginning, and discouraged and terrified. These feelings are universal for people in such situations. I really want people to know that they don't have to deny these feelings. These reactions are true and cannot be denied. I want people to realize the legitimacy of their emotions. It's not easy to have a catastrophic illness. Or any illness. It's not meant to be easy. There will be some bad days. Some very bad days, when people are very discouraged and terrified. We cannot successfully pretend to ourselves that we are already the *tzaddikim* we read about. There's no shortcut. The fact is, there are some very special people in this world, who are "superior" to the ordinary average person. Reading about them when I myself was struggling in the year after my diagnosis, I would say to myself, *Why can't I be like that?* This used to make me feel terrible. When people are in crisis, they cannot afford to deny the truth of their feelings.

SS: *To other people or to themselves?*

NL: To both. To others and to ourselves. We have to get to know who we are, and not be afraid of what we'll find. At the same time, there is an objective truth that there are *tzaddikim* who really are greater than the rest of us. That is their role in the *klal*, to be greater. They can inspire the rest of us and pull us higher.

When I feel ashamed of myself for having a difficult time, I have to remember that we always have a choice, a human being is always given the choice. It is in our nature that we will sometimes question our whole existence. We need constant *chizuk*. In the times of the Talmud, one of those famous deathbed stories has the great *rav* on his deathbed, and the *talmidim* ask him what's important. And he answers, I wish for you to have as much fear of G-d as fear of man. So I always think of that and see from this that it has always been this way. People have always needed strengthening. It's very hard to be dependent on other people, on your family, and it's very hard for the family members. Very hard for everyone. It's not easy for my husband to take care of me. He is a brilliant *talmid chacham*, and I think that this is what enables him to do what he does for me. To tolerate and understand the weaknesses of a spouse takes wisdom and patience. The ill spouse and the caretaker spouse need to be matter-of-fact about the illness. We're condescending toward people who are helpless. People whom we identified once as being strong and capable, and who saw themselves that way, too. There is a stigma connecting these infirmities with old age, and no one wants to be like that, no one can imagine ever being like that. So people feel, "That's not me." *Those old people. Those sick old people. Those dying people, so out of it. I'm not going to be like that.*

SS: *Like what?*

NL: Seemingly not *with it.* Parkinson's patients walk slowly, we talk slowly. We slur our words. Parkinson's patients don't have a choice about these physical developments. The person will eventually get to the point of needing help to move around. Most Parkinson's patients get to a point where they need some help walking. A wheelchair or a walker is a common thing. The stigma we feel about disabilities. Of needing to use a crutch, or a walker, or a wheelchair. There is a basic stigma about being needy. Of being helpless sometimes, maybe even most of the time.

I think that there is something about interviewing that is intrinsically phony. It creates a false impression. It is a blown-up picture. I feel you're making me into someone I'm not. If anyone who's ill is going to be reading this article, and there are a lot of people who are ill—I don't mean an illness that is temporary and is expected to get better or even go away, I'm talking about one of the catastrophic illnesses, one of the progressive illnesses, that they have not found a cure for yet and which is not expected to do anything but get worse—if those people read things I've said here and see some quotes that sound strong to them, and spiritual, and optimistic, then even though those particular quotes are accurate, an interview with someone in a magazine can't give the whole picture. The interview will most likely end up conveying a false impression of how I'm dealing with my situation.

It's a damaging distortion. I used to read things around the time my illness was diagnosed, when I was going through a real identity crisis, when I felt that I had lost my identity, when I felt I was nothing. I'd read things about how other people were dealing with serious illnesses or with other extreme situations in life—it wouldn't have to be about illness—and I'd feel that I should be like that. But I wasn't. So I felt inferior.

SS: *Is that why you keep asking me to take things out? So that no reader anywhere will end up feeling inferior as a result of this interview?*

NL: Part of the reason. Some of the things I say, when you read it back

to me, I think they're ridiculous. Like some guru dispensing wisdom.
I sound like such an arrogant know-it-all, very full of myself.

SS: *Well, at least if people read what you've just said, you'll get credit for being*
a very humble know-it-all. [We laugh together, and I'm wishing I could
convey, with words, Naomi's hesitations and silences.]

SS: *How do you expect to remove the stigma of being ill and weak? I think*
it's ingrained in human nature, to be scared of physical deterioration and
aging. A lot of things that the Torah forbids are ingrained in human na-
ture. The art of seeing and relating to the person who is still there, inside
a changed body, is not so easily mastered.

NL: Whether it's ingrained in our nature is not the issue. Our society
needs to remove the stigma. I believe it's possible. The stigma should
be removed.

SS: *It's another impossible question. But I'm asking. How does a mobile per-*
son come to terms with immobility?

NL: With any progressive disease there get to be a lot of limitations on
people's capacity for living. It's almost self-understood that there will
be some bad moments.

SS: *Bad moments? Or very bad moments?*

NL: OK, and feelings of despair. There are many, many changes brought
about by the degenerative diseases, and they are frightening. They
change a person's life completely. Many small daily things that
I never used to appreciate suddenly become a source of anxiety.

SS: *Such as?*

NL: When my husband goes to *daven* three times a day, I sit here by myself in the living room, and many times people knock on the door
and I call out, "Who is it?" and they don't answer. So it's unnerving.
It's scary, no matter how often it's nothing. I get scared that it's a
terrorist, or a burglar. At the same time, there's something else that
changes—a strengthening of *emunah*, because it becomes clear, it
becomes obvious, that we have to connect to *Hashem* much more
than we did in the past. We need to carry on as best as we can, and
not worry, and just keep going. We have to keep going, knowing that
there are going to be some difficult times.

I was born to a *frum* family in Williamsburg, in Brooklyn, and was an
ordinary Bais Yaakov girl. I was brought up to value the Torah and

davening and was taught to keep mitzvos. I had my training in high school and seminary. I wasn't unusual in this respect.

But this illness has brought new meaning into my prayers, and I began to have a much closer connection with *Hashem*. I find myself talking to Him all the time, about everything. I tell Him what I think, good or bad, and I make deals with Him.

SS: *What kind of deals?*

NL: Did I ever tell you about the time I needed a cleaning lady?

SS: *I don't think so.*

NL: I had to fire my cleaning lady, but I hadn't found another one. I was lying on the couch, so discouraged. The floor needed sweeping, and I remember the torment I felt of not being able to get up and sweep the floor—something I realized now that I had never appreciated adequately at all. I was lying there so depressed. I cried out to *Hashem*, "*Hashem*, You can't do this to me. You cannot give me Parkinson's and leave me without a cleaning lady. What's going to be with me? I understand that Parkinson's is here to stay. But please, send me a cleaning lady!" That night I found a cleaning lady.

SS: *How?*

NL: I was still on the couch when I noticed an old address book on the shelf next to the couch, under a pile of books and newspapers. I took it from the shelf and opened it, and there was a flap, a sort of pocket in the address book for stray addresses and miscellaneous phone numbers. There was a little strip of paper sticking out of the flap, and when I opened it, there was a number written on it, no name. I dialed it, and it turned out to be the number of a cleaning lady. I asked her if she had any time available, and she came that night. She came that night to be interviewed and started work the next day. She worked for me until very recently. And did I ever tell you about my husband and parking?

SS: *I don't think so.*

NL: OK. So my husband always has to run many different kinds of errands every day to keep the household running—things that I used to take care of—and for my illness, all kinds of things. If I have to go somewhere, he has to push me there in the wheelchair when we get out of the car. He cannot leave me home alone very long, and I enjoy going out for a drive with him in the car, even when we don't have any errands for me specifically. But also I cannot stay seated in the car too long, neither in the cold of winter nor in the heat of summer. I said, "*Hashem*, you gave me Parkinson's. So please, kindly give my husband a parking space whenever we have to go somewhere." When we're looking for a place, I'll ask him, "Why don't you look on such-and-such a street?" He often says to me, "We'll never find a parking spot on that street." It's uncanny, but a parking spot always opens up for him at the right moment.

I'm not going to say it's all fun and games. I have some very dark moments. There are times I think, *I can't sit in one place for so long. I can't live like this. I can't go on. I can't go on anymore.* Then an hour later I find myself thinking it could be worse. And I feel so lucky. On some days, I can go up and down and up and down like that all day long.

One of the hardest things about all this is that the situation does not allow for any privacy.

But this Parkinson's has made me look at life differently. When I see people in pain, physically or emotionally—even though their pain is different from mine—I feel their suffering more than I did before. This illness is teaching me to be more grateful and happy for ordinary days, and for the little things I can still do, like hold the telephone, and read.

SS: *Can I ask you if you can hold a book in your hands?*

NL: Some books I can hold.

SS: *Do you still feel obsolete?*

NL: No.

Wait. Yes. I do still feel obsolete. It doesn't have the same meaning for me as it used to. I have stopped expecting my life to stay the same. I'm not waiting to be the way I was before, or to be the same person tomorrow as I am today.

SS: *Can you say how you deal with not writing?*

NL: I have stories in my head and words in my head that I think would make a good essay or story, and then after mulling it over for a few days, I always end up thinking, *Oh, that was such a silly idea.* Whereas in the past, I would have written it down right away and the words would have taken me on a journey.

I have learned that there are many things I can no longer do. But there are many other things that I still find pleasure in, in this life. And sometimes, I have moments of such sweetness that the feeling rises up inside me and I tell *Hashem*, "Thank You for creating me, for this alone it is worth living: this absolute happy moment in time."

Last night after you left, I remembered the poem I wanted to read to you.

SS: *A poem by you? I'm so glad, Naomi!*

NL: No, no. It's a famous poem. I don't remember who wrote it, but it's from the early nineteenth century, and it's in a lot of anthologies of American poetry; I might not be remembering it exactly, but it goes like this:

> Jenny kissed me when we met,
> Jumping from the chair she sat in.
> Time, you stealer of all good things,
> Put that in.
> Say I'm weary, say I'm sad
> Say that health and wealth have missed me
> Say I'm growing old but add.
> That Jenny kissed me.

Sometimes I feel like the person in the poem. There are so many difficulties, but the wonderful moments make up for everything.

SS: *For everything?*

NL: I look for those moments. Many times I think to myself, "For this alone it is worth living."

Last week we went to the *erusin* of one of my grandsons. A friend of his who got up to speak was making everyone laugh. I couldn't hear what he was saying. Usually I don't care that much, but I would have loved to understand what he was saying. Without my telling her anything, one of the people in the hall very unobtrusively got up and moved my wheelchair closer. The way she did it was sensitive and very kind.

And so it is with other things.

Sometimes I will see someone I don't know doing something kind, and I feel, *just for this it is worth living.*

This illness has changed me in that way.

SS: *I remember when you used to tell me how sitting in your backyard and watching the hummingbirds would fill you completely with joy.*

NL: Yes.

There was something I wanted to tell you—something I wanted to write about. I was sitting in the car while my husband was doing an errand in the Ungarin neighborhood, in back of Meah Shearim, waiting for him to get back, and I was looking around and I noticed a woman hanging out her laundry. She was hanging her family's clothing with great precision, as though there were a regimented system of how to hang laundry. All the men's shirts were hanging together, all the socks were in a row, linen with the other linen and baby clothes with baby clothes, and the children's shirts. And so it went, on and on. And I realized that that's one of the things that makes me feel so good about living here. The people and how they live and the symmetry in their lives. I always enjoy seeing laundry lines out. It's part of Jerusalem, part of the aura of the people and the orderly rhythm of their lives, and their good nature. It's a symbol of the serenity of how the families live. The precision and the constancy of their lives are revealed in their laundry. In the midst of terrorist attacks and missiles, life goes on. Even when we're poor or when there's danger all around, we do our best. We don't give up. And these families, the Jerusalemites, they live in tiny apartments. Most of them have many children, and the cleanliness in their apartments is unbelievable, and their children are always turned out beautifully when they go to their various schools. And this is one of the things that I feel when I live here, the souls of these people who live in the ways of the Torah. This cannot be explained. It's something in the air here. It's in the street, it's in the yeshivas. It permeates everything. The *kedushah*. There's a lot of good in people.

So I live each day, one day at a time, and I hope it will be a *berachah*. I'm going to take the good things and be happy

My favorite time of day is night, because that's when I can say, "Thank You, *Hashem*, for getting me through this day." But when I close my eyes, I often feel that I'm not worthy. So I think of one of my favorite passages in *Avinu Malkeinu*. It starts off with "Please give us life, we're entitled to it. Because of this, surely because our ancestors have done this, this one and that one, this one went through fire and died *al kiddush Hashem*, so please." Then we come to the last line and we say, "*Avinu Malkeinu, Hashem,* You know we don't deserve anything, You don't have a reason to judge us favorably regardless of what we just said. Please do it out of *chessed* and do it as a favor and please don't analyze it too much, just grant us a kindness." And if we want *Hashem* to give us *chessed* without analyzing it too much, then when we do a *chessed* we should not analyze and wonder, *Why do I have to do this?*

SS: *If there was only one message you could tell people, what would it be?*

NL: Many people try to accept what *Hashem* gives them. We can become great, each in our own real way, and become very close to *Hashem*. That's what can happen during terrible sicknesses, *lo aleinu*. There will be times they feel it's the end of the world and they don't want to go on having to fight so hard. They'll feel they'd rather give up. They needn't feel guilty or lowly about feeling that way. It's a universal feeling, and maybe it's exactly what we're meant to feel.

When people are faced with a major illness that will change their lives forever, they should try to get on with their lives as well as they can. Ultimately, people will be amazed to find strength and courage inside themselves that they had never even known was there.

There will be ups and downs, and they will feel very good about themselves when they find the way, their own way, to cope.

People can cope with illness. They can. And they do. They have the means to cope with it.

Last night I dreamed that I was out on the street and I could walk again, like other people. I myself was surprised by the fact that I could walk, but in my dream, I figured that the diagnosis of Parkinson's disease had been a big mistake. I walked up and down the block, reveling in my newfound ability. When I woke up from the pleasant dream, I expected to be devastated that I was back in my old body. I knew all too well that the reality was different from my dream. I thought, "Too bad it was just a dream." But strangely enough, I wasn't devastated.

And when one morning I couldn't brush my teeth anymore because my hands had lost their power, I couldn't believe that I could go a whole day without brushing my teeth.

And so there were milestones all around, until I got to the point where I couldn't walk unaided in the street, and then I couldn't

*walk, even aided, more than a few steps outside my house. Then
came this past Rosh Hashanah, and I couldn't go to shul to hear
the shofar. Someone had to come to my house to blow the shofar
for me, even though the shul is only at the end of our block. As
I said my prayers alone, by myself in my house, I had a wake-up
call, or an epiphany. I was crying about my deterioration and my
life, and my love of writing, which had now been denied to me because I could no longer use my hands, and was saying the prayer
of Shema Koleinu, "G-d, do not forsake me when my strength
gives out." I was crying bitterly, and I heard a voice inside my
head, saying, "Hey, wait a minute, lady. Could you please stop
crying right now? G-d did not forsake you, and He did not leave
you alone."*

Naomi Lobl

NAOMI CALLED ME THIS EVENING. There was a lot of traffic noise in the
background. She was outside somewhere. "Sarah, hi. Can you talk? I have
to tell you something." Her voice sounded unusually bubbly and light, but
I braced myself.

"Naomi, what are all those cars honking? Where are you?"

"In Geulah."

"Naomi, listen, if you're calling about the cleaning lady, I'm not going to
delete her, I'm sorry. It doesn't sound like you're preaching, or like you're a
know-it-all, not at all. So last night after we talked, I reread that story and
put her back in. I'm sorry. OK? Naomi? Naomi? Hello? Are you there?"

The line had gone dead. I hung up the phone, and it instantly rang again.
"Sarah, can you hear me now?"

"Yes, where are you?"

"Wait a minute, there's a *ram kol*. Just a second."

A loudspeaker swelled and roared to a crescendo, then passed. "What is
it saying?" I asked her, with zero hope of being heard amid the blasting
assault. I dislike those car-borne loudspeakers. They're either advertising
something, which I feel is an intrusion into other people's lives, or they're
announcing the time and place of a *levayah*, which makes me nervous.
"Where are you, Naomi? Is your husband driving?"

"No, I'm in the car waiting, I'm outside a store." Naomi's voice was
fairly trilling.

"It must be so hot in the car. Do you have air-conditioning?"

"I'm fine. We're under a tree." She wasn't laughing, exactly, but her voice sounded buoyant with good humor. What came incongruously to mind was an easy river laughing its way downstream, in sunlight. *Row, row, row your boat, gently down the stream.* "He parked right outside the store, and I'm under a tree."

"You sound so happy. What are you so happy about? Did you hear what I said about not deleting the cleaning lady?"

"It's hard to hear you, so I just want to tell you something."

"Is it about the interview? I'm sick of changing it. And I'm so mad at Google Docs. I want to finish."

"No, no." More bubbly happiness. "Nothing about the interview. You know what it's like on Thursday in Geulah around 5 p.m. or 6 p.m. during *bein hazmanim*, trying to find a parking space?"

"No, not really. I don't have a car. But yeah, go ahead. So?"

"So anyone who has a car will know exactly what I'm talking about. It's impossible to find a parking spot at this hour on the corner of Malchei Yisrael and—wait, I'm looking at the street sign—Rechov Amos, and my husband had to go into a store by six o'clock to pick something up, and it was important. He was going around and around, so he turned up a side street, and way up by Zephania there were two spaces, but I knew he'd never make it if he parked all the way up there, and it was so hot out, I didn't want him running on foot all the way down to Malchei Yisrael. And he'd never make it on time anyway, so I said, 'No, don't park here. You'll find one closer.' And when I said that, he looked over at me with such an expression—I won't even try to describe it. But I said, 'Just keep going and you'll find a spot near the store.' By now, after all this driving around in circles around Geulah, he only had four more minutes until his appointment, and you should have heard what was going on in my mind. I was *davening, Come on, please, don't pick this time to teach me a lesson—I'll never live it down. Please...Please, please, please give him a parking space close to where he has to go! Please don't choose this time to be stringent with me, please, Hashem...*And to my husband I was saying, "Don't worry, just keep going. Keep going, keep going. You'll find one, don't worry, just keep going...keep going..."

יֹשֵׁב בְּסֵתֶר עֶלְיוֹן בְּצֵל שַׁדַּי יִתְלוֹנָן:

אֹמַר לַה' מַחְסִי וּמְצוּדָתִי אֱלֹקַי אֶבְטַח בּוֹ:

O BRIDGE: A FRIENDSHIP

From a distance of mist, I saw at dawn
threads
of nothing
     strung across the water.
Thread-thin cables,
a bridge
upon a time.
Magical   shimmering
cables of steel, gossamer threads.
At dusks and at dawns
we held on tight
to its light.
What heavy lives it supported! For thirteen years,
back and forth back and forth we strutted, back
and forth, transporting loads. We could've driven a Mack truck
on those gossamer threads. Lightweight as light, on nothing at all,
Two hearty laughing ladies
shouting *l'chaim!*

Once or twice the threads dissolved, twinkling, faltered,
failed in thick nights opaque.
How we rejoiced when the lights came back on
into our two lives, one by one, little ones, coming back on.

Pains dissolving in understanding
waters, infinite reflections mirroring face to face
in this life and another, pains melting to illusion, O Bridge
upon a time
    magical
        shimmering

At dusks and at dawns, through nights
sick, opaque, thick with solitudes, thirsts, angers,
children, grandchildren,
illness, divorces, deaths, relatives, sorrowing, weeping, weddings
Crossing the darkness
and then,
>through the mist
>lights
>coming back on! One by one little ones, coming back on! Coming back
to life, into our two lives. *L'Chaim!*
Necklace of necklaces strung twinkling over the water,
lightning striking us, lightweight as light!
>>*O Bridge!*

Your cables swung twinkling
wildly over the water in
storms and in snow,
What heavy, heavy lives you supported!
What heavy hearts you supported, for thirteen years!
Back and forth back and forth back
and forth, we trudged back and forth, back and forth.
Nothing could break you. Back and forth, back and forth.

Another time, once
when the twinkling failed, again we were walking on air, but
still! We kept going, who cares!
Driving across in our Mack truck, shore to shore, back and forth two of us,
>two laughing old ladies,
>shouting *l'chaim*
>to nothing at all!
High over the water
L'chaim!
Dissolving all
in understanding
waters, infinitely mirroring,
not understanding how it could be
beyond our understanding.
>What turns one into two
>>And me to thee
>>Face to face
in this life and another.

>>*Now the frame has gotten bigger*
>>*and the waters wide*

We always said it was a gift
of words,

        So
Now
we'll leap
off into thin air
        Shall we?
Once again:
Yes. Now we'll leap
Each singing her song
shouting thanks to the bridge
that was there so long

      So long!

And letting go of the bridge
All at once we see
Who was carrying you and me

A CONVERSATION WITH
DR. GISELLE CYCOWICZ

"I have a friend," began Dr. Giselle Cycowicz, "who was together with me in Auschwitz. She works today for a Holocaust museum in America. We speak on the phone frequently—we're still close friends—and one day she called to ask my opinion about something.

"One of her coworkers at the museum where she works—who is also a Holocaust survivor—had recently gone on a lecture tour to promote the idea of reconciliation with the Germans. Why? Because the woman maintained that it would be better for us to forgive than to carry this anger all our lives. This woman had invited my friend to serve together with her in a panel discussion that would address this subject, and my friend wanted to know what I thought of the idea.

"Before telling you my answer, I will give you a little background."

"FIRST IT MUST BE SAID that by temperament and nature, my friend is, in general, not a forgiving person, and after the war, she had always been very hard on the Germans. She could never look at them as regular people; could never imagine that a German woman could ever be a real mother, etc. She did not, *could* not, see Germans as human beings.

"My friend and I were together in Auschwitz as children. She was there from 1943 to 1945, from age eleven to fourteen, and I from age fourteen to seventeen. Whereas I and my family—because of the way things turned out for Hungary—had been sent to Auschwitz directly from our own home, she and her family had already lived for three years in a Polish ghetto before being deported to Auschwitz. And in the ghetto, from the age of eight, it was she whom her family had sent out to search for food, since the SS paid less attention to young children. So by the time she and her family arrived, she already had two or three years of extreme trauma and starvation behind her.

"Some years before she addressed this question to me, I once mentioned to her that I was leaving for a lecture tour about the Holocaust, and she said, "I don't see what you have to tell anyone about your *sojourn* in Auschwitz." As far as she was concerned, my experience in Auschwitz was like some kind of pleasure trip compared to hers, because in her eyes, she still was looking at the image of me and my family immediately upon our arrival in 1944. To her we looked like normal human beings. We had some flesh on our bones.

"So she was very, very badly traumatized. But there was no one who was not. I told her that to arrive in Auschwitz and be there for just two hours was enough to give anyone a trauma for life. You didn't need to be there one more minute for this to happen. But I don't know if she believed this.

"What immediately came to mind when she asked me about reconciliation was the many groups from abroad, many of them from Germany, who regularly visit Israel. They're brought to me because of my work with survivors, and because I speak English.

"And it was one group, in particular, that I thought of, AMCHA, the Israeli Center for Holocaust Survivors and the Second Generation. Its name comes from the fact that *amchah* was one of the codewords that Jews used to recognize each other during the Holocaust. It means 'your people' in Hebrew.

"There were eleven or twelve of them, young Germans between the ages of twenty-five and thirty. They said they wanted to know the truth about Auschwitz, really, the truth, as it was. We had only an hour in which to speak, so when the hour was up, they asked if we could continue the discussion later, at my home. They arrived at 9:30 that night and stayed until about 2 a.m. I could see they really wanted to know, so I told myself not to pull any punches. I would tell them what it was like to the best of my ability.

"I didn't know where to begin.

"I found myself speaking first of the latrine.

"THE HUNGARIAN WOMEN'S BARRACK in Birkenau was located in what was known in Auschwitz as C-Lager. C-Lager was one long street with two rows of barracks, sixteen on each side. Each barrack held more than a thousand women. More than thirty thousand women all together.

"One of these thirty-two barracks was the latrine, one was the washroom, and one was the infirmary.

"We spent many hours in the day standing in line for roll call, and we all had dysentery. Try to imagine it. After standing in roll call for four hours, standing in the sun or the cold—and many times there was a curfew imposed, so we were standing hours longer—what was on our minds? To get to the latrine. This was always on our minds. But much of the time it was impossible to get there. After using the latrine, we longed to get into the washroom to wash ourselves a little bit. That was our other overriding concern. It was a constant anxiety.

"Inside the latrine barrack, running along the whole length of the building, were four long concrete blocks with holes in them. These holes served as the toilets. There was room for two hundred people to use the toilets, and at any given moment, about thirty thousand people needing and wanting to get in. To get inside that latrine was our big preoccupation.

"One thing that always hits home with the survivors I work with—it is the subject of toilet paper. Why is this? We knew about hunger, we knew about deportation. But any ordinary person, even in the most primitive parts of the world, does not live without something he can use as toilet paper.

"Our camp was surrounded by electrified barbed wire. On the other side of the barbwire was a walkway about five meters wide, with an electrified wire running along both sides. This was where the new transports walked when they arrived at Auschwitz. When a new transport arrived, the SS would order us to go into our barracks and lock the door. They didn't want us to see them or for them to see us.

"When you go through all these inhumanities...I told the group of young Germans whatever came to my mind. I didn't hold back.

"WHEN WE WERE TAKEN to a labor camp, we girls worked in twelve-hour shifts every day. We worked very hard. In another camp, there were two hundred of us working in an airplane spare-parts factory.

"It was at this point that my mother was taken away. They said she was too old. She was in her forties.

"The SS were watching us all the time. In the factory they were all around, and in the camp itself they were watching us all the time. In the snow and in the rain. The Germans went beyond the call of duty; they took whatever opportunities came their way to do cruel things. For example, when we came back after our twelve-hour shift, sometimes they wouldn't let us go to our barrack, but would make us carry buckets of water into the kitchen.

"There was a little oven in our barrack and a big pile of coal outside. One Sunday, when we weren't working, it was incredibly cold, and an SS guard came in and said, 'Why is it so cold in here?' The answer was obvious, but I said, "Because we don't have heat.' She said, 'There's coal right outside, why don't you light a fire?' So another girl and I lit a fire. The guard reported our infraction, and the next day this girl and I were punished. We didn't get the daily bread ration.

"In the factory, when the day shift ended at 6 p.m., the SS would start yelling, 'Out! Out! Out!' because the night shift was supposed to come in. Our coats were on an upper level. They would chase us up the staircase. It was a broad staircase, and I remember them chasing us up the stairs, screaming at us, 'Animals! Animals!' Many of us would fall onto each other, and when we fell, they would beat us and strike us with their whip.

"My sister, who was then nineteen, had a pair of wooden shoes. I got a pair of men's shoes that were too big for me. We didn't have stockings.

"After liberation, an SS guard was assigned by the Allies to guard us—we were young girls—and it was snowing. It was incredibly cold. All of a sudden, the guard got very upset because he discovered that his boots had disappeared. He was very, very upset. He was in a big overcoat and a winter hat and gloves, and we were in rags. And I remember looking at him, a man suffering because his boots had been stolen, and I couldn't help but feel for him. I felt sorry for him.

"AFTER SPEAKING FOR SOME TIME, I invited the group to express any comments or questions they might have. One young man, around twenty-one or twenty-two, said, 'You don't know how grateful I am that you're telling us about the concentration camps, because there is no way I can hear about these things. My grandfather was in the SS. I want to know. There is a law in Germany that students must learn about the Holocaust. But we learn in a very sketchy manner, without many details.'

"Some others asked about the mezuzah on the door. They said they had seen these things everywhere and were embarrassed to ask. I told them, 'I'm religious.' And I told them what's in each mezuzah, and what it means.

"The same young man who had spoken before then asked me—hemming and hawing—how I could reconcile being religious with the horrors I experienced during the Holocaust. I said: 'What happened to my faith during the Holocaust? I never lost my faith. I never for a moment thought G-d was not there.'

"This young man stayed in Israel for two months as a volunteer at AMCHA. I would take him with me to the therapy groups at the old-age homes, and he learned fluent Hebrew. When it came time for him to leave, he said, 'I'll be back,' and a few months later, I met him in the street. He said, 'I'm back, and I'm staying. I cannot live there any longer.' Now he's undergoing conversion. He's wonderful, he is becoming very knowledgeable. He is a darling boy.

"So...to return to my friend's question. When she asked, 'What do you think about my serving on a panel about reconciliation?' I thought about it a little. And then I said, 'You know what I think? The idea is ridiculous. It's garbage. Who are we to forgive the Germans? We're playing around with our feelings. We, who are still alive, can we ask the six million who died if they want us to forgive?'

"I believe that anyone who went through the Holocaust is incapable of granting forgiveness for what he went through. Yes, we can go on living. We can create lives for ourselves. We can put aside out feelings. But the moment we sit down to discuss the Holocaust, it bursts open like a geyser.

"I see this in my work with Holocaust survivors. I treat many of them in individual therapy up until their time of death; I literally accompany them to their deaths. I am with them however they are, no matter how disabled or demented they are, because for the most part there's no one else to be there for them, and in many cases, if they have offspring, the children are not close by or do not come often to visit. They went through horrendous events that no one can understand. Many of them are not fluent in Hebrew. But if I come and speak in their native tongue, or in Yiddish, eventually the stories emerge.

"I also do group therapy for Holocaust survivors, both at AMCHA and at an old-age home. We say to these people that they may bring up any issue in their lives—children, health, practical needs—but when a memory comes up from the Holocaust itself, time suddenly collapses and we're back to the 1940s. Reconciliation with Germans in general is one thing. With G-d, it's another matter.

"One Yom HaShoah, there was a show on television entitled, 'Where was G-d?' They had religious people and nonreligious people, and I was supposed to represent the person who had not lost his faith. They sent a crew with cameras. They asked me for a strong memory of Auschwitz, then they put the light on me and said, 'If you would meet G-d now, what would you ask Him?'

"This question came as a shock to me, and I couldn't stop myself, I started crying. I answered: 'Of course, I have questions for G-d. My father was taken away. We don't know what happened to him. My mother...The million children who were killed...My uncle who arrived in Auschwitz with sixty relatives, including his wife and ten children, all of whom were married, with children of their own. Of the sixty, he alone survived. And all my other uncles and aunts, along with their children. They all died. Even in my own family, it's impossible to count exactly how many were killed. I would ask G-d and would complain and would yell. But whatever G-d does is for our good. We cannot always appreciate it because we are too close to it. We only see it during the time we are on this earth. We don't have the perspective to see it otherwise.

"'G-d is infinite. G-d sees it all, from the moment of Creation to the future that has not yet occurred. I can see only what is before my eyes and what is behind us. Only G-d knows its meaning in the whole of time.'"

WRAPPING MY MIND
AROUND IT

All men, like all living things, were once rain, air, sunlight and soil...The most important component of our entity is the immutable Soul, but the body passes through...miraculous metamorphoses...Even the rose...is difficult to consider as a form of the mud from which it grew. The metamorphosis of materials is a miracle of the highest order, second only to the supreme miracle of Creation from Nothing.

Rabbi Avigdor Miller, Sing, You Righteous

My two youngest children are parents now themselves: the mother and father, respectively, of a boy and a girl. To employ pop-culture lingo (the kind of expression that annoys me until I start using it myself), *I can't wrap my mind around it.*

One day my daughter, daughter-in-law, and I were looking on from the couch as the firstborn babies of my babies, both of whom at the time were eleven months old, were crawling around the living room floor. At their previous meeting a month or so before, the children had been occupied with multiple roll-overs, and with propelling themselves forward with a variety of body-dragging maneuvers, and with getting stuck inside chair legs, resulting in a recurring imprisonment that elicited from both the same high-pitched, heart-stopping, ear-splitting wails of bafflement and terror, and elicited from the two young mothers two similar little smiles of pleasure and amusement. Whereas back then, the infants had been unmindful of each other's presence, engaging independently in their separate activities (with their mothers repeatedly repositioning them on the rug face-to-face, eager to awaken some mutual interest), at this encounter now they were both as intrigued by the *other* as they would have been by a colorful electronic toy.

"What must it be like, being eye-level with a chair?" I remember my father wondering aloud when my crawling ten-month-old son, during his first morning in his grandparents' Los Angeles home, got stuck under the dining room table. *What must it be like,* I the grandmother was wondering now, if you're a close-to-the-floor sort of person in a world inhabited by giants—with furniture rising up all around you—to be suddenly confronted eye-to-eye, for the first time, with a moving, noise-making mirror image? A four-legged object that appreciates all your nonverbal jokes and speaks your language, and is interested in all your favorite activities: clapping hands, putting things in its mouth, banging on things, pulling itself to a standing position...

"It's so funny," observed my daughter-in-law. "They do exactly the same things."

"That's just what I was just thinking," said my daughter.

"Me, too," said I.

Though it's usually the differences between their personalities that we notice—one more on the quiescent side, and the other more rambunctious—the three of us were struck on this occasion, in virtually the same moment, by the way these two small human beings were operating according to a standardized, pre-installed timetable—a multifaceted, multidimensional, multipurpose pre-set program. It was like witnessing in fast-forward a movie of the precisely calibrated, petal-by-petal opening-up beneath the sky of the delicately pale pink, exquisitely complex, automated roses out on my *mirpeset*. The babies' mental, emotional, and physical powers were blossoming methodically as we sat watching.

"Maybe we're still like that," said my daughter, "and we just don't realize it."

I WAS PERCHED ATOP a tiny plastic chair (having asked G-d as I stepped up onto it to please not let me fall; I know now what I was oblivious to as a girl: the risks of taking my equilibrium for granted, and what it means to fall), craning my neck to peer between the heads of the mothers and grandmothers who were blocking my view. To make matters worse, my glasses were in my purse, and my purse was somewhere down on the floor, hidden in the crowd of feet. I tried to catch sight of the Chanukah party in one of those miniature movie screens inside the forest of handheld phones surrounding me—cameras I haven't learned how to use, and don't want to learn how to use. I refuse to fall into the habit of self-deception whereby one imagines that one permanently acquires life's fleeting moments, like winged things preserved in amber, by storing them safely away in one's cell phone and forgetting about them.

In years past, I too brought along my camera to such parties, with a full load of film. But no matter how I tried, I didn't succeed in making life stand still. Time kept flowing and flowing, a river, a tsunami, an ocean.

How could it be?

My little girl—whose own Chanukah party in *gan* I particularly remember because she was my firstborn, and her *gan* party my first—is the woman at my side, standing on a miniature chair like the one on which I'm balanced, smiling at Batsheva with the smile I once smiled at *her*. I remember so clearly being unable to grasp that I had a daughter old enough to be in school, who understood Hebrew, and who was singing Chanukah songs that I myself as a Jewish child had never heard. Unembarrassed tears of joy streamed down my face unchecked at that party.

How could it be that that little girl was now my adult companion and friend, who in many ways takes care of me now?

I've always wanted to catch up with time, to preserve memories with words, in writing, but am coming to understand—if not to accept—that I will never catch up and will not grasp life. Time flies! How can it be that my little girl has become an adult who became the mother of my grandchild singing in a Hebrew-speaking *gan*, and my mother and father have flown? All the sweetness of the children singing in one voice, each of us absolutely different from all the others, and all of us all alone, singing *Al HaNissim*.

RAIN

...And what is the reason that He did not make it rain [until the Sixth Day]? Because there was no man...to recognize the benefits of rains...And when Adam came...he prayed for them and they descended.

Rashi, Bereishis 2:5

He Who sets the ear, does He not hear?

Tehillim 94:9

My sister Julia was always kind to me, throughout my childhood. Sometimes I'd see the older sisters or brothers of my friends bossing around, teasing, even tormenting their younger siblings. But not Julia. Known unofficially as the beauty of the family, a brilliant student consistently at the top of her class, held in high regard by teachers and, of course, by my parents, Julia was beloved even by her peers (and by me), in spite of such jealousy-provoking virtues.

I remember one of my other sisters telling me how so-and-so, an exchange student from Switzerland, had said of Julia: "I've never known anyone else who is at once so beautiful and also so kind."

Exactly.

I was so proud of her. To my mind, she was perfect.

Appointed by the high school's English faculty to serve in her senior year as editor in chief of the yearbook, Julia selected as that year's theme a quote from the Lebanese poet Kahil Gibran: "Say not that you have found the truth, but a truth." Having puzzled over those words as deeply as I possibly could at that age—I was in elementary school—here I am, more than half a century later, visualizing that italicized line in the lower right-hand corner of the yearbook's opening two-page spread. The black-and-white photograph that I associate with the quote (though I think it might have actually appeared elsewhere in the yearbook, not on the title page, or even in a different year altogether) was of one of the boys in twelfth grade (the older brother of one of my other sister's friends; I even remember his name) standing dramatically aloof and solitary in a windblown field, under wide and empty skies. With one hand slipped casually into his jeans back pocket, teenager Teddy Thompson—in confrontation with an impersonal, unresponsive cosmos—was as cool, calm, and collected an existentialist as one could hope to find, and as indifferent to the universe as was the universe to him.

Anything my eldest sister presumably espoused or approved was something I took as a guidepost to my own future happiness. So though I didn't yet have an ability to conceptualize such a thing—or the vocabulary to articulate for myself what I thought Gibran's words meant—the inchoate message I took away with me nonverbally was this: *To be smart, to be spiritually sophisticated, to be in the know, don't believe in anything. Because nothing is there.*

My sister epitomized for me everything exciting and beautiful that life had to offer. To say I looked up to her doesn't do my adulation justice.

I idolized her.

Julia was born in the early 1940s, when the destruction of European Jewry was on the rise, yet before the term "Holocaust" had been coined. Even when she graduated high school in the late 1950s, what had happened to Jews in World War II still hadn't moved into the forefront of America's public discourse. Especially in upper-middle-class suburbs such as ours (where, as far as I knew, we were the only Jews around), there was certainly no great, overwhelming inclination to investigate or confront—much less verify—such unfamiliar, uncomfortable things. Quite the contrary. The reports of satanic cruelty were too outrageous and obscene to be believed, especially by those who would much rather dismiss them as unsubstantiated rumors. That which historian Martin Gilbert would later call "the most horrible of horrible horrors" was subject not only to the skepticism of Americans, but even—as recorded in autobiographical accounts by Holocaust survivors—the skepticism of many European Jews, until such time as they themselves were caught in the firestorm.

This phenomenon shares some roots with the perversity of official "Holocaust denial," as exemplified today by the Iranian government. That denial is increasingly back in style nowadays among those who would like to bury our history.

WHEN JULIA GRADUATED COLLEGE and it was my turn to enter junior high, then high school, the foul-smelling cloud—which in the Holocaust's immediate aftermath had been successfully kept out of town, out of sight, and out of mind—was drifting along now across municipal boundaries into manicured backyards, and country clubs, and classrooms. I smelled something, and knew my friends did, too. Words such as *concentration camp...ovens...cremated...gas chambers...the Nazis...*had gained some currency among the children of our town—the stuff of a kind of prurient fascination and ghoulish speculation. I heard from some kids at school that their parents said, *Jews went like sheep to the slaughter.* I felt contaminated—an object of vague, unvoiced suspicions—and was scared, and ashamed, of something for which I didn't have a definition.

Like most children, I wanted to be like everyone else. But there we were, as different as could be from our neighbors and friends, a distinction only made worse by my nonconformist parents, who had chosen—for their children's sake and their own—a big, drafty old concrete house that no one else wanted, in the middle of wild, untamed fields and woods.

Amid the snowy Connecticut winters that smothered us in dreams, and the annual blossoming of spring...Amid the lush blues and greens of summer...and autumnal rains, and falling leaves, I did not know who I was.

BEFORE GOING FURTHER, I should ask you, the reader, to please bear in mind that whatever you read here about Julia's experience of our hometown is based on perceptions and assumptions made by the child I once was. As adults, my sister and I have never talked about it.

But having offered that disclaimer, I'll assert that as far as I the child and I the adult can see, Julia emerged from childhood essentially unscathed and unscarred by anti-Semitic hatred, and remained comfortable and at ease with gentile society, while just a decade or so later, when I was growing up, I felt identified with darkness, bafflingly so, almost as if I wore the yellow star.

Maybe the stark divergence in our two life trajectories is indicative of the great difference one generation can make. Or maybe it's a matter of personality; as the baby of the family I'd always been on the insecure side, anyway. Maybe I was just naturally self-doubting. Maybe my trepidation, and uncertain sense of identity, aroused a sort of bloodlust on the part of certain children.

Or maybe—among the countless theories mankind spins about the purpose, or lack thereof, of its journey through *Olam Hazeh*—there's some other, more convincing explanation.

At least we can all agree on this: that every individual's life, however insignificant it may appear to himself or his contemporaries, is a thread woven into the vaster tapestry. Each life affects other lives in myriad, invisible ways.

Who aside from G-d knows how two sisters born and bred in the same family can end up in such radically different adulthoods—I in Jerusalem, an Orthodox wife, mother, and grandmother, who ran away from America without even accumulating enough college credits for a bachelor's degree, and Julia, a practicing, Harvard-educated psychoanalyst, with not one but two PhDs in her portfolio? Politically on the liberal left, Julia is a compassionate universalist, an active protector of any creature that comes to her attention—whether it be a spider in her kitchen or a harpooned whale in a distant sea. The animal's innocence is paramount. At one time, I remember her calling herself an agnostic, reserving final judgment regarding the existence of G-d, but for years now, she has decisively redefined herself as an atheist. She believes in every human being's absolute right to justice and freedom, and in her youth, fought and marched for civil rights. Though I think she herself would no more bow in prayer in a synagogue than genuflect in a Christian church, there are rituals whose origins may have been Christian but which to her mind are secular, and they're precious to her. Card-sending and gift-giving, Thanksgiving dinners and tree-decorating and carol singings...in these communal traditions she invests time and care in honoring. She attends Sunday services at her local Quakers Friends Meeting House, which imposes no dogma or demands upon its congregants other than to sit in silence during group contemplation hours, and listen in silence when a fellow attendee rises to share his thoughts. Among the Quakers, agnostics and atheists are as unquestioningly respected as anyone else, be she or he Muslim, Christian, Jew, Buddhist, or of any other persuasion.

What is it that my sister can *not* tolerate?

Each so-called "organized" religion's claim to an exclusive monopoly on Truth.

As for me, well...as I said, I'm an Orthodox Jew. And if you know anything about halachic Judaism, you'll know pretty much what I strive to believe. Nor will you consider it a contradiction if in the same breath I admit my growing awareness, as years go by, of how very, very, very little I understand.

The universe is said to be expanding faster and faster. My awareness of not knowing is expanding right along with it.

JULIA STILL LOVES NEW ENGLAND, and she ultimately settled there. And we still love each other, more than ever, I think. I, the little sister, continue to look up to her, continue hoping to impress her, and hoping that something, someday, will awaken her to G-d's immanence, and His availability for communication. Whether I harbor this hope more for her sake than for mine, however, is hard to tell.

To this day, elegantly petite Julia is kind, and graceful, and beautiful, and modest in demeanor. Unlike me, though, she's never shown signs of needing to convert me to her point of view. Surely she'd be happy were I to one day be relieved of what she regards as my misguided religious belief, and of what she once called my "overactive superego." But since I show no signs of awakening to my error anytime soon, she seems content to let her little sister go on believing as I please.

Since our perspectives on life have grown so radically apart over the years, our conversations with each other—whether by e-mail or by phone, or while visiting each other in person, in her environment or mine—are confined to topics about which we see eye to eye. Chief among those safe territories is the centrality in our lives of nature, and its incomprehensible magnificence and indescribable, perfect beauty. The endless wondrousness of this world, before which we both stand in awe, is an aspect of the moral, cultural, and spiritual worldview we inherited from our parents, and is an aspect of our love for each other that can be shared always.

Out of consideration for our hearts, and blood pressures, I don't talk to her about G-d, Israel, or American politics—left, right, or otherwise—or the Holocaust.

As for the subjects she refrains from discussing with *me*, I can only surmise. I haven't asked.

Within these tacitly agreed-upon borders, we lovingly try our very best to make room for each other, pretending in each other's presence (though neither of us genuinely believes it) that though on the larger questions of life we don't see eye to eye, our respective North Stars are small truths, and can comfortably coexist intact, side by side. We make believe that Truth—as in *The* Truth, with two capital T's—is just in the eye, and I, of the beholder.

JULIA'S ELEGANT LITTLE LOG HOUSE, situated far off the road at the end of a long rocky driveway, stands in a rise of meadow adjacent to dense woods. After a celebratory *l'chaim* with the kosher wine she'd bought in anticipation of my visit, we were sitting together on her front porch, the evening I arrived, looking into the pale quietness of the late summer day, listening and marveling together at the squirrels and the blackbirds, the noisy woodpecker and quicksilver sparrows, and bluebirds, and robins, and two tiny, shimmering hummingbirds. She knew the species of all of them, and was familiar with each one's habits. At one point, much to our delight, we caught sight in the same moment of two wild brown rabbits, hopping tentatively along in the lengthening shadows of twilight at the far side of her lawn, where grass meets forest.

She told me a story.

Something interesting had happened to her that week, she said, after work one day. She'd been about to turn right out of the Medical Center Building parking lot downtown, where her office is located, and was inching carefully forward into the lunch-hour traffic, when a car, speeding so fast from the left that she didn't see it coming, came so close to hitting her before swerving away wildly into the next lane that for a fraction of a second she expected death, but in the same fraction of a second the speeding car had vanished, and with a sudden burst of tears, she cried out, "Thank You, G-d!"

"I sat there in the driver's seat," said Julia, "I couldn't move. I was just trembling uncontrollably. My heart was pounding, and my hands were shaking so hard—I was gripping the steering wheel. That's when it came back to me, what I'd said, and I was shocked. As shocked by what I'd said as by the near-accident itself."

"What do you mean, Julia? He didn't hit you, did he?"

"Right, no. I mean, yes, the accident didn't happen. I sat there, devastated. I was so deeply disappointed."

"What do you *mean*? Disappointed in *what*?"

"In myself." Julia was speaking quietly. "I had suddenly become aware of a deeply implanted belief, that apparently I'm carrying around with me subconsciously. I was unaware of it until those moments. It contradicts everything I believe, and live by. I am holding onto something inconsistent with what I know to be true."

THE NEXT DAY, having stayed up late with Julia, talking into the wee hours of the morning, I was now looking tiredly into the predawn darkness from the rocking chair on her front porch, catching sight of the tip of the giant orange fireball sun rising up behind the trees. And I was watching Julia as she fetched the *New York Times* from her mailbox, cleaned and replenished the birdfeeder, watered her flowering bushes and lawn, and attended to various other of her daily chores. In a few minutes, we'd be having morning coffee together—morning coffee, another strong area of agreement—and in a half hour or so, on her way to work, she'd be driving me to the train.

I'd visited my other sister in California, and my two children and their families, and now that I had stayed overnight in Julia's cozy, artistically renovated little house of logs in Massachusetts, I was ready to go home. My flight to Israel was due to depart late that night from Kennedy.

A few years previously, my sister had bought a two-cup electric percolator, which she keeps stored in the back of a high kitchen cupboard—along with a can of Maxwell House and two *toiveled* coffee cups that I had provided—for use during my annual visits.

Petite Julia's quick little footsteps, crossing and recrossing her kitchen as she got the coffee ready, reached me now through the open windows, along with a flute sonata on NPR's Classical Music program. I was gazing around at the meadow, and up through Julia's newly installed skylight, when I noticed at my feet that the plants growing alongside the raised platform of the wooden porch were all curled oddly inward, their leaves blackened around the edges.

The screen door opened, and out came Julia, bearing our mother's big antique serving tray from the Connecticut house, with its lush clusters of faded white roses painted upon the tray's red-painted background. Everything Julia serves—even when she's by herself—can be counted on to be aesthetically harmonious. I'd known that her arrangement of our morning coffee would be in keeping with her usual artistry.

But as Julia set down the tray, resurrecting in memory a thousand Sunday teatimes in the house we grew up in...with the coffee cups on two white linen napkins, and a slender glass water vase holding three sprigs of pink flowers, like an Impressionist painting by Manet...to my chagrin there was also a paper dish holding two delicious-looking, big round cookies, and an unopened container of fresh cream.

How could I surreptitiously check the container of cream without her noticing? And could I find out about the cookies? If only the packages sported a good *hechsher*! Call me a coward if you will—you wouldn't be mistaken—but the fact is, during the last hour of my visit, I just wanted so much to avoid all differences between us. So there we were, side by side, she on one chair and I on the other, as she undertook the careful pouring of the coffee. I don't remember anymore how I handled the cookies and cream crisis—whatever I did, I hope it was with grace. All I recall is that the cookies returned to the kitchen, and that when Julia came back with a carton of milk for me, instead of cream, I changed the subject by asking about the blackened leaves.

"Oh," replied Julia. "I didn't tell you? There's been a terrible drought for more than two years. Almost three. It's very bad."

"Oh. I see." Thoughts jumbled up in a traffic jam in my brain. The *parashah* that week was *Noach*, so I'd just recently reread *Rashi's* commentary about *Bereishis*, in which he says that the rains couldn't fall since there was no man yet to pray for them.

I thought to myself: *Boy, I bet there's not even one believing Jew in this whole town.* In my mind's eye, I tried to visualize someone with a yarmulka and *peyos*, walking along the sidewalk outside Julia's Medical Center Building.

I dared not do it in front of her—she'd think I was crazy—but I knew I should pray for rain, and that I *should* do so in Julia's presence.

"Oh, wow," I murmured inanely. "That's really something. Three years. Wow."

I prayed in silence.

Pray out loud!

Are you kidding! What'll that accomplish? She'll look down on me, she'll think I'm crazy, thinking I can talk to G-d.

But you can.

I know! You don't think I know that already?

***Do** you know?*

Of course, I do. But if she hears me, then when it doesn't rain, she'll be convinced she's right.

Coward! said my *yetzer hatov.* *Let her hear you. The important thing is to talk to G-d, not to see the answer.*

"Oh, wow," I mumbled. "I hope to G-d it rains."

You're a coward.

Don't bully me!

I prayed in silence.

Oh, dear G-d, which voice is which? They're intertwined like a Havdalah candle!

Julia went back inside again, her steps crisscrossing back and forth in her kitchen. "Sarah, dear," she called through the window. "Don't you want to check the guest room upstairs, to make sure you're not forgetting anything?"

"No, no, I did already. All my stuff's down by the car."

"All right, I'm going to get my things together, and let's be down by the car in, let's say, seven minutes. All right? Sarah? Did you hear me?" called Julia.

He Who sets the ear, does He not hear?

"Yes, fine. Seven minutes."

I tipped back my head, looking up through the skylight.

THE MINUTES PASSED.

"All right, dear, are you ready?" asked Julia, the screen door closing behind her.

"Yes, I'm ready. Julia,"—I rose from the rocking chair—"I just wanted to ask you, what are those little spots on the skylight, in the dust? Are those rain spots?"

She looked up. "Maybe, yes. Those spots must be from a few years ago."

She locked the front door behind her, adjusted the purse straps on her shoulder, and looked around to check that all was well. As she stepped forward onto the flagstone pathway leading down to her garage, with me at her heels, she was pressing the electronic doodad to open the garage door when she said, "You know, I think you're right. I think it *is* raining a little."

I looked at the flagstones. Little drops of rain were visible by my shoes as I stepped along.

By the time we got down to the garage in about ten seconds, the light rain was falling noticeably. And there was a wind. We hurried into the shelter of the garage and got quickly into her car. By the time she was driving out along her rocky driveway toward the road, the rain was drumming down on the car roof, as if some huge brimming bucket overhead had tipped to its side. She turned on the windshield wipers. "Oh," exclaimed Julia, "this is wonderful. We really need this."

By the time we were out on the road, about half a minute later, she had to drive quite slowly, for the rain was coming down so hard, it was hitting the street in shining slanted sheets.

I told myself to thank G-d, *and to do so out loud.*

But Julia was right there next to me, and I was her little sister, more scared of her than of the *Ribbono Shel Olam.* "Wow," I said as casually as possible, as if I weren't talking to Him. "Wow, thank G-d."

"Yes, we really needed that," said Julia.

Past tense, for the rain was already stopping—just a summer shower, that's all, as unnatural as all natural things. And the sun was already coming out, as if nothing had happened.

I promise you, my reader, that this is a true story, though I myself find it incredible.

You find it hard to believe? I reprimand myself. *Every morning, so you're just parroting it when you read in the siddur:* "Posei'ach es yadecha u'masbia l'chol chai ratzon...Karov Hashem l'chol kor'av, l'chol asher yikre'uhu v'emes—*You open Your Hand to fulfill the desire of every living thing...Close is G-d to everyone who calls Him, to all who call upon Him in truth.*"

For a long time after that visit, I kept wishing I'd had the courage to pray out loud, whereupon my beloved sister would have witnessed a prayer being answered—impossible as it seemed to me, as well.

But she was spared that test, as I was not.

And now...If only I had the courage to send Julia this story.

LOVE

My neighbor Hilda Mendelson called this morning to say goodbye, have a good life. "Don't let anybody destroy you," she added. "A person has the right to live without being insulted. When are you coming over?"

I'd planned on getting my phone bill paid that day, before the kids came home from school—the final warning before disconnection had already arrived—but this was a matter of life and death. I wasn't used to it. "Now," I said.

Hilda's nurse answered the bell. Mrs. Freed, around sixty, an angular, dignified woman, sported a well-pressed white uniform and a white halo of thin hair. She was of fair height and had heavily lidded pale-blue eyes, so people could be excused for imagining, in her presence, that she looked down on them. She and Hilda were relatives—second cousins, Hilda once told me—and Mrs. Freed used to be an RN in Minneapolis, where they both come from. So when his wife got sick four years ago, it was Dr. Mendelson's idea to have Lorraine Freed brought in as Hilda's professional full-time caregiver. She was a widow already, and retired, so it seemed like a nice arrangement for both of them. But not long after her arrival, Dr. Mendelson himself passed away from some long-standing heart condition, not before expressing his relief—according to the Mendelsons' son—that his wife's competent, level-headed cousin was already installed in the household and that everything was in place for Hilda's convalescence.

Mrs. Freed closed the door behind me as I stepped inside, and turned to say something, hands clasped at her chest. As usual, she was leaning forward a little. She looked sometimes like a line on a slant, as if she were walking against the wind.

She gave her head one slow, grave shake, lips pressed together. "She's taken a turn for the worse, I'm afraid," she confided in a lowered tone, pointing with her chin toward the bedroom.

"Can I go in?"

She lifted her hands palms up, a gesture of resignation that said, "What can I do?"

The Mendelsons' bedroom, like the rest of the house, was well-appointed and comfortable. Hilda had always been an excellent homemaker, everyone said so. She really had a talent for that sort of thing. Twin beds in dark walnut, each with a highly polished, moderately majestic headboard. To the right of the beds, a wall-long matching chest of drawers and atop it a tall, four-paneled mirror. Ruffled Bloomingdale's-style sheets in a luxuriant floral pattern—a satiny feel to them—with pillowcases to match. Her bed was the one by the window, and the window had been opened out onto Hilda's flower garden. A well-pruned rosebush was almost coming in through the window, its glossy green leaves sprouting forth from young branches. I got a glimpse of some of those sultry summer roses: velvety pink, over-large, petulant.

Hilda's head was a small gray thing on the pillow.

"Hilda?"

She opened her eyes. Without lifting it off the blanket, she opened one hand to receive mine. I sat down right next to her, my weight sinking up against hers in the plush bed—whatever weight was left of her, now that she was so fragile. Her body had grown so frail, it sometimes seemed translucent. I leaned against her drawn-up legs, not shy the way I was last year at a similar deathbed scene. We were already good friends back then, but feel more comfortable with each other now. The bed had joined us together.

I could hardly make out her lips, they were so pale; her mouth was just a dark line. *So,* I thought, *is this what a person on the verge of death looks like?* "How do you feel?" I asked, instantly realizing how stupid that was.

Each end of that dark line lifted up a tiny bit. It was her laugh. A moment went by. "How do I feel?"

"I'm sorry, Hilda. How stupid of me."

"No, no. It's all right, *mammale.* It's a good thing it ends."

My face must have given a questioning look.

"Life," she said. "A very good thing." She smirked. "How are you?"

It seemed so frivolous to talk about anything in my own life that I just gave her hand a squeeze, and she gazed back at me with eyes that were dull, dark slits. They looked like the eyes of an American Indian chief. Their black gaze took me in. She said, "You look pretty."

I was quite glad to hear that, and was instantly disgusted by my wondrous capacity for pettiness, caring about something like that at a time like this. Then I snuck a glance in her mirror and was surprised. I did look pretty. Full of life.

A few minutes later, after I'd sat there absentmindedly stroking her arm, she said, "Your hands are so kind," and I liked that comment, too. Liked it too much. I was too stupid and too full of life. Then she said: "I could die peacefully like this, holding your hand." I felt honored. I thought how I'd mention to my husband that she'd told me that. Some more minutes passed as I sat there stroking her arm, then she said, "Don't let them take me to the hospital."

"It's up to you, Hilda. You're the one who knows what's best." I chided myself for these pat words of support, uttered as they were in my pride that, apparently, she considered me capable of influencing events. "You have to follow your own instincts."

Her face turned slightly into the pillow. Those chalk-pale lips parted, and I saw the small, stale dark cave in there, in her mouth. "Who knows what they're going to do to me this time." She murmured something else I couldn't make out, then stretched out one arm behind her, up over her head, catching on to the top edge of the headboard as if the hand were a long metal hook. "I can't take more pain." The sleeve of her nightgown slipped down along her ravaged, gaunt upper arm, its gray crepe skin hanging lifelessly, and all at once I noticed how ghastly she looked. I wondered: *My goodness, is this death coming? Am I sitting here on the day of...in the very hours before...? Later I'll say: "I was there!" I'll get the phone call (they'll say, "Someone has to call the neighbors"), and I'll cry, "I was just there with her! She held my hand!"* I saw a picture of myself in my mind's eye, head fallen forward, heavy with tears and loss. I saw people discussing how hard it must be for me. Then I thought, *What a curse to have started out as a suburban American child!* No matter what happens, you have your roots in its vanities. Academic competitiveness, getting your legs tan, and your hair right...Oh! To be sentenced to such a mentality! No matter how much you hate it, no matter how far away you get from it in life, nothing else is ever quite as real as it should be after growing up in that artificial soil. Not even a deathbed.

"Yesterday I felt better," she was saying slowly. "I had an enema. Lorraine gave me a garlic enema. She says it works for some people." Hilda's eyes seemed to be closed. "*Ich veis*. Garlic enema. Did you ever? Some people say organic coffee enema's better. I'm going to try it this afternoon. I don't know." Now her eyes seemed open. "And that woman in Har Nof—you know the one I mean? I don't know how many times I've been to her. She says visualize this bright strong happy light absorbing the weak negative dark stuff. But I don't know, it doesn't seem to work for me. The only thing I can visualize is the end."

"Hilda—"

"So what, then? Chemo again? I don't think I can. That's what the oncologist says I should do, but I just don't have the strength. G-d knows I don't."

"Rabbi Zissman says that maybe you—"

"I can't take more pain."

"Of course not. Anybody would fe—"

"So what's going to be? How am I going to get to that door? How am I going to walk through that door? Yes, I know. Rabbi Zissman says I should just say to *Hashem*, 'I'm in Your hands, whatever You do, it's all right.' He says to fight, yes. To keep on fighting, if I can. But also to say, 'Whatever You do, I go along with it.'" Hilda looked at my face blankly for a long minute, and I listened to her breathing. "It won't change anything anyway, if I don't. If I don't go along with it. Except maybe make it harder. So I might as well. Right?"

I nodded.

"But how to get to the point of saying that, that's what I'd like to know. It's all very well to say, 'Hey, see that cliff you're standing on? You might fall off any second into that bottomless black ravine down there, and no one knows exactly what's down there. Just trust in G-d and everything'll be all right.' Very nice, let me tell you! Somebody comes along who's nowhere near the edge himself, and he says, 'Trust!' You bet! Easier said than done! I want to trust, believe me! I know he's right. If you don't have *emunah*, you've got nothing. Nothing. You can have your health. You can have a nice husband, and good children. You can have money. And a house. But if you don't have *emunah*, you have nothing. Absolutely nothing. And if you do have *emunah*, you have everything. It doesn't matter what you're lacking, you have everything. But it's scary, being on that edge. It's no picnic."

It was nice hearing her anger again.

"*Ach*, who knows." She sighed. "If I could just close my eyes and say, 'Goodbye, world!' maybe that'd be better. You know that Yiddish expression? No answers down here, no questions up there? It's like that. The thing is, though, I don't want to leave yet."

"You don't, Hilda? I'm so glad to hear that!"

"What, that surprises you?" She eyed me sharply. "Of course I don't want to leave. Nobody wants to leave! Even a worm doesn't want to leave. A cockroach. You ever see the way a cockroach freezes up when you want to kill him, and then zip! He's outta there like a madman! Like lightning! You better believe it! And the way he glares at you with those tiny little shiny black eyes of his! He knows what he wants. He wants to live! But why? Tell me! What has that little bug got to live for? Can he smell a beautiful flower? Or enjoy his meals? Does he see the moon? Does he like the warm sunlight on his little body? Does he have friends and relations? Tell me! Ha! But the way he runs for his life!"

I felt ashamed, suddenly. I sat there, quite still, leaning against her thin, drawn-up legs.

"I'm just like that cockroach, sweetheart, except suddenly someone comes into the kitchen and turns on the light and I go '*Aaaarrgh!*'" She stuck her hands out in front of her face, fingers splayed, and made a comical face of petrified terror. "And I can't run anywhere! Can't move an inch!"

It filled me with gaiety suddenly to see Hilda fooling around, and I threw back my head with laughter. She smiled pleasantly. Then she lay her head back down onto the pillow and turned slightly toward the window. "I had a dream this morning."

"You did, Hilda? What'd you dream?"

"Yeah." Her upper lip twitched slightly. "The most beautiful dream."

I waited.

"I was walking behind this woman, and she was leading me to a place completely covered with snow. The whitest snow. White, white snow. But the strangest thing, all over the ground there were these branches sticking up out of the snow with green leaves on them."

"If you could just speak a little louder, Hilda."

"I said, the branches all had green leaves on them. Right there in the snow."

At this moment there was a brisk little knock on the bedroom door.

"Come in, Lorraine."

Another knock. Hilda raised her head. "Come in, Lorraine!"

Mrs. Freed entered, carrying a tray. "Here's some soup, sweetheart. Green pea and vegetables. You'll like it, I think, if you give it a try." She set the tray down on the bed table, and moved the book Hilda was reading to the dresser, to make room.

"Thank you, Lorraine. It smells good."

"Of course it smells good. The question is, will you eat it."

Mrs. Freed carefully moved over the lamp, and the electric alarm clock, and the box of tissues. "Dr. Sherman called this morning and says the crucial thing is, they've got to find out what's going on so the medical team can decide what direction to go from here." She turned in my direction. "You know, she doesn't eat, then she wonders why she's weak. Everyone says the important thing is to keep her strength up, and she picks at her food like a bird. There's more on the plate when she finishes than when she starts."

"Lorraine."

"Well, it's true. For some unknown reason, you don't do what's in your best interest." She tilted her head back toward me. "She was supposed to go in for tests this afternoon, but Hilda says no, she doesn't want to. What's that supposed to mean, *want* to? What in heaven's name does wanting have to do with it?"

Hilda grunted.

"If she'd get over this irrational stage where her emotions are getting control over the decision-making, then we could get somewhere. But no! She picks this time to play games. First she wanted acupuncture, when the doctor says they have absolutely no proof whatsoever that it's effective. No research at all. Then wheatgrass therapy, whatever that is, then she went in for this reflexology business. And all those months with that macrobiotic cook! We were just wasting precious time! Time we should have been spending on the established medical procedures! Leonard didn't leave her money for it to be squandered like this, but no, Hilda thinks she knows better than the doctors! Dr. Sherman's a very smart man. A very experienced man, and she's just groping her way along. Whatever she heard about, that's what she wanted."

"Lorraine, would you please stop it."

Mrs. Freed shot her a disgusted look. "And then that Rabbi Zissman was foolish enough to tell her that his sister decided to stay home in the end, so ever since he told her that, Hilda's gotten it into her head that she's going to stay home, too, when his sister was at a completely different stage of the disease. A completely different situation. Oh. By the way. Mrs. Ettner called to wish you *refuah sheleimah*. She wants to know if tomorrow afternoon would be good."

"Yeah, fine."

"There's fish, too. First finish the soup."

Mrs. Freed turned around and walked out.

"You see that?" Hilda whispered. "See how happy she is? All this makes her feel good. She feels important."

I nodded knowingly, but wouldn't say that that's what I was feeling, too: important. Sitting there, her hand in mine. Hilda's friend in the last days, perhaps, of her life. I was proud.

"Forget what I just said, OK? The last thing I need is more *aveiros*. You know, I always thought that eventually, one day, I'd learn how to keep my mouth shut. But I guess time's running out. You're not allowed to believe anything negative I say, you know that? Lorraine does her best, G-d bless her. You know...," Hilda gave a little guffaw, "that reminds me. Did I ever tell you, at my son's wedding, this guy came over during dessert. He looked like some great sage about to impart the wisdom of the ages, and he said, 'Mrs. Mendelson, remember. The secret of being a good mother-in-law is to wear beige and keep your mouth shut.'"

We grinned at each other.

"Hilda, I was just at a *shemiras halashon shiur* where the rabbi said it's all right to speak about someone if you're doing it for a purpose. And if you're not repeating it over to different people in a random manner. And also, right, just what you say, if the one you're talking to doesn't believe you."

"Nu, so what's my purpose?"

"To let it out."

Hilda snorted. "Ha! I've let it out, believe me. I wrote her a nice long letter forgiving her for all the good things she's done to me."

"You did?"

She nodded.

"So what happened?"

Hilda rolled her eyes. "Nah. I put it in my drawer. She'll find it after I'm gone, when she cleans up. Remember that time that naturopath told me not to eat nuts? During that time, he said no tomatoes and no milk, no fish. No sugar, no salt, no this, no that. *Ich veis*, no air. No nothing. A diet of nothing.

"Well, anyway, Leonard arranged for Lorraine and me to go to this recuperation place in Switzerland. They give the chemotherapy and then you rest up and get your strength back. Anyway, on the plane trip over, the stewardesses hand out those little packets of salted nuts, you know what I mean, and I thought, OK, I'll cheat a little. Live it up. I'll have a salted peanut. You know, live, laugh, and be merry.

"Well, boy oh boy, did I get it. *Oy*, did I get it! You should have heard! All the way over the Alps! A salted peanut! I was bringing this down on myself through my own immaturity. I had no one to blame but myself, I'd always been irresponsible and impulsive, even in Minneapolis. Even as a child! Blah blah blah, all the way to the get-well party.

"How many hours was that plane ride? Four, maybe? Well, by the time we got there, you can imagine, I was really in a positive frame of mind, all gung ho to get my immune system going. You bet! My immune system had a workout it'd never forget. *Ich veis*.

"She kills me, this woman, to save me. Because of her great abiding love." Hilda looked down at her hands, folded lightly upon her chest. "Deep love." She sighed. "Oh, I'm incorrigible. Me and my big mouth. I make myself sick. Sometimes I look in the mirror when I'm angry and I say, 'Not even G-d could want me, I'm such an ugly person.' Believe everything I tell you, lady, and both of us are in big trouble. Just consider me a big old windbag. Just a sick old woman letting off steam." She stretched out her long fingers, then pressed them together, palm to palm. "Oh! I didn't finish telling you about that dream I had!"

I love Hilda.

"I was telling you, I was following along behind someone in a fur coat. She was walking into this field, and the whole field..." Hilda's eyes closed for several moments, then she continued. "It was really a big meadow. The entire thing was completely covered in snow. Everything was sparkling. It was shining like..." She pursed her lips. "I've never seen anything like that before. So brilliant, I can't describe it, I don't have the words. And sticking up out of the snow all over the place were these lovely branches of green leaves. It was so lovely. I was following her and getting excited about going to this beautiful place, and then—are you following me?"

I nodded.

"When suddenly the woman stopped in her tracks and turned around. I hadn't seen her face till then. She said, 'You go back. You can't come with me.'"

Hilda's gaze drifted up to the ceiling. "I wonder whether everybody has to go through Gehinnom when they get there."

Thinking she'd smirk, I retorted lightheartedly, "Oh, I don't think you'll have to, Hilda. You already have."

Now, talk about wanting to feel important. Talk about wanting to influence events. At this point, upon hearing these clever words of mine, these effective, lighthearted, well-meaning words, Hilda's mouth dropped open, literally. She got an astonished look on her face. And then, from out of the depths, from out of the dry, cavernous depths of her, rose up a long, low moan. It was gravelly and strange. Then she flung both arms back up onto the headboard. They hit against the polished wood with a scratchy thud. She yelled out, "That's right! I've already been through hell! That's right! I've already been through hell!"

Then she was sobbing deeply and coughing, trying to catch her breath. It was awful, a loud rasping, very grating, almost animalistic. I couldn't stand the sound. In my mind's eye, I saw again the picture of myself, like a little movie, walking in the future one day past her door, after she had died. I saw my head lowered under the weight of the infinite loss and my face collapsing in a paroxysm of weeping. Thinking about it now brought a knotted-up sob to my throat. It would be horrible, it would be too lonely, to walk past her house if she had vanished from our midst. I'd rather cry for her now, when she was there to know I'm loving her. A silent little thought slipped by just then like a furtive minnow in shadowy water: *So I can get credit for it.* It was so quick, I could have missed it. I would rather have missed it.

"No more pain!" she was screaming. "No more! I can't! I want to die in my own bed! G-d! Take me home!" Something within me recoiled. "Take me home!"

Mrs. Freed hurried in. She patted Hilda on the back, and when the coughing stopped, I rose and gestured that I wanted to talk. She led me into Dr. Mendelson's study and offered me his soft black leather recliner. I wasn't about to sit down if she wasn't. We could hear Hilda in the other room groaning, "G-d! Take me home!" We discussed the situation back and forth for a few minutes, and I felt very adult, and chided myself: *Of course you feel like an adult, you idiot, it's about time. You're middle-aged.*

"Mrs. Freed," I intoned somberly, "it would be so much better if you would support Hilda's desire not to go back to the hospital instead of fighting her on it. If this is…coming near, the…end, then maybe the best thing to do is just make the time that remains as beautiful as possible."

Mrs. Freed regarded me through her heavily lidded eyes; leered down upon me as if from some great distance with what looked like amazement as much as disdain.

"What do you mean?" she said quietly. "My cousin's not going to die now. She'll get over this stage. She can live five more years if she does what the doctors tell her. It's easy for you to talk. It's easy for Rabbi Zissman to talk! I'll never forgive that man! All of you!" She caught her breath and clapped one hand flat to her chest. Her eyes had filled suddenly with glittering tears. "You're not the one who will miss her the most." She glared at me. "I am."

This scene passed, and I made my way back to the bedroom. Hilda's bed was empty, the flowery pastel sheet drooping down onto the carpet, and I heard water running in the bathroom. She was probably trying to do the organic coffee enema. I wondered if my telephone had been turned off. I looked at my watch. I didn't know how long Hilda was going to be in there, so I rose, guiltily, and went out into the living room, where I told Mrs. Freed that I was sorry I had to go, so please tell Hilda goodbye for me and I'd call later.

WHEN I CALLED LATER ON, Hilda picked up the phone after a few rings. She sounded faint but glad to hear me. "Hello, *mammale*. How are you?"

"I'm fine, Hilda."

"And the family?"

"Fine, *baruch Hashem*."

She paused. "Sorry about all the commotion this morning."

"That's all right, Hilda, really."

She gave a little laugh. "You know, I had the funniest thought when I woke up a while ago. I went to sleep right after you left, and when I woke up I thought at first it was the morning, so I was just about to say *Modeh ani*. But I found that actually I didn't want to. That had never happened to me before. It felt hard, to thank G-d for returning my soul to me in kindness? Can I say that, I mean, with sincerity?"

I wasn't sure if she expected a reply.

"You know, I think happiness is a very important concept. Very important. It's the main thing, but it's so simple. A choice. Yes or no. I'll be happy or I'll be miserable. Regardless of everything that's wrong. But you know, maybe I'm wrong."

I wasn't following her. "Wrong about what, Hilda?"

"Oh, all those years it seemed to me I was right. I always wanted to move mountains. But under every mountain was a scorpion. It's not so simple.

So this line came to me this afternoon, I heard it somewhere, but I couldn't remember exactly how it goes. Either, 'She's so scared of dying, she stopped living years ago,' or, 'She's so scared of living, she started dying years ago.'"

"That was the funny thought?"

"What funny thought?"

"The funny thought you had when you woke up?"

"Oh, no. That was something else. I just thought to myself, Hilda, get a hold of yourself. You're going to feel pretty silly if you get well, after making all this noise."

THE MYSTERY
OF THE WALTER TILE

To satisfy my curiosity as to whether the tile I had liked in my brother-in-law Walter's apartment was the same tile delivered by the store, or whether the store's inaccurate ID number in its window display had brought about an incorrect order (as I knew was the case), Walter kindly brought over a spare sample of his bathroom floor tile on his next visit. He happened to have an extra of that particular tile, he told us, because of a newly discovered error made during the installation of his and his wife's master bedroom shower stall drain, which had recently forced the workers to tear out that bathroom floor and re-lay it. How fortunate (for me)!

Even though there was no practical purpose in determining conclusively whether it was my mistake or someone else's—the store's or the interior designer's; the contractor's, by virtue of his secretary, who could have sent the wrong ID number, or the contractor's when he asked his supplier for that information; or the supplier's, when he gave over the information to the interior designer—I was pursued by keen disappointment ever since I first turned on the light in our new dark-brown bathroom. The keen disappointment was accompanied by an equally keen desire to demonstrate (to my husband) that it wasn't *I* who'd made the mistake. But I didn't want to appear to be hung up on my pride, which actually was the case. How could I show I was right without appearing to be petty? How could I uncover the wrongdoing without appearing to be a small-minded woman who preferred uncovering someone's—anyone's—mistake, rather than take the blame herself for something that wasn't her fault? It was complicated, but luckily, I was in the right. I'm more sensitive to visual things than most people, I explained to all of them involved in the bathroom's renovation, and to my husband. Very sensitive to color. The tile I'd admired in Walter's house was not the same one that had been delivered and laid down in ours. Could my eyes have tricked me, as the secretary had suggested with a kind little smile, a little condescendingly, as if to indulge the client's harmless insanity?

The stakes were getting higher.

Could the light in Walter and Rivka's bathroom really have made their floor tile look different than it did later on, when the tiles arrived in our apartment? I knew this wasn't the case. (My husband wasn't much help in this department, since he hadn't noticed; he just wanted me to be happy. For him, a dark-brown bathroom and a light-brown bathroom are indistinguishable, and of equal beauty in the grand scheme of things.) I didn't want him to think that in his wife's eyes, one tile appeared lovelier and more desirable than another because, G-d forbid, she was the type of unpleasant woman for whom the neighbor's grass is greener. I also didn't want him to think that I was behaving irrationally or unconsciously; I wanted to show that I was very self-aware, and prepared for the possibility that I might have made a mistake (I knew I hadn't).

I wanted to lay down in our home a lasting foundation for our marriage, of uncompromising truthfulness, full self-disclosure, and insightful self-knowledge.

I wrote him a note in which—since I knew I was right—I could humbly acknowledge the possibility that I was mistaken, and with magnanimous good humor, concede that I might be proven wrong. I wanted to build my credibility in my husband's eyes, and demonstrate that in spite of my humility, I'd be proven right after all. I would forgive the one who had erred, and thereby store up forgiveness for myself in the future, for surely I, too, would make mistakes sometimes.

> *Dearest,*
>
> *I know it's only for the sake of my pride that I want to know the answer. Please don't worry that I will demand that a new floor be laid down if we find that they delivered the wrong tiles, though I do think that if and when they see their mistake, they could very well offer to correct it.*
>
> *It's not important who was right and who was wrong. I am well aware that there's nothing to be gained in practical terms except*

a little embarrassing self-knowledge for somebody somewhere at this late date, and how nice, how lovely, how self-affirming it will be, after all, if that somebody were to be somebody else.

But I'm prepared to discover that I'm mistaken.

Love,

S.

YEARS HAVE COME and years have gone since that bathroom came into being, and the old bathroom clock goes *ticktock*, *ticktock*, relentlessly, counting time.

What did we see when Walter placed his sample tile on the floor, side by side with ours?

They were the same color.

Oh, for the mysteries...for the pains of this world!

ON HER SIDE OF THE FENCE
IN BERKELEY
She Considers What She Has

She on a chair, her glass in hand,
tilts her face back from the sun.
Though this for sure is no promised land,
nor those her children who, screaming, run
across the grass, it *is* her yard,
    though the neighbors', too,
as are the flowering trees, and the hard
little barks of someone's dog in the blue
              dusk blooming
                   softly   all around.
The sky, too,
is communal property.
Hers, but not hers alone.

Her glass in the light, tinkling in ice and lemonade...
Only the breath on her lips is hers, made
of the same stuff as summer's vaster

breath.
So if the wife next door and her daughter-in-law and son are laughing now
    at quiet jokes,
around their table in their promised land, so what? To each his own!
Who cares!
Can they be enjoying more than she the sun, wan in their glasses
    as the daylight fades?
So *what* if they possess one another unto death.

Isn't she equally blessed, who can't
   depend on anything
      but her own next breath,
         and the pink sky spreading
        gently
                overhead?

Besides, she knows their secret: *together's* never as cozy as it seems.
Even on lawn chairs around their table, shooting the breeze,
aren't they still just a bunch of *me*'s?
During lulls in their conversation, she sees
how the wife gazes absently around, or surveys her nails,
'till the husband comes back out, with drinks and sandwiches on a tray.

It can't be denied totally, of course:
Unlike the wife, she's on her own,
in a life where questions don't die down.
If, on the other hand, it were she
On the other side, and life were going
as she'd planned, with ivy curling round the door,
and children, one and two. Three. Four....
If what the neighbors have were hers
And she were the wife, pitying the nice gal next door...
Would she still hear the roses on the table implore
Thank G-d for our beauty! the way she does now?

        So whose life is better,
        whose more hard?
        For all I know, it could be I, she thinks,
        Awaiting the buzz of her cellular phone,
        fearing the huge oncoming unknown,
        who owns this moment more.

She pauses in some buried doubt and decides to take the garbage
out,
but sits there staring a moment more
as the orange sun sets. *In the grand scheme of things, so whose life's more real?*
       Is there such a thing as a better deal?
       I have the void all to myself.
       It's better than nothing. Is it not?

She smiles to herself at her own funny thought,
and takes her glass to go back inside,
calling cheerily as she passes their gate,
left slightly ajar, "Hi, everyone! *Hot enough for you?*"
A chorus of *hi's, how ya' doin? Be well!* They smile in return.

She enters her kitchen.
Sets her glass in the sink,
When through the open screen door—*Oh!*
                            She jumps!

The neigbors' cat, arranged in black on white, has entered, and *slinks* along
her leg!

                    And vanishes!
                    And reappears!

"Get out! Get outta here!
OUT!"
                    A chance to cry out.
                    (And who's to say
She'd have it any other way.)

THEIR POTATOES

De kluger nemt. De naar geet—The wise one takes. The fool gives.

The Talmud

One potato, two potatoes, three potatoes four, five potatoes, six potatoes, seven potatoes, more.

Children's rhyme

This past *Tishah B'Av* fell on Shabbos, so as prescribed by halachah, the fast was moved to Sunday. An oppressive heat wave had settled over Jerusalem earlier in the week, like a vast overturned cup of oven-breath, and the weatherman predicted it would be three or four days before Jerusalem would get out from under. Even our air-conditioner couldn't take the heat; it went on strike.

What all this meant for me was that I was already lethargic, enervated, and inclined to irritation even *before* Sunday's fast. Just taking a small bag of garbage downstairs that morning had left me heavy-limbed and headachy.

At least I knew what to make for after the fast. I always serve baked potatoes: easy to make, easy to get down, and healthy. So around 2 p.m. on Friday, when I suddenly saw we were all out, I was so annoyed. I'd have to venture out again. And our regular fruit and vegetable store would be closed by this hour.

I was girding myself with strength and caffeine for my mission when the phone rang. "A *gutten erev Shabbos!*" my husband exclaimed. "We're just finishing up over here. Can I pick up something at the store on my way home?"

Against my better judgment, since I knew he'd agree unhesitatingly (a tiny movie appeared in my mind's eye of a black-hatted figure searching for potatoes in the heat, from one neighborhood to another), I hinted guiltily, "Well, I was going to make potatoes for after the fast...but..."

"No problem! Sweet or white?"

"White."

"Fine! How many?"

"Oh, I don't know. It's for the two of us. And Eliyahu." (Our grandchild.) "And Randi." (Our friend.)

"Fine! Anything else?"

"No, I think that's all."

"You have everything for salad?"

"Yes. Just the potatoes."

"Nothing else?"

"No, just the potatoes."

A while later, my husband arrived home, the back of his neck dripping, forehead shining, red-faced from the sun. Characteristically (as anyone who knows him can attest), he was grateful for this opportunity to serve the Creator.

As for me, I felt like a dove who'd been turning around and around in her nest and could now settle down. Even the air-conditioner didn't bother me.

LATER THAT AFTERNOON, about forty minutes before Shabbos, there was a knock at the door. Through the peephole, I beheld the young daughter of our neighbor.

But not just any neighbor, *bli ayin hara*, because for the first time in my adult life—actually my whole life—I've been given a neighbor who shares with me not only a living room wall but a friendship. If the idealized stereotype of neighbors is that of two housewives who don't have to be shy anymore to ask each other for a cup of sugar, the ideal is real.

My friend's daughter, who along with her sisters likes trying out new recipes for Shabbos, was looking at me expectantly. "Do you have any potatoes I can borrow?"

"What?"

She repeated the question.

My mouth was hanging open. I instructed myself to close it. "White or sweet?"

"White."

Neither lying nor selfishness was possible.

Nor self-sacrifice.

"Oh," I said.

From the kitchen, a voice exclaimed, "Who's there?"

I told him.

"Does she need something?"

I told him.

"Wonderful!" he exclaimed. "How many does she need?"

My lips were shut. I told myself: *speak*. "How many do you need?"

"Do you have seven, maybe?" she asked.

"Seven," I called out glumly.

"Just a minute!" I heard the chair move in the kitchen, and then my husband counting aloud. "One, two...three...four...five, *six...seven!*" He was now at the door, the bag of potatoes on a happily outstretched arm. "We have eight! Would you like eight?"

They're mine. I thought.

My friend's daughter was looking at me worriedly. "No, just seven. Thank you."

"*A gutten Shabbos!*" he exclaimed.

Back in the kitchen, my husband was sitting at the counter, his lunch mat surrounded by a number of *seforim*. "Isn't that interesting," he said. "They needed exactly what we had. In the store, I thought I was getting them for us. I didn't know whom I was buying them for." He threw back his head with a joyful laugh. "Those seven are theirs. Don't worry, I'll find you more."

As things turned out, he didn't need to. My neighbor's daughter, alerted abundantly by my facial expressions, had had the same idea, and somehow found seven potatoes more, and brought them to us to break our fast.

As eight flames burned in the menorah last week, my husband spoke of the Talmudic axiom at the beginning of this story. The wise one knows that when he gives something away, it's he who takes something more precious, even, than potatoes.

THE NEIGHBORS

I don't favor one conclusion over another for the story that follows. I'll just say what happened. Had a secret listening device been uncovered afterward in my hosts' living room, that would have been fine with me.

FOR DECADES, the incident has sat idly in some neglected corner of my mind. It was a question back then, and remained a question, with no apparent relevance to the Jewish life I would come to know as a young *baalas teshuvah* in my early twenties. A new arrival in Israel, I stayed for a time with a Yemenite family in the Jerusalem neighborhood of Geulah. The whole scene was so foreign to me. Radios on buses were talking in Hebrew or Arabic—I couldn't tell the difference—and milk came in plastic bags. And it was so deadly hot. The heat was brutal. Everything was uncomfortable.

Why had I come to this...this...Middle Eastern country?! And there was no air-conditioning! I should have stayed and finished up my degree in summer school at NYU, the way I'd planned! The people in the neighborhood...women with black scarves, or even wigs...men in long black frock coats and curly hair hanging down around their ears...What was I *doing* here? And what did I know about Torah?

The sum total of my knowledge came from a volume entitled *Judaism*, by a Rabbi Meir Meiseles, along with another book I'd come across a few years before, on a shelf (surprisingly enough) in my father's office in midtown Manhattan. The black Hebrew letters were on the right side of the book, with English translations on the facing pages, and commentary in small print down at the bottom. It was about Genesis in the Bible—that much I understood—but it was the first time I'd seen a book like that, and those black letters...gave me some sort of good feeling, strange and familiar at the same time. That's the only way to describe it: they gave me *a good feeling*, and that good feeling made me (for lack of a better word) want them.

But I didn't think this to myself. It was too preverbal and ephemeral a feeling to articulate, nor did it occur to me to try. The letters just *attracted* me, and were (again, for lack of a better word) beautiful. They seemed to be evidence of an alternative place, a Jewish realm apart and different from the world I knew.

The last time I'd seen Hebrew letters was when my grandfather used to recite them at our annual Passover Seder, and back then, I certainly had *not* wanted them. They were old and out of it, like Pop, and uncool, like Pop, and inscrutable, as we grandchildren surely were to him. If anything, I wanted to be disassociated from those old black letters in the little Manischewitz Wine Haggadahs, and from the sweet grandfather with his ever-gentle smile and his hearing aids. The letters were like an invisible chain trying to lasso themselves around me, in spite of the fact that I had absolutely no idea what they were. I must have sensed the Covenant laying claim to me against my will; I was involuntarily bound. It was mandatory to throw it off.

But now I was a young woman who'd made a big mistake by coming to Israel for the summer, and now that I was here, the only place I liked going, the only place I felt comfortable, where I felt I belonged, where I didn't feel like an outsider, was the Kotel. Everything else in this country excluded me, but those stones were as much mine as anyone's.

Up Rechov Yechezkel I'd walk each morning at 5 a.m. to get the #1 bus to the Wall, and afterward, to Geulah's main street, Rechov Malchei Yisrael, for cappuccino at Gerlitz's coffee shop.

Whom did I see, aside from the Yemenite family? The strangers walking up and down Rechov Hoshea, where I was staying, and the neighbors in the building—the American family up on top, the Americans one floor up, and the Americans across the hall.

It might sound, with all those Americans around, that I should at least have felt at home in the building, but they were all from Brooklyn—Boro Park, for the most part—and were therefore as foreign to me as any Yerushalmi.

There was one Israeli family across the street whose daughters I'd noticed with some envy: two teenage sisters with long braids, a few years younger than I. Long braids, long skirts, placid faces. I'd see them walking along quickly and quietly, sometimes in the company of their determined-looking, black-scarved mother. One of them, the older one, was especially self-contained and graceful.

I mention them for a reason.

ONE EVENING, a couple of weeks after my arrival in Israel, I walked in to the Yemenite couple's apartment, and the pretty American wife from the top floor was sitting at their dining room table. My hostess gestured to me to take a seat, hardly acknowledging me, which was so unlike her. She was usually very solicitous of my well-being, her young American houseguest, and would offer me something to eat or drink as soon as I came in. Something was going on. They were all very tense.

The woman from upstairs, around thirty, was, as usual, in her hat and wig (the significance of which, as Chassidic garb, was still an unknown to me). She sat stiff and straight-backed, unsmiling.

She and the Yemenite couple all seemed very agitated and were speaking Hebrew, so I didn't know what they were talking about. All of a sudden, there was some kind of shout outside, and the neighbor fell silent, eyes wide and lips parted. Something terrified her. She whispered, "*At shamaat?*"

I didn't know what that meant.

From somewhere outside, it came again: a rough, gruff, animalistic voice, sort of like a bark, or growl, with an indescribable twist to it that was somehow crude and mocking. "*AT SHAMAAT!*"

The three people at the table stared at each other.

What did that mean, *hashamat*?

After a taut silence, the conversation resumed, back and forth, in a hushed undertone. What was going on? Suddenly came that same brutish noise outside, breaking into the stillness of the violet-blue summer evening like a cannonball. To me, of course, the words were meaningless, but I could hear that it was a shouted repetition of whatever the woman at the table had just whispered. Then it happened again, and again. For example, if she'd whisper, "*Kol ha'yom hayah kachah,*" this would be echoed by, "*KOL HA'YOM HAYAH KACHAH!*"

The neighbor's face had gone pale. In a tinier whisper now, she asked: "*At shamaat?*"

"*AT SHAMAAAAAT!*"

My hostess rose nervously, walked across the room, shut the windows that faced the street and drew the curtains. Then she came back in and sat down, still ignoring me.

All three were whispering now, but whenever the neighbor whispered something, outside in the night came its furiously raucous echo.

In a little while the neighbor's husband arrived, and she no longer needed company, so the two of them left.

The next day my hostess told me that one of the girls in the house across the street—the older of the two sisters—had a dybbuk.

I asked what that was, and upon hearing her reply, thought, *What* in the *world?*

Through the night, every once in a while, I was awakened by the voice, and heard it a few times in the two days that followed. Then it ceased.

My hostess told me that people had brought the girl to a rabbi who performs exorcisms. A few days later, I asked what was going on with that girl, and my hostess told me that the dybbuk had exited through the girl's fingernail.

What in the *world?!*

The girl's family was keeping the whole thing a secret, she said, for the sake of *shidduchim.*

Shibukim?

Months passed.

One day, I saw the girl on the street for the first time since it happened, walking along Rechov Yechezkel between her mother and sister, and tried furtively to see evidence of some sort. But with her long braids and graceful bearing, she just looked the same.

FORTY-SOMETHING YEARS WENT BY. I was getting off the bus one morning at the Kotel and found myself behind a woman in hat and wig. From the back, her profile rang a bell, and I hurried a little to catch up. "Hello? Excuse me?"

She turned her face halfway, smiling faintly and inquiring with her eyes. Yes, it was she, the upstairs neighbor, except that she looked like a grandmother now, as do I. "Yes?"

"Hello! I stayed downstairs from you for a while, in the 1970s. Remember, Sarah Cousins? I'd just come to Israel?"

She nodded politely, trying to place me.

"Remember? You came downstairs to the Yemenite couple, and I was there? That time when the girl across the street was—"

Suddenly her face closed down like an iron gate. "*Hashem yevarech otach!*" she murmured, and walked quickly on ahead.

"LECH LECHA"

For an American Jew who has made aliyah, taking a trip "back home" has its dangers. Not, of course, the same kind that prevail in the Middle East, but, rather, the possibility that he might have too good a time. Depending on how deeply his roots have grown in *Eretz Yisrael*, the land of his birth can still exert a magnetic power.

Years ago, it would take me weeks—sometimes months—to recover from a visit to my parents in Los Angeles. Not that I loved LA, particularly. I did savor immensely its creature comforts, but my parents had moved there after my own move to Israel, and it never felt like home.

It was the East Coast I loved, the kingdom of my childhood.

The worst time to visit was in the fall. Such outrageously potent, jubilant beauty, when the leaves are turning, and the fragrant air carries elusive memories and inarticulate yearnings that only autumn can evoke, with its trees aflame. My mother used to drive along the Merritt Parkway and say, "See that yellow tree over there? It's yours."

I remember being small on the front seat, and pointing. "Is that my tree?"

"The red one? It's yours."

It's not that I have ever been tempted to move back to the United States, not in the slightest. Even in the first months after making aliyah, the re-planting of my life felt irrevocable; there was no question in my mind.

But Israel (like LA) didn't have a real autumn, not to mention the other seasons—at least not that I could see, accustomed as I was to more blatant glories than are apparent in the Middle East.

Our next-door neighbors from London took a trip one summer to Passaic, New Jersey, for their son's engagement—this must have been about thirty years ago—and upon their return, showed us pictures of the *simchah*.

I looked at the *chassan* and *kallah*, the two sets of parents, the grand-parents, the siblings...this alone was enough to arouse my ever-present, latent longing and sense of impoverishment, separated as we were from all our relatives. But what got me most of all were the wide, lush green lawns and towering trees, full-headed and luxuriant, and what seemed to be dark woods in the background—an extravagance of riches. Why was it my fate to have to separate myself from everything that had been imprinted on me?

"You took the pictures in a park?" I asked.

"Oh, no," she replied. "That's the *mechutanim*'s backyard."

"Their *backyard*?" My heart collapsed in upon itself. I thought of my *mirpeset*, with its assorted flowerpots and struggling geraniums.

"Yes," she said, "but all the backyards over there are like that."

Suddenly I was struck by a horrible possibility. These neighbors didn't know it, but I had already grown quite attached to them, in spite of our having moved into the building not long before. A few times a week I'd run into them in the elevator and we'd exchange British pleasantries. Now I'd probably lose them, too; they'd probably move to New Jersey, to be close to their married son. Why not? With a backyard like that, who wouldn't?

"Are you thinking of moving there, too?" I asked sadly.

"Moving?" inquired Edna.

"Yes, to Passaic. To be close to Eli. And to have a backyard."

I can see her now in my mind's eye (so very English in every way), and how she seemed momentarily taken aback. "Oh, never," she said daintily. "Not at all. I'll take Israel and its dry twigs any day."

I'VE LONG SINCE DEVELOPED an eye for the visual beauty of *Eretz Yisrael*, and am as attached to it, I think, as I ever was to the topography of my childhood. The country's architecture, on the other hand, is nothing to write home about, generally speaking. Not for us, centuries to design our own Buckingham Palaces, nor, for most Israelis, enough space for a backyard. Housing's constructed on the run, in a rush, to accommodate the ingathering of Jews from around the world, in an unnaturally compressed time frame.

Yet there was a moment one spring, walking along a rocky shore in Maine (surely one of the most beautiful spots on earth) that I noticed for the first time, after living for most of my life in the Jewish State, that I was missing a different, ancient beauty. I couldn't put my finger on it. Apart from the Kotel, it wasn't something I could visualize.

If I ever find myself driving north again along the Merritt Parkway—let's say I'd be showing a grandchild the leaves—I'll think of my mother, and my father. I'll pass Exit 38 to Silvermine Road.

All the trees will be singing praises.

But no matter where I turn, I am going home.

UNNATURAL THINGS

I was hurrying along to catch a #27 to the hospital, thinking about the cappuccino I'd get at the old bakery on Rechov Strauss, right near the *tachanah*, when something weird down on the sidewalk caught my eye, and I stopped.

Half an inch closer to my shoes and I would have squashed it: a tiny oblong strip of—wet cardboard? Or silver foil? About the size of a paper clip, but narrower. And this little paper-clip-type object was moving forward in a purposeful, aggressive-looking manner, as if it were alive.

On closer examination it appeared to be a primitive, teeny-tiny caterpillar. But it had neither head nor fuzz. Just two teeny-tiny reptilian-style legs, one on each side, sticking out from...could that be a torso? It was like a fanciful five-year-old's drawing of some imaginary animal from outer space. It wasn't a worm, exactly, either, or like anything else I could identify without my reading glasses. And this headless, oversimplified little thing, as unrealistic as a paper cutout done with the same child's scissors, possessed nothing to differentiate one end from the other. No tail, no whiskers. Or eyes. And it was squiggling and scurrying crookedly along, stopping and starting as if on a jerky conveyor belt.

If whatever I'd ever witnessed thus far on earth could serve reliably as a point of reference, the thing was moving in a fashion consistent with the emotion of terror. And sure enough, when I took a step closer, the headless thing froze in its tracks.

So...apparently it was alive, a living creature with intelligence, or a nervous system, that perceived...me...and was unnecessarily terrified of me—a Giant Shadow obliterating the sun—for whom any thought of squashing such an inscrutable thing with my heel was actually too yucky and disgusting to consider.

After half a second, the thing resumed its panicky progress, setting off once again on its path. Could it be a he? Or a she? Hurrying home to...the children? She (or he) obviously had some very important business to attend to, but I felt like saying, "Hey there, Mama, what's the rush?"

Maybe she just wanted something to drink. As did I.

I turned and continued on, to get my cappuccino.

But where was the bakery? It took me several moments to absorb the fact that where the bakery had once reigned, there was now a fluorescent-lit discount children's clothing store. The little café-cum-confectioner I used to frequent when I lived in this neighborhood, years ago, a remnant of the twentieth century, no longer existed.

Much more time had passed than I'd realized.

The bakery was gone.

ONE OF THE LAST TIMES I'd been in this particular ward had been to ask Rabbi Avraham Baharan, *zt"l*, some editing questions about his book, *The Two-Way Channel*. "People think that death is abnormal," Rabbi Baharan had commented that morning from his hospital bed, a few days before he died. "But it's not death that's abnormal. It's life."

My friend, whom I will call Bracha, greeted me now from her hospital bed, some thirty years later. Shocked, frightened, and demoralized by the huge change that had suddenly befallen her (she who was known for doing, doing, helping, smiling and spreading good cheer), Bracha showed me how her left arm hung limp at her side and was without sensation, as was one side of her face. One side of her mouth pulled downward slightly, sagging.

She wouldn't have believed me, so I didn't say it, that her beauty had not been lost. I'd been scared to see her, but her eyes and her smile still expressed the goodness that I now understood had been the source of her beauty, built *middah* by *middah* throughout a difficult life.

When we're young, our growth comes about by way of everything we increasingly acquire on the way up, step by step, from babyhood on: new skills, new capabilities, more and more as time goes by. We reach the mountaintop, spend whatever amount of time we're granted up there as time flashes by, then set off on the climb down. Now our growth comes about in just the opposite way. As our skills, capabilities, and talents...our energy, vigor, and sometimes even our much-prized intellectual understanding, with which we're so identified, fall painfully away from us, like the tail of a comet, our essential selves are sent now on a new trajectory, transported into a different life, different from what we've known before and are leaving behind.

As a Hungarian teenager, Bracha and her mother had spent two years in Auschwitz.

"Do you know of Rabbi Lazer Brody?" she asked at one point in our conversation.

I replied that yes, I'd heard of him, the translator of *The Garden of Emuna*.

"His wife came to visit me yesterday, and you know what she said? She said: 'We tell *Hashem* about our *tzuris*. Let's tell our *tzuris* about *Hashem*.'"

THE NIGHT AFTER my father's funeral, my mother and I couldn't sleep. I wish I had a recording of what we were talking about for hours and hours as we lay on her bed. One day years later, the two of us would try to remember, but we had no idea. We talked and talked nonstop, on and on, all night long. At some point in the wee hours, suddenly my mother sat up in bed.

"What was that?" she said.

I said nothing.

"Is someone else in the house?"

A shiver ran right through me, for this reminded me of something that I'd read as a teenager. In James Agee's autobiographical novel about his 1930s childhood, *A Death in the Family*, the family, mourning for Agee's young father who has just died in a car accident, is sitting in their living room the night after the funeral, when suddenly, all of them—including the stone-deaf, somewhat senile grandmother—sense something's entrance, a presence that then flitters through the house, upstairs, downstairs, and in a few seconds…is gone.

"No, Mommy," I said. "We're alone."

"Are you sure, Sarah?"

I didn't answer.

She lay back down, we resumed talking, and then again, she sat up and listened. She was looking at the door.

In that conversation years later, I asked her about it.

My practical, down-to-earth mother, not inclined to believe in anything you can't see with your own two eyes, said, "It was Daddy. He was outside the door, in the hallway. He was worrying about me."

I dared not make a peep. I held my breath.

"It was him, all right," she said. "I've never felt anything else as real in my life."

AT OUR MOTHER'S BURIAL in the same New Jersey cemetery, in the plot next to my father, my sisters and I stood looking down at her freshly dug grave, clinging to one another. She was in the ground. And our father.

It was incomprehensible.

They were finally together again, side by side.

Later that day, we sisters discovered in conversation that during those minutes standing together at our parents' graves—his with its covering of rain-fed green grass, and hers of gray, packed dirt—all three of us had been crushed and flattened by one and the same thought: our history as a family, which for us was the history of the world, ancient and modern, an immense reality in time and space...thousands upon countless thousands of fragments of sights and sounds...an immense empire of emotion—was gone...evaporated into nothingness. We were children, by ourselves now in the big, empty house. A vanished empire, with only three impoverished orphans to serve as witnesses that it had once been.

And as close as the three of us were, we knew, also, that the house we shared was not one and the same house. There was no way to bridge the distance between our memories and between us.

JERUSALEM HAD JUST HAD three days of pounding, freezing rain. I loved it, but was hoping it would turn to snow.

On the icy downpour's third day, I was relieved to see through our living room's sliding glass doors that the recently planted flowers out in the window box hadn't died in the deluge. And the next morning, as the last clouds chased each other to the stormy horizon line, there they were—their serene, open little faces, pink and yellow and orange—turned up to the sky.

How could that be, that such delicate blossoms weren't destroyed? Why weren't they drooping, wilted and sodden? Like everything else in this world in which we find ourselves, the little flowers—like our own selves, here on this planet—were unnatural phenomena totally beyond our comprehension.

> So, my dears, our flowers taught us...
> First, that we die
> according to a fixed timetable
> And get old

According to a fixed pattern, endlessly repeated
No matter how hard we try.
That generations come and go and
there's nothing we can do about it
Nothing to do to stop the flow
Of time, and we can't find out why
from the same root
the same seed
the same dirt
the same sun
some of us thrive
and some
don't, and no matter how we try
not to,
we die. No matter how beautiful
we were, or that we still want to sing
And then, something
else, too:
that when
we disappear
we're born.

THE MOON
OVER MEXICO

Rabbi Shimon ben Pazi pointed out a contradiction. One verse says, "And G-d made the two great lights," and immediately the verse continues, "The greater light and the lesser light…"

Chullin 60b

"You should start out by quarter of." My son-in-law placed my suitcase by their front door. "Three at the latest. And you'll need time to return the rent-a-car."

"You set the alarm clock?" asked my daughter.

I had.

"You have both passports? Israel and America?"

I checked. Yes, I did.

We were saying goodbye on my last night in San Diego, and in a few hours, while they slept, I'd be leaving for LA. My El Al flight was at seven.

"You filled up the tank?"

I nodded.

"There's an all-night Starbucks on the freeway," said Mimi. "You know how to get to the on-ramp?"

"Umm…"

"You take a left out of our street and at the top of the hill, you turn ri—"

"Oh yeah, yeah, right, I know. Thank you. Thank you so much."

They stood there, hesitant, going down a mental checklist. Not infrequently on previous visits, I had found new and creative ways to mess up.

"And when you get onto the freeway," said Dovy, "make sure it's 205 North. If the signs say South, you're on your way to Mexico."

"Oh, come on!" I laughed, and he smiled. "I'm not *that* ditzy."

THERE WAS A PULLING on my heart as I passed their room, then the children's room...Feeling my way along the hall and down the stairs, tiptoeing through their dark house...lugging and dragging my suitcase through the front door...and then, outside...into the immense and misty Californian night.

Across the street, the neighbors' towering eucalyptus was vaulting upward, its black, shadowy wings lifted up toward the starry firmament.

Turning the key in the ignition, backing out cautiously, trying to keep the car from raising its hoarse and husky voice...navigating the little cul-de-sac, home after little home of dreaming little families...and then...taking a right out of the neighborhood, now I could relax.

All alone in the big, soft darkness before dawn, when mankind was fast asleep, I set sail through San Diego's empty streets, all my senses alert and on edge. There was the turnoff! *Up* onto the on-ramp and I was on my way, gliding free.

The radio at this hour was mostly static, but I spun the dial until I landed in some sort of New Age interview program—catering, apparently, to all the insomniac, restless, solitary souls strewn out over the somnolent American heartland like tiny points of light. An amiable moderator with a faint hint of Midwestern twang was just introducing Dr. Christopher Knight, a British astrophysicist, who from 3 a.m. to 5 a.m. (great!—they'd get me all the way to the airport) would be sharing some peculiar facts about...the moon.

"IT IS A PUZZLING quirk, indeed," said Dr. Knight in his clipped English accent, "that the disc of the moon should seem, from an earthly perspective, to be exactly the same size as the sun. While we casually take it for granted that the two main bodies seen in Earth's skies look the same size, the probability of this being the case is virtually nil."

"But isn't that just because the moon's so much closer to us than the sun?"

"That's certainly the case, Jim. But the question remains: Why do moon and sun appear to us on earth as precisely equal discs? The remarkable answer is that while our planet's moon is exactly 1/400th the size of the sun, its distance from the earth is exactly 1/400th the distance of the sun from the earth. While the surprisingly neat number of four hundred for relative size and distance is apparently an amusing coincidence of the decimal counting system, the odds against this happening are huge. Experts have always been deeply puzzled by the phenomenon. Isaac Asimov, the respected scientist and science-fiction guru, described this perfect visual alignment as being 'the most unlikely coincidence imaginable.' That kind of mathematical correspondence does not occur anywhere else, on any of the other planets in our solar system. Furthermore, this perfect fit of the lunar and solar discs is an optical illusion."

"An optical illusion?" said Jim. "You mean, not real?"

"By *definition*, optical illusions are 'unreal.' The perplexing thing about *this* optical illusion is that it would seem to be *designed*, remarkably enough, especially for a human being's perspective, because it only works from the viewpoint of a human being standing on the earth's surface."

Traffic was pleasantly light. For a second, I scanned the night sky, but if the moon was up there, the freeway's occasional oncoming headlights were the only visible luminaries.

"Another incomprehensible coincidence," Dr. Knight continued, "is that the moon precisely imitates the perceived annual movements of the sun. When the sun is at its lowest and weakest in midwinter, the full moon is at its highest and brightest, while in midsummer, when the sun is at its highest and brightest, the moon is at its weakest. It would be easy to dismiss these sun-mimicking performances by saying that it is simply a consequence of the moon's distance from the earth and its orbital characteristics. And indeed, this is what most scientifically trained people *will* say, because it is self-evidently true. To the scientifically trained mind, these phenomena absolutely must be understood, again, as inevitable coincidence—a result of the virtually incalculable vastness of time and space, because otherwise, it would suggest the intervention of a creative intelligence."

"Oh, you mean G-d?"

"We shall consider that possibility shortly, but before we do, let's first take note of a few of the other interesting quirks of nature related to our moon. Tell me, Jim, why do you think that one of the features of our planet is seasonal change?"

"Well, let's see. Gotta think back to elementary school. I know it's got something to do with how close the earth is to the sun."

"That's a common misunderstanding, Jim. It's actually due to the angle of the planet in relation to the sun, which is about 22.5 degrees from what might be described as a vertical position. If the earth were, instead, in the upright mode, life would be almost impossible across much of the planet, with extremes of temperature providing only a narrow band suitable for mammals such as humans to survive. Even then, the sea and air currents would move wildly between the hot and cold zones, causing catastrophic weather conditions with regions of permanent rainfall and others with none at all. Hurricanes and tornadoes would ravage many areas, and overall, it seems highly unlikely that higher life forms would exist at all were it not for the 22.5-degree angle relative to the sun. How is this angle maintained? It is maintained by the moon, which acts as a gigantic planetary stabilizer.

"Now let us turn our attention, for a moment, to the sun itself. The diameter of the sun is estimated at 1,392,000 kilometers, and as the average diameter of the earth is 12,742 kilometers, it follows that 109.245 earths could be placed side by side along the diameter of the sun. This is not a number that stands out for any reason, but when we looked at the number of sun diameters in the earth's aphelion (its greatest distance to the sun), we found that there are 109.267, effectively an identical value because the estimate of the sun's diameter is within this tiny margin. How strange. There are the same number of earth diameters in the sun's diameter as there are sun diameters between the earth and the sun. This is a near-perfect echo that does not work for any other planet in the solar system."

Interviewer and interviewee sallied back and forth for who knows how many miles about the immeasurable unlikelihood of this and other related phenomena. Every quarter hour or so there'd be a commercial break, and I'd spin impatiently through the channels while waiting for the interview to come back on. But it was a lovely ride. I had the freeway almost to myself. At one point, I tuned in just as Christopher Knight was saying that no other known planet has such a narrow temperature band.

"Our earth is subjected to a range of temperature that permits water to be liquid most of the time. In fact, water is a very curious substance altogether. On earth we can see it at the same time in its three states—as solid ice, as liquid water, and as a gas in clouds. Each water molecule is composed of just two atoms of hydrogen and one of oxygen and yet it acts as a universal solvent with a high surface tension. As everyone knows, warm water rises as convection currents—but it is also true that ice floats. Other planets in our solar system may have ice or steam, but only the earth is awash with life-giving liquid water. Liquid water has been absolutely crucial in creating the world we know today, and as far as is known, life cannot exist without it.

"With only a small change in the overall temperature of the earth, or an alternation in the seasonal patterns, the nature of the water on our planet would change. As we have seen, a more pronounced planetary tilt would lead to a freezing of the oceans. On the other hand, if the earth were not tilted at all, the equatorial regions would become unbearably hot, and weather patterns across the planet would be radically changed. It is therefore vital for our existence that the tilt of the earth has been maintained at around 22.5 degrees, yet this is a very unlikely state of affairs. Venus is the nearest planet to earth and the most similar to ours, but it shows signs of having varied markedly in the tilt across time. The earth is very active internally and highly unstable, yet despite a few periodic wobbles, it keeps the same angle relative to the sun.

"The moon has a sidereal rotation period of 655.728 hours, which means it rotates once every 27.322 earth days. Given that the moon has an equatorial circumference of 10,920.8 kilometers, this means that the moon is turning at four hundred kilometers per earth day. So consider these facts as a whole: The moon is 1/400th the size of the sun. The moon is four hundred times closer to the earth than the sun is. The moon is rotating at the rate of four hundred kilometers per earth day. The earth is rotating at forty thousand kilometers a day, and the moon is turning at a rather precise one hundred times less.

"Some people would not get to the point of recognizing the patterns in the ratios within the sun-earth-moon system. And a scientifically trained person looking at any one of these points would almost certainly respond that all numbers are equally valid. A value such as a hundred or forty thousand dropping out of the mix is just as likely as any other number. We absolutely agree with this view, and we would ignore such results if they were only happening once or even twice, but we are confronting a whole list of non-random-looking values. If we look at the available information logically, the moon appears to have been inserted into the sun-earth relationship with the accuracy of the proverbial Swiss clock. In our view, anyone who dismisses all of these points as coincidence is being either very illogical or downright dishonest. As the astrobiologist Paul Davies once said, 'Most people take the existence of life for granted, but to a physicist like me it seems astounding. How do stupid atoms do such clever things?' To which I'll add the following: It's true that if someone tosses a coin a hundred times and it comes out heads every time, the chance of the next toss resulting in another head is exactly fifty-fifty. However, if this ever happens to you, I would suggest you check that the coin is not double-headed."

"So what you're talking about," said Jim, "is the science of probability."

"Yes. Virtually all scientific discovery is a process of identifying patterns that stand out from the chaos of random events. When something varies markedly from the norm, there is usually a reason. One thing is certain in all this: no moon would mean no humans. The more we have looked into how our planet developed into a paradise for living creatures, the more surprised we became. Opinions vary among myself and my colleagues, but the common thread is that we recognize evidence of intelligent design."

"Oh, so you mean...a benevolent crea—"

"Let's put it this way: what these facts indicate is that the moon was engineered by an unknown agency to act as an incubator to promote intelligent life on earth."

"Oh, so, *umm*, I presume this...that this means you *are* talking about..."

"Most of the American population who state that they believe in G-d would probably assume coincidence. Only a minority might claim that it is the grand plan of the Al-mighty. Let me point out that such a conclusion cannot be dismissed out of hand as religious fanaticism or self-delusion. Have you heard of Anthony Flew?"

"The *How to Think Straight* author?"

"Exactly. At the age of eighty-nine, after sixty-six years as a leading champion of atheism and logical thinking, Professor Flew has been led by the accumulated mass of new information over recent decades to state that science appears to have proven the existence of G-d. Flew's reason for this monumental about-turn is the discovery of evidence pointing at some sort of intelligence that must have created the world we inhabit. He has particularly cited the biological investigation of DNA, which has shown an unbelievable complexity of the arrangements needed to produce life, leading to the conclusion that intelligence must have been involved.

"Now, Flew is a man of principle, and when he was asked if his new ideas would upset the scientific community, he replied by saying, 'That's too bad. My whole life has been guided by the principle of Plato's Socrates: Follow the evidence, wherever it leads.'"

"Hasn't he been discredited, though?" asked Jim.

"Indeed he has. In response to his deviation from basic scientific dogma, his colleagues in the scientific community have regretfully concluded that Professor Flew is suffering either from Alzheimer's or dementia."

"Excuse me for pressing you on this point, but what do you th—?"

"I will answer as follows: Nature abhors a vacuum, but we scientists abhor a vacuum even more. Something must be found to explain the inexplicable. We are talking about many factors here that logically should bear no relationship to each other at all. Taken in isolation, any one of these strange associations might be considered a coincidence, but there comes a time when coincidences become so frequent that something else must be at work."

"And that *something else*...?"

"A superintelligence. Some people, as I have said, regard this entity as an omnipotent, benevolent G-d, Who answers prayers, an idea to which I personally cannot subscribe. For our purposes here, we shall designate it, 'UCA,' which stands for Unknown Creative Agency. I have concluded that the only possible answer to the question of what, or who, was capable of creating the moon is that a contingent, or network, of humanlike time travelers—aliens, if you will, at such an advanced point in the technological development of their civilization that we cannot conceive of it—conducted visitations to our planet billions of years ago."

So taken aback, so entertained was I by this, that sitting there all by myself in the car, I laughed right out loud and exclaimed (whether to Jim or to Dr. Knight, I didn't specify): "Well, what do you know about that!"

Suddenly it dawned upon me that the sun was rising, and I'd better keep my eye out now for the airport exit.

A huge sign was coming into view overhead:

"*NINGUNOS ARMAS PERMITIDOS SOBRE LA FRONTERA! NO FIRE-ARMS ALLOWED OVER THE BORDER!*"

I turned the car around in a panic. After explaining myself to the mustachioed, gun-toting policemen and heading back through the customs checkpoint with a screech of the tires, I glanced up at the sky and there she was, sailing high, serenely vanishing into the sun's first light.

SHABBOS SUNFLOWERS

All of a sudden, the flowers died
after more than two weeks,
but I was still so surprised.
They'd been standing up straight, so yellow and bright
long beyond what's normally right
for the life of a flower.
From what unseen source grew that joyful power?
They'd held on tight ever since Janey's visit.
Certain creations are so exquisite,
we can't let them go without a fight.
Like the sun and the moon, we need their light
As I poured out the water and threw them away,
my heart gave a cry
as I heard someone say
in the softest of whispers that was really a shout:
Don't be so sad that you're throwing us out!
This isn't goodbye! From Above is this treasure.
The light that died here is alive forever.

THE GARDEN
IS THE ONLY PLACE

G-d-awareness is much, much more than that which the intellect can envelop. [It] is a combination of whatever the intellect can know, melded with intellect's own awareness of what it can never know, what it is not made to know.

Rabbi Ozer Bergman

The garden is the only place there is, but you will not find it
Until you have searched for it everywhere and found nowhere that is
not a desert.
The miracle is the only thing that happens, but to you it will not be
apparent
Until you have studied all things carefully, and nothing happens that
you cannot explain.

W. H. Auden

"Look, you know me already," said Janet. "I would love to believe. But I don't think this proves what you think it does."

The item I'd just showed my friend had appeared that morning in the Tuesday science section of the *New York Times*, spread out now between us on a small table at a Manhattan coffee shop. "Scientists," it began, "have discovered an altogether new creature."

It is a centipede—which may be the world's smallest—and is the first new animal species found in Central Park in more than a century. Museum researchers found the new centipede, along with many other tiny beings, in leaf litter—piles of broken twigs, fungi, and decomposing plant and tree leaves mixed with soil. Leaf litter is perhaps the "richest and most complex community in the woods," said Dr. Eleanor Sterling, director of the Natural History museum's Center for Biodiversity and Conservation. "It is," she said, "predators, scavengers, vegetarians living together in a very complicated system."

"Leaf litter accumulates very quickly," said Liz Johnson, the director of the museum's biodiversity program for the New York region. "In one year, five tons can pile up in two and a half acres of woods. Invertebrates consume it and keep it from burying the forest, and there they are as numerous as litter. There are, for instance, some 50,000 springtails (an insect) in one square yard of litter, and that is only one of the hundreds, or perhaps thousands, of invertebrates found there. If they rake all the leaves, remove all the fallen twigs and branches, new species—and the regular guys—will not survive. The whole system will cease to function."

Janet read the passage through again and shook her head. "Yes, it is amazing."

"Wait a second, there's something else in here..." I hurriedly turned the pages. "Something about astronomers who are trying to save federal funding for the Hubble Telescope. They wanted to show what it can do, so they focused the telescope on one little spot in the night sky that they'd never looked at before, and you know what they found?"

She grinned. "Angels?"

"Come on, Janet. They turned up the Hubble to its highest capability, and...oh, here it is! When they examined that one little inch, they found two new galaxies. Plus a black hole that's in the process of swallowing up *another* galaxy. And one of the galaxies is four times the size of our Milky Way! See the way the stars whirl around like that in a spiral? Doesn't it look like water going down a drain? Or like a seashell?"

"Yes, it's amazing. But what's your point?"

"I'm not sure. But for one thing, size has no meaning. An inch of soil in Central Park is as infinitely complex as one inch of sky. And there's something else in here, too, about a new physics book that shows how the existence of our earth is dependent on the existence of stars, that life on earth couldn't exist without them."

"Amazing."

"Haven't you ever wondered, why all the stars?"

"Of course, I have. Everyone does at some point. And that reminds me. I'll show *you* something now. There's something really interesting in here—maybe you saw it. About Charles Simic's latest book." Janet took out the *New York Review of Books* from her large over-the-shoulder bag, and now it was her turn to leaf through pages, explaining as she searched that as a child in Czechoslovakia, Simic had been orphaned during World War II. As a result of all he suffered, he eventually wrote a poem referring to truth and justice as "The Famous No-Shows."

"OK, here it is," said Janet. "Listen to this. 'Any sentient adult knows, whether admitting it or not, that life has no explanation: that truth and justice do not reign on earth, and that there is no one governing earthly events.'"

My friend looked over at me now with an expression that I interpreted as meaning: Remember, this is the *New York Times*. The *Book Review* section. You can't just *disagree* with it. "That's basically my position, right there. I'd like to believe, but I think anyone in his right mind eventually outgrows the need for some kind of Supreme Being. Oh, Sarah! I'm sorry! Did that insult you?"

"No, but you know what I really think, Janet? That you believe in G-d, intuitively, but can't rationalize it to yourself."

"Ha. That's interesting." She gave a laugh and glanced at her watch. "So convince me! I *wish* you'd convince me. Come on. Why don't you just make that your new little project. Convince me and Sam."

AND THE ANSWER to that is that I see all too well through Janet's eyes. The reality my friend inhabits is the same one in which I grew up; as one would expect, my surroundings formed my outlook. And in spite of the fact that at this point in my life, the non-randomness of nature seems too obvious to be denied, I identify easily with anyone who doesn't see it that way. It's as easy to block out the existence of an Intelligent Creator as it is to casually block out galaxies with one hand held up to the night sky. To my coreligionists who have never inhabited that secular reality, it's inscrutable, inexplicable, foreign, unfortunate, while for me, it's just the other side of a windblown, diaphanous veil.

If I knew how, I would brush it aside for her. But something has to prompt her to do that herself.

I knew from prior experience that I'd soon be thinking in retrospect of other things I could have, should have said. I would wish that I'd had the presence of mind to say: wherever we direct our gaze, Janet, whether to the dirt under our feet or at stars millions of miles away, we behold an infinitely perfect system; that there's no such thing as *big* and *small*, and that we ourselves—in our every molecule and cell, our every thought, every wish and impulse...we with our noblest deeds, our brightest hopes, our dark emotional conflicts...we with our purest and sweetest ideals...and our humble and shameful failures...are the central purpose of the created universe. No matter where we stand at any given moment, the structural patterns—more vast and more perfectly wired and interconnected than we can hope to imagine—is at our fingertips, and within us. Peer into a single atom and you'll spy our solar system in exquisite miniature, its central nucleus precisely like the sun, and the surrounding planets spinning in elegantly precise geometrical balance. Pry open the energy within that tiny atomic building block and you access enough explosive radioactive power to entirely destroy our planet in the fraction of a second...the very power which in the Creator's Hands gives life to the centipede and the springtail, to fungi and broken twigs. *Predators, scavengers, vegetarians*...each and every inch of Creation is inhabited by a *rich and most complex community.* Frogs and daffodils, viruses and tears, thunder and lightning, *all living together in a very complicated system* along with bacteria and sharks and oceans and volcanoes, ice and rock and birdsong...

And all is reflected by the mirrors of our minds.

I recalled the image of a branch of green leaves. When I was a Jewish teenager who hadn't yet been introduced to Judaism, that recurrent thought-picture served silently as a dim but eloquent reassurance of the prevailing, mysterious orderliness of nature. I held on mentally to that bough with its glossy leaves as evidence of *something*...but my eyes were closed. The possibility that there could be such a thing as G-d seemed too good to be true, like a fairy tale. Belief in G-d was equated with wishful thinking.

There must have been trees with that type of leaf outside our house in Connecticut, and having nothing—aside from the harmonious beauties and unlikely congruities of the natural world—to buttress my persistent instinct that G-d existed, the mental image of those leaves, equidistant and symmetrical, served to summarize the cosmos. The living branch in my mind's eye defied chaos, defied bedlam, defied human cruelty and craziness and the black void of emptiness surrounding our tiny, helpless planet.

When all else failed, with all the nonsensical human societies on the verge of catastrophic nuclear extinction, there was always that image. I fell back on it many times, reflexively: a single curving bough with its two rows of green leaves, each glossy identical leaf pointing to either right or to left, and one single leaf standing on top, pointing straight to the sky.

SO...IN THE COFFEE SHOP half a century later, I knew exactly what it's like to stand in darkness in a place flooded with light, because that's the world that bore me. I imbibed a reality, a reality where people live by their doubt, whether they refute the desire to believe or embrace it.

That conflict is at the core of our humanity. For Jews, it seems like a genetically inherited inner struggle, implanted on purpose within us, ensuring a certain level of spiritual discomfort. It's written that even as we stood before Mount Sinai, moments after hearing G-d's voice, a spirit of skepticism entered Jewish hearts.

What's the result of all the myriad small actions that an observant Jew engages in each day of his or her life? Washing hands upon waking up, saying blessings over food, saying a prayer at night before going to sleep...Physical acts and gestures carried out in relation to G-d gradually establish an ongoing relationship. Otherwise, He would remain an abstraction to be pondered, rather than experienced on a practical level. We have to reestablish *Hashem*'s existence for ourselves day after day, since blindness takes over naturally, like a proliferation of weeds, or cataracts. His creation is visible everywhere but He remains unseen, though we're bombarded incessantly by evidence of His Presence.

SITTING ACROSS THE TABLE from Janet, I was at a loss now for words, in spite of all my traveling—by which I mean not traveling to India and Russia and Spain but traveling through my life from the kitchen to the supermarket, from one child's room to another's, until a grandchild was in my arms.

I recalled what a rabbi and his wife had told me one day years before, when I needed politically correct excuses to be observant. It seemed like a good thing to say now to a person who's ecologically aware, and worried about global warming and nuclear power, recycling and climate change, governmental corruption and inhumanity. "Shabbos is our weekly celebration of the Creation," I said. "There are things we don't do on Shabbos in recognition of the fact that the world exists without human intervention. It's like an oasis."

We'd arrived at this point in our conversation many times, on each one of my visits to New York. "Look," she replied. "I'd love to do Shabbos, I really would. You know that. But I know I won't. The thing is, there's so much pressure all week long. The weekend's the only time I can get things done."

What would it be like, I thought to myself, *if we knew that we could speak to G-d and that He hears us? He Who created the ear, does He not hear?*

"G-d is alive, Janet."

"Well, could be. Who knows."

"You can tell Him, in case He exists, that you don't believe in Him. You know, Janet, I don't believe in Him either."

"You don't?"

"Of course not. That's why I talk to Him."

"Hmm. That's clever." She checked her watch. "Oh wow, it's quarter of. The kids get home at one." She rose to her feet, adjusting the purse strap on her shoulder. "Sammy's home with strep, did I tell you?"

The two of us—with our brains that can worry and wonder, doubt and fear, love and speculate and grasp language...with our mouths that speak words and our ears that hear...with our ability to get up out of a chair—we were serving in these moments as eloquent proof of the Creator in Whom we don't believe. "Janet," I said now, "what would you do if you knew G-d is as real as...Sam?"

"Well...if that were really true...it would be...wonderful." She stood there a moment, thoughtful. "Then I could just sort of...turn to G-d." Janet's gaze moved over to the window and out to the busy street, where she lingered, then returned. "You know, I'm happy for you that you believe the way you do. Religion gives a very positive outlook, I think. It's a good way to live. But I can't convince myself of something *because* it would make me feel good. I can't trick myself into believing something I know intellectually isn't real."

We gathered up our stuff and left.

THAT NIGHT, after the Meal Mart takeout I'd gotten on 72nd Street had been consumed, we cleared the table of plastic plates and forks and knives and ended up having one of our long Friday night discussions.

Her candles and mine were flickering.

"My intellect is one of the only things I can really say I *have* in life," said her husband, who like Janet is a successful writer and editor in the general market. His mother had kept a kosher home, and he retained some details from his Hebrew school education. "I remember what it was like, when I was about ten, or twelve, lying in bed at night wondering if there was a G-d, and if He would save us from the Commies. But any hope I had in that department, that G-d would keep the human race from spinning out of control—I lost that when I started reading about the Holocaust. As far as some kind of Supreme Being is concerned, I still feel that way, that nothing is there."

When I apologized later on that we hadn't been able to heat up the food, Janet assured me that it didn't matter. "The kids were happy. We were, too. The togetherness, and no one rushing off anywhere. The challah and the chicken, and that babka cake. It was great."

Janet had gone out of her way—way out of her way, as always—to make me comfortable, and on Shabbos afternoon, I was in their guest room reading when Janet went out to do some shopping. Upon her return, she told me about having met up with Mr. and Mrs. Grunwald, her elderly neighbors two flights down, as they stood outside the locked electronic entrance to the building. She'd been eager to be of help and was holding open the door, when their awkward expressions reminded her that they were waiting for a non-Jew to come along.

"I told them about my *frum* houseguest from Israel—I'm so proud, my little Orthodox friend!—and they invited you to come down about five for *shallashulaf*. Something like that. They said you'd know what it was. I think you'll have a good time. They're a very sweet couple. When Michael was born, Mr. Grunwald asked if we were having an Orthodox *bris* and we said we hadn't really made plans yet. He organized the whole thing for us in their *shul*. I don't think they like me so much. He always looks the other way when I'm around. I think it's the way I dress."

MR. GRUNWALD HAD FINISHED with Havdalah and the three of us were talking. In response to my questions, Mr. Grunwald was recounting some of his experiences in Auschwitz.

Upon arriving there as a nineteen-year-old, he had claimed to be an electrician—a field which he then tried to master. One painfully freezing day, an SS Guard ordered him to follow him out to one of the watchtowers at the edge of the huge camp yard, to fix a light that wasn't working.

The two marched out to the far edge of the camp yard, he in his thin rags, and the Nazi, with his rifle, in his overcoat and winter hat and high black boots. The Jewish teenager climbed up the ladder to the platform and had crouched down to work on the broken light, conscious of the guard standing behind him, when he noticed off in the distance an enormous pit of fire.

The wind up there was so fierce that the young Mr. Grunwald was struggling to control his hands when a weird, shrill, unidentifiable sound reached his ears. Suddenly, from over to the left, an enormous dump truck sped by, packed with a load of about a hundred naked, screaming Jewish children.

He couldn't move his head, which would have angered the guard; he followed the truck only with his eyes. The screams and cries were already swallowed by the winds.

The truck stopped at the pit, backed up, and like any dump truck emptying its load, upended its cargo.

"I can't get that picture out of mind," said Mr. Grunwald. "I live with it every day."

I asked what to me was the obvious question: "Didn't seeing that make you doubt the existence of G-d?"

Mr. Grunwald looked at me, startled. "No." He seemed about to say something else, but after a long silent moment he looked over at his wife. "I wouldn't even let such a thought enter my mind."

"You know," said Mrs. Grunwald, "we would like to ask you something. Your friends upstairs, they don't want to keep Shabbos?"

"They do, but they come from a very different world. It's the world I come from too."

"I must tell you. My husband and I are disappointed. You visit them—and we told them about Shabbos years ago."

"Yes, I know, they would like to believe. It's hard for them."

Mr. and Mrs. Grunwald looked at each other. He shook his head slowly, baffled. "Hard? It's *Hakadosh Baruch Hu*'s Torah."

SHORTLY AFTER ARRIVING for a visit at my friends a few years later, I eagerly ran down the two flights to knock on Mr. and Mrs. Grunwald's door, but someone else answered.

"Oh!" said Janet, when I came back up. "I forgot to tell you. They moved to Monsey."

"Janet, really? They moved?"

"Yeah, to be nearer their children. I heard they were moving so I went to say goodbye, and when Mrs. Grunwald came to the door, all of a sudden," said Janet, "I burst out crying. I don't know why I reacted like that.

Just weeping uncontrollably. I couldn't believe it. Totally out of nowhere. She was as shocked as I was, I could see. So we were just standing there. I wanted to say I love you. But I...anyway...I just asked her to say goodbye for us to her husband, and to thank him."

"And then?"

"Nothing. I said goodbye. And when I went back upstairs, I really don't understand it, I couldn't stop crying."

JUST ME AND MY SHADOW

Through the predawn darkness, Riverside Drive beckoned. It was 5 a.m., but for me it was noon. I was on Israel time, and morning was taking a long time to arrive.

When I peered out my friend's guest room window way over to the right, I got a narrow glimpse of trees between this building and the next. I shouldn't do what I was thinking. Back home in Jerusalem, women catch the early buses to the Kotel before it gets light, day in, day out. The #3 passes through East Jerusalem—as much a hardcore Middle Eastern Arab neighborhood as anything you could hope to find in Egypt, or Iraq. Here in Manhattan, though, I knew you'd have to be nuts to go out strolling at that hour.

On the other hand, I was in the city for just four more days, and this was my last morning in Manhattan. And my hosts lived on the very street that I as a child, from the sheltered suburban boredom of my sheltered Connecticut suburb fifty miles away, had longed for from afar. With its hundreds of majestic old trees, block after block, and the acres of park down below that stretched gently down to the Henry Hudson Parkway...and its shining view of the blue or gray river, under summer or winter skies, like an Impressionist painting extending all the way out to the twinkling George Washington Bridge...was where I expected my Real Life to begin one day. Romantic Riverside Drive—the trees, the park, the graceful brownstones, the racially and culturally integrated neighborhood—had in my preteen and adolescent mind epitomized the moral enlightenment of feminism, the righteousness of the civil rights movement, and the glamor and excitement of growing up.

After graduating from college, my two older sisters had rented a room together in the International House—from their windows you could get a slice of sunset and a view beneath the stars of New Jersey's Palisades. By the time I entered high school, the two of them were working in a program to strengthen public school education in Harlem.

Many decades later, it's still one of the most beautiful streets in the world, so for a horse chafing at the bit, the decision wasn't long in coming. A few minutes later, down I rode in the spacious, old-fashioned elevator, and the all-night doorman was bidding me good day. "Cold out there! You goin' for a jog?"

I, in my high heels, nodded happily. "Sort of!"

NOT A SOUL WAS OUT. The leaves and branches overhead were a misty canopy…the sound of my footsteps on the sidewalk…Hands in my coat pockets, looking off down toward the river…and to the right, all the distinguished old stone buildings with cornices.

No reason to be scared, after all.

An old song came to mind—my father used to play it on the piano:

> Just me and my shadow
> Strollin' down the avenue
> Me and my shadow
> Not a soul to tell my troubles to…

Beyond the low stone wall, down in the dark park, huge trees huddled together in groups, or were positioned singly. All stood graciously in place, exactly where they'd been for years and years.

"I need money."

I jumped out of my skin and spun around.

She was taller than I, and gaunt. Hazel eyes—crazed, empty. A drug addict! Did she have a knife?! She'd materialized out of nowhere. Chopped-off blond hair, a long, skinny arm outstretched.

"I have to get downtown right away. All my stuff's down there. I need twenty dollars for a taxi. The social services took everything. I don't have anything left. They took it all." Her long fingers opened out flat, palm up.

I searched my mind for the right thing to do. Maybe she had a gun!? I turned slightly, holding my purse away from her, and rummaged around for my wallet. "Here."

Her fingers snatched the bill from mine, like one of those exotic flowers that trap insects—a Venus flytrap.

"A dollar?" Her voice was flat, desperate. "No. That's not enough."

"Okay." I extracted a five.

"No," she said. "Five's not enough. You don't understand. I have nowhere to go. I'm homeless. I have to have twenty. I have to get a taxi downtown."

I looked off furtively toward Janet's building, hidden now from view. Where was the morning?

Her pale eyes were fastened on me. "I can pay you back. Give me your email address and I'll pay you back. I promise."

I turned slightly again, to keep her eyes out of my purse, opened the wallet carefully in the yellow light from the streetlamp. "OK. Here."

"Oh, thank you. Thank you very much. Bless you. I'll pay it back, I promise."

"Are you Jewish?" The question had surfaced without warning.

Her eyes stopped short, like an animal caught in the headlights. "Why did you ask me that?"

"I don't know. I just—"

"Yes. I am. I'm Jewish. My name is—" It ended with *stein*. "Are *you*?"

"Yes."

And with that she fled.

THEN OUR MOUTH WILL BE
FILLED WITH LAUGHTER

A song of ascents. When *Hashem* will return the captivity of Zion, we will be like dreamers. Then our mouth will be filled with laughter and our tongue with glad song…Those who sow in tears will reap with glad song. Walk on, he walks weeping, carrying the measure of seeds, but will return in exultation, a bearer of his sheaves.

Tehillim 126

One day I answered the phone and couldn't quite catch, at first, what the caller was saying. It took a few seconds to tune in to the musical curve and lilt of an Indian accent, and to understand that someone was inquiring if I was the daughter of Norman Cousins.

I said yes, I was.

"Oh!" he exclaimed. "How lovely! This is marvelous!" The man said he was founder and director of The International Laughter Club and had just arrived in Israel to give a series of workshops and seminars throughout the country. He said that Mr. Cousins's book *Anatomy of an Illness*, and the programs Mr. Cousins initiated to promote the use of humor in hospital wards—his voice seemed to be bobbling around buoyantly along a quickly running, giggling stream, as if he were being tickled—had been his inspiration, and the guiding light of his own career. Had I heard about The Club? No, I hadn't. Well, then, it would be his pleasure, he said, to have me as his honored guest this evening at the first seminar, at Hebrew University. In the meantime, would it by any chance be possible to visit me in my home in person, along with his wife and colleagues?

"Certainly!" That was my father's word. Without thinking, I'd reflexively shifted gears and was already trying to sound like him—upbeat, cheerful, self-confident. I didn't want the man on the phone to be disappointed, though as usual I feared he would be. "When would be good for you?"

He consulted with some other voices in the background.

"In ten minutes? If this would not be inconvenient?"

Rushing around with the vacuum cleaner before my guests arrived, I was immersed in the old familiar quandary. Since my father's death in 1990, we who were fortunate enough to be his family members have occasionally been called upon to represent him to the public. For me, it's a role and responsibility which has often evoked pervasive feelings of inadequacy.

It was my father's tendency, even under the most difficult circumstances of personal suffering (of which he got his abundant, fair share), to see the upside, the possibility, the beauty, the hope. If the sky went dark, he'd give it a spin with his mind and the sun would rise. He was an emissary from the Bright Side, a spokesman for light, an ambassador from the land of Yes. My inner compass, on the other hand, swings readily to *No*. With parents as bright as noon and as energetic as bees, how I got my pronounced vulnerability to gravity's pull, G-d only knows. All I can say, now that neither he nor my mother is in this world, is that the problem isn't that the two of them didn't bequeath to their youngest daughter a large capacity for joy; indeed they did. But for whatever reason, the baby of the family got a generous share of darkness, as well. And I knew that whoever this was on the telephone, he was hoping—perhaps without being aware of it—to meet my father by meeting me.

The doorbell rang. I stashed the vacuum in a closet and opened the front door with a grand, welcoming flourish. There in the hallway stood four men, three of whom my antennae recognized instantly as Israelis. The fourth looked just the way you'd expect of someone with the director's job description—a beatifically smiling fountain of serenity, with merry dark eyes, and at his side was a diminutive, almond-eyed lady, attired in a pink and silken sari. First it was the director who entered, then his wife. The Israelis followed, filing in one after the other, each in turn beaming his best grin expectantly my way.

ANATOMY OF AN ILLNESS AS PERCEIVED BY THE PATIENT, published in 1979, told how in early middle-age my father was abruptly felled by a mysterious ailment which his doctors could not initially identify. One day he was indefatigable—a nonstop editor, writer, lecturer, diplomat, and activist—the next he was paralyzed, and confined to a hospital bed. It was when the condition worsened relentlessly and he overheard his doctor say, "I'm afraid we're going to lose Norman," that he decided to take matters into his own hands.

He followed his intuition (as he had his whole life). Something told him that if—as had long been acknowledged in the medical community—negative emotions can affect the body for the worse, perhaps positive emotions can affect it for the better. Perhaps, he suspected, happiness had an effect biologically, on the cellular and even on the molecular level. He checked himself out of intensive care and into a nearby hotel, chucked his painkilling medications, had an intravenous installed whereby he was giving himself an around-the-clock injection of vitamin C, to combat infection, and had my mother rent out Marx Brothers movies and old reruns from the 1960s' TV show, *Candid Camera*. (This was before the Internet era.) My mother set up a movie screen at the foot of his bed.

Then he went about the serious business of making himself laugh.

Comedy was his self-prescribed daily regimen, and he would later call laughter "internal jogging." He found that for every twenty minutes of laughter, he'd get two hours of pain-free sleep.

I remember those times. They were terrifying. Not because I as a girl feared he was going to die—how ridiculous, of course my father couldn't die—but because seeing him bedridden, quiet, fading, wincing with pain, not joking around, not even working, he who had always worked and always played, he who was the stable pillar of our world, was to have life as I knew it turned inside out. Worst of all was to catch a fleeting glimpse in his eyes of discouragement, and even, sometimes, fear. Because in Daddy, there was no such thing as discouragement, and certainly—*certainly!*—not fear.

The illness literally came over him overnight. The cure didn't. Little by little, month by month, the swelling went down, the inflammation subsided. Little by little he was spending more time sitting up than lying down, more time in his chair than his bed, more on his feet than in his chair. Slowly through the weeks, and months, regaining the use of his hands, and arms, his legs, his feet...gradually, as mobility was restored, finally, he became himself again.

My father had written more than a dozen books before *Anatomy of an Illness*, but this account of that gradual recovery from what doctors had regarded as a terminal progressive disease, was his first (and only) book to stay for months on the *New York Times* bestseller list. After thirty-five years as editor of the *Saturday Review* magazine, suddenly he was known as the man who healed himself with laughter.

The story people heard was true, as far as it went. With ease I can summon up the mental picture of a laughing Daddy, still in the depths of illness, throwing back his head with joy, and that's still the abiding afterimage. But the whole story (like all whole stories) is more complex. My father had been honing the art of positive thinking ever since his first decade, when as a little boy during the Depression, he contracted tuberculosis, was quarantined in a sanatorium, and had to consciously find his way back to the carefree mentality of childhood. His sense of humor arose from a consciously cultivated optimism, the bedrock from which his happiness sprang. "Optimism is realism." That's a line I've been attributing to him for years. But some time ago it occurred to me that maybe he never actually said it. Maybe it was just the message he emanated.

MY FATHER HAD ALWAYS LOVED telling jokes, playing elaborate tricks, and making up stories to astound and delight. For instance, in a packed hotel elevator, he'd turn to my mother and say something like, "Did you see that gorilla in the lobby?" But my mother told me that she could always ask, "Norman, are you serious?" and she could get a straight answer.

In the Personals Column of his magazine, items such as the following would regularly appear:

> *COMPUTER ERROR HAS CAUSED us to manufacture 320 marine compasses, needles pointing West only. Strictly for the weekend mariner who knows his way around. Westroads Marine Compass Co., SR Box BB.*
>
> *I AM CAPABLE OF ELEGANT and soaring thoughts under the gentle stimulation of a South Pacific island sun. Is any book publisher curious about my unborn masterpiece? SR Box SP.*
>
> *TO MY THREE SONS AND TWO DAUGHTERS: Eighteen years of unexplained absence is a long time, but I am now back and eager to tell you what happened. Please let me know where you are. Your loving father, R.E.T. Jr. SR Box TE.*
>
> *ARE YOU LOSING OUT because you are making yourself too clear? We can help give you an impressive ambiguity that can*

*command the respectful attention and admiration of your col-
leagues, customers, and business associates. SR Box LO.*

*IMPORTANT NOTICE: If you are one of the hundreds of para-
chuting enthusiasts who bought our course entitled "Easy Sky
Diving in One Fell Swoop," please make the following correction:
On page 8, line 7, change "state zip code" to "pull rip cord."*

*I WOULD LIKE to go around the world and promise to write
fascinating, luminous letters about it in exchange for tickets and
other expenses. SR Box KJS.*

*COMPUTER ERROR HAS RESULTED in large supply of electric-
powered swivel chairs that make approximately 150 high-speed
revolutions per minute as soon as body weight hits the seat.
Excellent bargain for the nausea-resistant. SR Box SC.*

*WONDERING WHAT TO DO if your waterbed freezes this win-
ter? Our trained hamsters (sold in pairs only) skate for hours to
the tune of the beautiful "Blue Danube" waltz. Pair sold complete
with 33 LP record and 8 extra miniature skates. WM Box D.*

My father's love of laughter was part and parcel of his *ayin tov*—his
positive outlook on himself, others, and the world—and was consistent
with all the ways he worked on himself. Above all, it was with an integrity
in regard to words, both spoken and written, that he kept himself on the
side of light. Without exaggeration, I can say I have no memory of him
putting another person down. I have not one single recollection of his ever
speaking of anyone in a demeaning way, even of politicians whose policies
he criticized and deplored.

He gave others words of encouragement, never discouragement, and
I believe he did the same for himself. When in the early 1980s he suffered
a massive heart attack, I'll never forget what he said when I called him on
our upstairs neighbors' phone in the Old City. (Bezek hadn't yet gotten us
connected.) I said something innocuous like, "Daddy, how *are* you?" but my
overwhelming fear must have come through loud and clear because he said,
"Don't you worry! I have a gr-r-r-r-eat heart!"

He actually seemed to forget wrongs done against him—and there were
many. I witnessed them myself when I worked for him as a secretary for
a few years at the *Saturday Review*. He wasn't just quick to forgive but eager to forgive, eager to let bygones be bygones, to let go of resentments

or grudges—anything small, narrow, confining, anything that made us smaller than he believed we really were.

I HAVE AN IMPRESSIONISTIC recollection of how my hour with The Laughter Club began. In memory, there was one long, drawn-out *hello* of mutual grinning and nodding of our heads, and mutual reassurances that we were all on the same team. If laughter were a political party, we were busy showing each other how we'd cast our ballots.

My skeptical inner naysayer, however, immediately went to work analyzing the Israelis, who ran their own branches of The Laughter Club in Jerusalem, Haifa, and Tel Aviv. To my mind, they seemed over-zealous about demonstrating to themselves and to Norman Cousins's daughter that they were *very, very happy*—with the biggest of smiles to prove it was so. Was I perversely negative (or maybe just projecting!) or were these dyed-in-the-wool Israelis trying to trade in their ever-so-Jewish natures for a Jewish-Lite model, fashioned after their Eastern guru?

He, on the other hand, struck me as an authentic master of mirth, true to his culture and his roots. Indeed, you had only to look into his laughing brown eyes and amusement would start bubbling up within you. He explained that we can access this inborn gift simply by letting the physical mechanism work its magic spontaneously. If in a group we induce each other "to laugh for no reason," he said, by chanting "ha, ha, ha" in unison, or mimicking laughter in any number of other ways, we trigger that automatic reflex. Contagion and person-to-person mirroring take care of the rest.

He gave a demonstration. Focusing his attention inwardly for a few seconds, the irrepressible merriment began visibly simmering up into his face, as if he were contemplating the funniest thing in the whole world. Before I knew it (I just couldn't help it!), I and his wife and his colleagues were cracking up until tears actually ran down our faces, and whenever we looked at each other, a new round of convulsive laughter started all over again.

Bearing in mind that we are made in G-d's Image, it struck me what a wondrous, strange, and inexplicable creation this is—the phenomenon of human laughter. We are surprised by something *funny*, we make certain barking-like noises, are jolted and shaken by certain rhythmic movements, and are filled for a few moments with *happiness*.

Yet somewhere along the line (and I really can't say if it was because of something he said, or something I read into his words), I started feeling wary. Maybe this Indian master had come to Israel in order to suggest—without saying so explicitly—that all we had to do was get Arabs and Jews together in Laughter Clubs, and our nasty penchant for war, and all our illusory troubles and useless grievances, would dissolve of their own accord. Had he ever heard about Eisav's hate for Yaakov? As the minutes went on, it seemed to me more and more that what this well-meaning man was advocating—and apparently what he mistakenly thought my father had advocated—was laughter as The Answer. Like so many others before him down through the ages, he had come upon *a* truth and believed it to be *the* truth, the solution to the human condition. Laughter appeared to be his object of worship. I was suspicious that he thought it could heal whatever ails mankind—not only the suffering and cruelty of unenlightened individuals but of wars between nations.

And he seemed to regard my father as his patron saint.

"Excuse me, Mr. V.," I interjected. "My father wrote that laughter is a metaphor for all the positive emotions—love, hope, faith. He didn't believe laughter is all we need, or the answer to all of life's ills. It's one aspect of life. We find that idea in Judaism. 'There's a time to laugh and a time to weep. A time to love and a time to hate. A time to—'"

His face fell.

I had avoided the word "Torah," but I'd clearly stepped on his spiritual toes.

The conversation sputtered on a little bit longer, then fell into an awkward silence, which we tried to fill, unsuccessfully. After a little while, he rose. "Well," he said, "thank you very much. The seminar is in two hours. We must really be on our way."

When I closed the door behind them, I felt—no surprise—inadequate. The man had come in memory of my father, and what had I done? I'd hurt his feelings. Was this yet another example of the darkness inside me leaking out? Why had I insisted on puncturing his balloon? After all, as crimes go, I thought, there are surely a lot worse ones that a non-Jew could perpetrate on Israel than to teach us to laugh for no reason.

I DID SHOW UP that night at Hebrew University, and as the seminar progressed, I found myself wondering if in all the years of living here, I'd ever beheld such a wonderful sight. In this country torn by terrorism and war and social conflict, more than two hundred Israelis of all types (observant and nonobservant, Sephardim and Ashkenazim and Yemenites, white and black, old and young) sat together in a great big room and laughed until we cried, without holding back, celebrating nothing whatsoever other than the simple, astounding happiness of being alive.

Simple…as long as you didn't look too closely into the Jewish eyes. For we can't totally escape it. *We're Jews, in Eretz Yisrael, and are still far from home…Far, far away from where we have to go.*

We can't laugh all the time, but we can sure laugh some of the time, as Daddy proclaimed. For to everything there is a season and we will have *orah v'simchah, sasson vi'kar*, at the appointed time.

THE POMEGRANATE
FOR LUNCH

A s I finish writing up the interview that follows, I wish to thank Dr. Dan Altura, author of *Biblical Oncology: The Hidden Bounty of the Seven Biblical Fruits*, for introducing me to current biochemical research into the workings of the human cell. Dr. Altura presents epidemiological and preclinical findings that demonstrate the potential use of the seven Biblical species of fruit, as delineated in *Sefer Devarim*, for the prevention and treatment of a variety of human cancers.

If this astonishes me, why should that be so? For a believing Jew, is it such a stretch? I question whether surprise is justified, whereupon I find myself slipping back spontaneously into my skeptical mind's default position, a leftover from my secular education: *It's too good to be true. Something so simple, natural, and easy to attain (and inexpensive) can't be the cure that mankind's been seeking.*

To be on the safe side, though...I've nonetheless modified my weekly shopping list to include the seven species of fruit, and am trying to influence my family and friends—and anyone who cares to listen—to modify their diets similarly. *Please eat fresh dates, fresh figs, cold-pressed virgin olive oil, wheat, barley, grapes, a moderate quantity (approximately three ounces daily) of red wine, and pomegranates.*

MY OPENING QUESTION after offering Dr. Altura a cup of hot tea—it was a cold, rainy day in Jerusalem—was how, as a chemical engineer, he had come to write *Biblical Oncology*.

"I'll start," he said, "with my background. At age twenty-five, I received my PhD from the UCLA School of Engineering and Applied Science. My master's degree and my doctoral thesis dealt with the chemical kinetics of a fundamental chemical reaction in nature called the hydrogen evolution reaction. The dean believed that any graduate from UCLA Engineering should have as broad a perspective as possible. So I've had a broad background, which has helped me throughout my career.

"My area of specialization is electrochemical kinetics, which I've applied at various points in my career to industrial processes such as the corrosion and failure of aircraft structures, the manufacture of memory discs for personal computers, and microanalytical processes. My understanding of chemical kinetics gave me a perspective into the microchemical workings of cancer cells and tumors, which in turn enabled me to delve into the complex arena of the human cell.

"The human cell is literally the most complex system in the entire universe, unless you're talking about a combination of human cells, such as a human brain, for example, or kidney, or liver, or some other combination of human cells.

"The workhorse of the human cell is the protein. It carries out almost all the functions—all the different biochemical reactions—that relate to biological systems. Each individual human cell has as many as twenty thousand different kinds of proteins that it uses for the cell to function. An enzyme constitutes a particular category of protein whose job—it's amazing—is to speed up a normal chemical reaction so that it can occur many, many times per second, by approximately one million times, or as much as ten million times. It's an amazing thing.

"The speed of chemical reaction was my area of specialization."

I ask Dr. Altura what's so significant about speed that it should be an area of specialization. "Speed," he says, "is absolutely necessary for the proper functioning of the cell. The cell's continued existence is totally dependent on all the different chemical reactions occurring inside it. Without enzymes, the chemical reaction would be so slow that it might occur perhaps once a week, or even less.

"Studying these phenomena has increased my belief in *Hashem*. The processes of the cell are amazing. Its complexity is unbelievable.

"Having said all this, now let's take a look at the seven Biblical fruits. They first appear in *Chumash* in *Sefer Devarim*, the last of the Five Books of Moses, after the end of the Israelites' forty-year sojourn in the desert. It was the last thirty days of Moshe Rabbeinu's life, when the Jewish People were about to enter the Land of Israel and Yehoshua was going to take over.

"It's precisely at this juncture that Moshe tells the Jewish People, 'You're going to go into *Eretz Yisrael*, and I'm not going with you.' Then, in *Devarim* 7:12–15, it states that if the Jews keep the mitzvos, they won't suffer the same diseases that the Egyptians, and also the Jews, suffered in *Mitzrayim*. Then, in 8:8, we come directly to the seven Biblical species.

"During this period, when the Jews were still in Egypt, members of the Egyptian royal class underwent the expensive process of mummification. Regular Egyptian citizens were buried in public burial grounds. The bodies of royalty, preserved inside the wrappings, remained intact, making later examination possible, and bones unearthed from burial grounds were examined, as well. Over the past twenty to twenty-five years, forensic scientists who were looking specifically for evidence of cancer have discovered that the Egyptian ruling class suffered from various forms of the disease, including prostate cancer, and that regular Egyptian citizens suffered from various cancers that metastasize to the bone.

"From the beginning of civilization and up until the development of antibiotics in the twentieth century, infection had been mankind's number one killer disease, and most people died of infections, viral and bacterial. The Black Plague, for example, which killed twenty-five million people in Europe, was a bacterial infection.

"Penicillin was the first true antibiotic. Until penicillin came along, people who got pneumonia, for example, frequently died from it. What does penicillin do? It attacks the bacteria that cause infection, and unless a person is allergic, it does so without harming the body.

"Our bodies are made up of trillions of cells, all of which have soft outer cell membranes, rather than cell walls. The bacteria cell has a structure that differs fundamentally from a human cell, insofar as it has a very tough outer cell wall. Penicillin targets only the bacteria cell wall, which weakens the bacteria and causes it to burst, then die. This doesn't happen to human cells because they don't have cell walls. They have membranes.

"It's on account of that success in treating infections that cancer subsequently surpassed infection as the foremost killer disease.

"In 1971, the American president, Richard Nixon, in his State of the Union Address, announced that he was launching a so-called War on Cancer. He sincerely thought that by the end of the decade, a cure for cancer would be found. But here we are, after forty-nine years—almost half a century later—*baruch Hashem* we're still here!—and there's still no cure on the horizon."

I ask Dr. Altura if a drug can be developed for the treatment of cancer that works the way antibiotics do.

"No. Because a cancer cell is a human cell, and it's 99 percent—or even more than 99 percent—identical, more or less, to normal human cells. So it's very, very difficult to target a cancer cell.

"Most of the chemotherapy drugs that are still being used today work by targeting fast-dividing cells. That's one of the problems with chemotherapy, because the human body, too, has fast-dividing cells such as skin cells and bone marrow cells, so those, too, are affected by the treatment."

"WHICH BRINGS US AGAIN," says Dr. Altura, "to the seven Biblical species. The seven species contain unique combinations of special biochemicals called polyphenols. Each of the seven fruits has a different combination of polyphenols, which is what gives the fruits the potential ability to prevent the development of cancer in the human body.

"A tumor is a combination of cancer cells. Preclinical research has shown that these polyphenols knock out cancer cells before they can develop into a significant tumor.

"Olive oil contains a polyphenol called ursolic acid. One study, carried out a few years ago, was of mice that had been genetically modified to develop prostate cancer. One group was fed a diet containing 1 percent ursolic acid. The other group's diet was identical, but didn't include the ursolic acid. The mice that ate the ursolic acid diet developed prostate cancer, but later than the other group. They developed a lower number of tumors, their tumors were smaller, and they lived significantly longer than the mice who did not consume ursolic acid.

"A prominent West Coast university conducted some Phase II clinical trials to test the effect of pomegranate juice on men with prostate cancer. Preliminary results indicate that the men who consumed the pomegranate juice have a much higher PSA [prostate specific antigen] doubling time than the patients who did not drink pomegranate juice. The higher the PSA doubling time, the less likely the prostate cancer will turn metastatic.

"In Spain, a clinical trial of olive oil was carried out for the purpose of researching its use as a preventative measure for heart disease. Six thousand postmenopausal women between the ages of sixty and eighty were given differing amounts of olive oil in their diet, some more, some less. The condition of all the participants was very closely followed for five years, a huge amount of data was gathered, and at the end of the five-year study, the medical team realized that aside from what they'd learned about heart disease, they had data in their possession that could be applied to the study of olive oil's impact on breast cancer development. They found that the group of women who had consumed the most olive oil had a 68 percent reduced chance of developing breast cancer, compared to those who consumed the least amounts of olive oil.

"Immunotherapy has become one of the newest types of targeted cancer therapy. Beta glucans found in abundance in barley, one of the seven species, is a natural immunotherapy agent. It stimulates the body's own immune system to fight cancer by activating so-called natural killer cells. Japan has already used a similar product for cancer therapy made from mushrooms. They've been using it in combination with conventional drugs for more than twenty-five years. The Japanese government has approved this product for cancer therapy. The difference between the barley's beta glucans and the newer immunotherapy drugs is this: the many thousands of dollars for treatment.

"The medical establishment in the US, and in some other countries, is primarily a for-profit business. The pharmaceutical corporations' most important goal is to maximize profits, with the saving of human life as its secondary consideration." Dr. Altura pauses, then continues: "I have a friend who suffers from kidney cancer, and is taking one of the new, targeted cancer medications. It costs more than seven thousand dollars per month. That means that each pill costs several hundred dollars. In Israel, the Kupat Cholim pays for this medication, and every citizen is covered. In America, if the individual doesn't have the right insurance coverage, he's out of luck.

"So the pharmaceutical companies are making tremendous profits from these new patented drugs. How eager will they be to have a competing, effective therapy made from olive oil that costs a few dollars a liter? Have you heard the expression, 'Follow the money'? There's a similar saying in Yiddish: 'When it comes to money, it's a different world.'

"I come from outside the medical establishment, so I'm looking at cancer prevention and therapy from a totally different perspective. Both epidemiological and animal preclinical studies have demonstrated that components of the seven Biblical species can help to prevent the initiation of cancer. So not only can they be used to fight cancer, they can also nip it in the bud.

"Prevention is always better than therapy after the fact.

"Because of a lack of funding, most of the cancer research on the seven species has only been done on either animals or in test tubes. It's grossly inadequate. What's needed are more clinical trials on human patients, to verify the preclinical results, but the drug companies aren't interested in funding clinical trials using the seven species because of the limited potential for profit. How much can you charge for a pomegranate?

"Conventional chemotherapy, and the newer targeted therapies, certainly have an important place in cancer therapy. But these standard therapies can potentially be used, also, in combination with the seven species as adjuvant treatments. This combination could be more effective than the standard therapies alone. Research carried out on animals has shown that components from the seven species, when combined with conventional chemotherapy, can have what's called a 'synergistic effect.' The combination is more effective than the individual components. This can even lead to a reduction in the quantity of conventional chemotherapy drugs—drugs that are very toxic to the human body."

I ASK IF DR. ALTURA has anything to add to a statement once made by Dr. Eliyahu Rips, a higher mathematics professor at Hebrew University, who—like Dr. Altura—is an Orthodox scientist. "Unfortunately, modern man has faith in science," said Dr. Rips, "so it is by way of science that we can reveal the miraculous nature of the Creation."

Dr. Altura thought about this for several long moments, nodding his head. "I would say this: I'm over seventy, and have been in science now for more than fifty years. I often see that the more we know, the more we realize we don't know. The human cell is too complex to be totally understood by humans.

"When it comes to Torah knowledge, more people are studying Torah today than at any time before in Jewish history. We are standing on the shoulders of the rabbis who lived before World War II, who were much greater in terms of Torah knowledge. Just as every step you take back into Jewish history, progressively more was known because they were closer to *Har Sinai*, what occurs as we move forward in time? *Yeridas ha'doros*, the decline of the generations.

"In terms of scientific knowledge, it is just the opposite.

"You know, a few hundred years ago, the amount of medical knowledge was limited, so therefore an individual could master all there was to know, all he needed to know. Then the industrial revolution opened up and gave us scientific knowledge. It opened up a whole new world. Most of what we know was discovered in the last forty or fifty years, sixty years, seventy years. Our scientific knowledge has increased by leaps and bounds. So today, it's completely impossible for any individual to know and to master all there is to know. Today, everything's a communal effort. Everybody has a little piece, and together, we can put all the pieces together.

"The most important part of medical research and practice is *pikuach nefesh*, the saving of human life. Chazal tell us, 'He who saves a single life...is as if he saves an entire universe. He who destroys a single life...is as if he destroys an entire universe.'

"We don't actually know how the seven fruits work to prevent cancer from developing. Recently some new evidence came to light, showing that the polyphenols in the seven species may interact with what are called micro RNA segments, which are coded for by the 97 percent of the essentially unknown part of the DNA. These micro RNA segments have just recently been found to control many critical biological processes in the cell. It could turn out that the interaction of the polyphenols with the micro RNA segments have a significant impact on the development of cancer in the cell.

"*Hashem* created man in His image, and each one of us is in the image of G-d. That's why we emulate G-d by giving charity, by being creative. Unfortunately, sometimes not only do we want to emulate G-d, we want to be G-d.

"Scientists are no substitute for G-d. We don't know G-d's plan, and we are presumptuous to think we do."

I ASK DR. ALTURA what distinguishes cancer from other diseases.

"The difference is that cancer is very, very human, and human cells are tremendously complex—actually, as I said earlier, the most complex system, literally, in the whole universe. And the cancer cell is smart. It's smarter than any of the medications that have been developed to fight it. And it's smarter than most doctors.

"The cancer cell is a type of human cell that divides uncontrollably. Most human cells divide only in a controlled manner, but cancer cells are the exception. They just go right on dividing and dividing.

"The last fifty or sixty years have seen mortality rates of heart disease go way down, both in Israel and in the United States, by about 70 percent. In Israel, heart disease has gone down even more than in the United States, so now cancer has replaced heart disease as the number one killer disease, while in the United States heart disease will still be number one for a few more years.

"Even though cancer mortality rates in Israel have declined over the past several years, it's still a terribly devastating disease. It's so complex that I believe they'll still be searching for a cure a hundred years from now. And they still won't come up with a complete answer.

"Usually, when you conduct an investigation into something, you know more when you finish than when you started out. But when it comes to the secrets of cancer, the more we learn, the more we uncover what we don't know. The more we know, the more we see that we really don't know, while the cancer cell is unbelievably smart. No matter what kind of chemotherapy is used, the cancer will effectively resist the drug. It's amazing. How does a cancer cell fight? It hijacks the DNA 'computer' in a human cell and then uses everything in the computer for its own benefit.

"How much do we know about what's in the DNA computer? We really only know, for sure, about 2 or 3 percent of its blueprint, which involves genes that code for proteins. So let's say you're going to build a 747 airliner. Can you imagine being able to build a 747 if you only have 2 or 3 percent of the blueprint? That's the situation we have now.

"Most scientists are atheists. A scientist who believes in the theory of evolution maintains that G-d does not exist, but that he himself is the next best thing. He's well aware that we only have the 2 or 3 percent, so he decides to dismiss the remaining 97 percent as 'evolutionary junk.'

"Some years ago, several hundred scientists got together to check the 97 percent, and they found that at least 80 percent is biologically significant, and that in fact, all of it is significant. With time, we may discover that every single part of the DNA is absolutely necessary.

"The way that the instructions in DNA result in the development of particular proteins is an extremely complicated process. For example: Two genes, BRCA 1 and 2, issue instructions to the cell to make the BRCA 1 and 2 proteins. The average protein can be compared to a necklace with about two hundred beads. Each bead is an amino acid. BRCA1 is also a protein, but instead of two hundred, it has over eighteen hundred amino acids.

"BRCA2 has a necklace of more than thirty-four hundred amino acids. These are tremendously complex proteins. So basically, why is that a problem for the woman who has one of these two genes, which are defective? Because the instructions from the defective gene produces defective BRCA proteins, which then can't function properly in the cell. This is what leads to the initiation of cancer.

"Most modern versions of Darwinian theory hold that in the beginning, there was one single cell, and that single cell, given enough time, 'evolved' into a human being. It's total nonsense. To illustrate the point, let's take the average protein, which consists of about two hundred amino acids. There are twenty different kinds of amino acids that are used to make a protein, just as you'd use twenty different kinds of colored beads to make a necklace. If each of the two hundred amino acids were to be chosen randomly, by accident, then according to Darwinian Theory, there would be a one in twenty chance for each of the two hundred amino acids in the protein to consist of a particular amino acid. We know that a protein won't work if even one amino acid out of the two hundred amino acids is missing, or in the wrong order. Mathematically, the chance of getting this right by accident—the right combination of amino acids in an average protein—is less than locating a single atom in the whole known universe. And this is only one protein from more than twenty thousand different proteins that can be found in the human cell.

"Did all of this happen by chance, and does it repeat itself by chance? It evolved, somehow or other, by accident? It's simply ridiculous. If an unbiased scientist looks at this phenomenon without bias, what will he see? That a human cell does not happen by chance.

"When the human cell was created, it was created with certain deficiencies which are actually necessary to the cell's proper functioning, for reasons beyond our understanding. Some cells could become cancerous, and that's a very serious problem. But *Hashem* simultaneously created a method, inside the cell, that limits or *prevents* the formation of cancer cells. How?

"To answer that, let's look again at the incredible DNA computer in the cell. It consists of a very long double chain of nucleic acids with three billion base pairs. Various factors in the environment—such as ultraviolet light, ionizing radiation, or cancer-causing chemicals—can create defects in the DNA, which can then lead to the initiation of cancer. But *Hashem* also created a very special protein called p53, which continuously checks the DNA in the cell for defects. If it finds a defect, it either gathers together other proteins to fix the defect, or the cell is destroyed by a process called apoptosis, to prevent it from causing cancer in the body."

"Dr. Altura, that makes me think of *Borei nefashos*, the *berachah acharonah*, 'Who has created all things with their deficiencies.'" I was thinking, too, by this time, about lunch, and about the pomegranate in the refrigerator.

"Yes," replies Dr. Altura, as he rises to take his leave, "imperfection is a necessary aspect of the perfection of Creation."

THE APPLE AND DR. OHR

When I was sick and lay a-bed,
I had two pillows at my head,
And all my toys beside me lay
To keep me happy all the day…
I was the giant great and still
That sits upon the pillow-hill,
And sees before him, dale and plain,
The pleasant land of Counterpane.

Robert Louis Stevenson

When she was sick and lay a-bed, most of the time she didn't feel like reading, especially not Torah. It was inexplicable: a distinct aversion to opening up any Torah books. She had no inclination or energy to look inward, nor upward. Nor was she bored. Answers didn't interest her, nor questions. She didn't feel like thinking, or eating.

She didn't want visitors, either, but at least that could be attributed to something physical, her physical weakness, at the time still undiagnosed.

Her conscience bothered her about the time and care her family was devoting to her, and she knew that the children, adults now with families of their own, were doing anything, everything, that they could to help. They went all together to the Kotel to *daven* for her week after week. She was so grateful. But the gratitude was heavy; it came weighted with guilt and indebtedness, because she alone knew that she probably wasn't sick. They were going so much out of their way for her, for no good reason. In her heart of hearts, she thought her condition, in truth, had to do with laziness, hence depression. She was tired, and slept a great deal, by day as

261

well as by night, more than she could recall having ever slept before. When she wasn't sleeping, she just lay in bed. Yet she wasn't bored, that was the strange thing. She would just lie there, looking out the window.

That whole summer, the tree out the window stretched generously toward her, a friend with great, long limbs, full of green leaves, and wind and breeze, and birds keeping her company all the livelong days.

For the first time in her adult life, she weighed what she'd dreamed of weighing in high school so long before, back when she first started envying that foreign species of delicate, ethereal girls who have waistlines and no appetites. She felt pretty. Just the thought of food sometimes repulsed her, and the pounds were melting away without effort, the numbers on the scale falling spontaneously, week after week. She'd heard of such things, but she herself had never had the privilege and pleasure of bemoaning the phenomenon.

Eating took effort. So far was she from normal instinctual functioning, she realizes now, with hindsight, that she can recall actually wondering, *What makes people want to keep chewing and swallowing? It's an effort: chew and swallow. Chew. Swallow.* Dieting was a thing of the past. It was lovely. The numbers on her bathroom scale kept giving better and better news, until one morning she caught sight of herself in the bathroom mirror at an unguarded moment and was taken aback. It was a shock. This thinness wasn't pretty; she could see her skeleton.

THE DOCTOR SCHEDULED A CAT SCAN, and one appointment after another, and sent her for blood tests. The numbers on the inflammation scale had gone up, up, up, out of the box. The crazily high count opened doors for her. Nurses were kind. If she forgot this or that official document, or came late for an appointment, they'd let her through anyway.

She slept. Things were strange. Morning would be afternoon, then night, then she'd wake up and it was night again, then morning, then the window by her bed would be shining, and dark. Sometimes the phone would ring, but she was tired. Once upon a time, she'd been a wife, and a mother. She'd been a friend, a sister, an aunt, and her grandchildren's grandmother. Once upon a time she'd attended Torah classes, and had loved learning and reading. She remembers that she'd been interested in things, but can't remember what that was like. Sometimes nowadays she'd take one of her longtime secular favorites off the bookshelf, but that sort of poetry and fiction that she'd once loved didn't ring true to her anymore, and the stuff by *frum* writers, including her own things, didn't interest her. What did ring true and was compelling? Only Holocaust literature: memoirs and histories. For her, these were the toys of Stevenson's poem, but they didn't keep her happy all the day. Just profoundly preoccupied and gripped by the horrendous, terrifying unreality of the Nazi era, and its echoes in the news today, until she'd be startled awake all of a sudden, when she'd doze off, by the dropping of a book from her hands.

One day, with mild surprise, she observed something about her state of mind: she realized, bemused and detached, that this was what's known (she thought of it with a kind of melodramatic enjoyment, as if she were a character in a novel) as someone who's *lost her will to live. Oh, so that's the story.* There was a certain satisfaction in identifying it. She had arrived at that famous bottom, where things didn't matter enough to worry anymore. One foot was in the next world.

The prolonged, pronounced aversion to Torah, however, was a spiritual deficit. Knowing this didn't help her to get a handle on it. She was ashamed.

THE CAT CAME BACK, and all of a sudden she was put on the fast track to surgery. The surgeon was named Dr. Ohr. *Hmmm!* Light! What a nice literary touch by the Author. First step after the CAT was a PET, a procedure in the hospital that required drinking down two tall cups of iodine to determine by way of high contrast if the unidentified thing had spread.

Sitting in the room where a number of subdued strangers were also drinking down the radioactive concoction, each individual in a separate enclosure, she read the PET information sheet. Among other things, she learned that for seventy-two hours (three days) after undergoing the scan, the patient was not to be in the presence of children or pregnant women. She was going to be *a radioactive object.*

And now I'll shift temporarily into first-person singular, which I've been avoiding until now, since what I'm about to describe was one of the finest moments of my life, no joke. It took something like this (talk about high contrast) to get me to think straight. For several prolonged minutes (my guess is two or three of them) ridiculous vanities and foolishness and insincerities were eliminated from my mind.

I looked up at the ceiling light and prayed to our Al-mighty G-d.

ON THE WAY to the hospital for the surgery, I was sitting low—I mean, *she* was sitting low—in the back seat of a cab (no particular reason to sit up straight) and was gazing up and out of the taxi window. All she saw was clouds and sky. There was no ground. Just clouds...empty air...

Clouds...

No ground.

A while later someone said, "Count to ten," then they were waking her up, and the surgeon was telling her, "Everything's fine." He was smiling.

TWO NIGHTS LATER, at 3 a.m., she felt an unfamiliar sensation. She wanted something.

One of the *Eidah Chareidis* people who circulate through Israel's hospital ward with carts full of delicious kosher food for any patient who wants it, was awake to meet the needs of just such creatures. And he had a sour apple, the kind she'd once liked.

The apple looks good, she thought with wonder. *I want it.*

Never in her life, not even once, had it ever occurred to her before that appetite is a miraculous creation, not some sort of natural, troublesome given, to be taken for granted as one submits to it or resists.

One sleepless night not long afterward, having been kept awake into the wee hours by murky torment and depression and deep confusion, unable to see the justification for her return to life—she was lost again. A more serious case of it this time around, for it hadn't arisen from illness now, but from regular dailiness. After all the commotion, the fall and the rise and the fall and the rise, why this Rescue Triumphant? There was a famous line that came to mind—was it from some Shakespeare tragedy? *"The sound and the fury, signifying nothing."*

The next day she got a phone call from a friend without family in Israel. The friend confided tentatively that she needed urgently for someone to visit her, and to do her a certain favor. Nothing spectacular—just to accompany her on an errand somewhere. *By any chance,* asked the friend, *do you have any time today?* The friend said that she had asked a neighbor, and had called a few of her other friends, but nobody was available.

"Yeah, sure," I said. "I have time."

I did what she needed, and as I left my friend's side, noticed the ground beneath my feet. My heart expanded and...nearly broke with joy and certainty, the kind that can keep us happy all the day, and that lives forever.

Appetite for the *parashah* appeared that Shabbos. And for chicken soup, with a matzah ball. And for dessert (apple crumble with brown sugar and cinnamon).

FOR EVER AND EVER

PART I

For my sixth birthday, my mother gave me *Now We Are Six*, by A. A. Milne. She took me onto her lap, opened the book, and began:

> When I was one, I had just begun.
> When I was two, I was nearly new.
> When I was three, I was hardly me.
> When I was four, I was not much more.
> But now I am Six. I'm as clever as clever.
> So I think I'll be six for ever and ever.

As usual when trying to remember childhood experiences, it's hard to identify what I felt, exactly, upon hearing her read those words aloud. All I can say is that it generated within me an undifferentiated happiness and inarticulate sense of special good fortune. Surely I understood, at least in theory, that I *wouldn't* be six for ever and ever, but the poem entered my mind intact and whole, undivided by skepticism or analytical thought. It was telling me that to be six years old was to be lucky. To be six was wonderful.

How far off was ten? Very far. And twenty, or thirty? Those numbers weren't relevant to anything real. Beyond them lay the far-off mist of Adulthood, an inaccessible place as safely removed from me as the moon. It would take as long to arrive in that science-fiction future as to travel backward in time to Christopher Columbus's discovery of America.

My father's armchair in Connecticut gave us a spin, the planet whirled through the blackness of space, and we were in a supermarket in Los

Angeles. My husband and children were in Jerusalem, and I was visiting my mother, in her eighties. Ill and frail, she rested one hand on the metal shopping cart, to steady herself as we inched along.

I had just steered our little parade out of the dairy section and was heading for organic produce, when, for no particular reason and without warning—like a malevolent shooting star arrowing down from outer space—an amazing thought struck: *In thirteen years I'll be sixty.*

I slowed, and stopped.

All along the air-conditioned aisles of Whole Foods Supermarket, the Southern California shoppers paused in sympathy, suspended in an ellipsis of time. My mother kept moving forward for a few seconds, then noticed, and turned around questioningly.

I wouldn't, shouldn't tell her what had just occurred to me. How could I do it to her? I was her baby, the baby of the family. That was my identity.

HOURS AND YEARS DISSOLVED in the ether.

One morning—an exultant, lovely morning when the unsuspecting sun had risen as innocently as ever and my own baby had gotten engaged the night before—I boarded a #2, asked the bus driver for a new *kartisiyah*, and was looking on absentmindedly when I realized that he was punching a hole in a reduced-fare seniors' ticket.

My soul staggered. I could have collapsed in the aisle. I said, "No, a regular ticket, please," then proceeded on back, nose in the air. I needed a seat by myself, away from peoples' eyes, to absorb the blow.

Outside the dirty windows, where Jerusalem's streets were floating by, springtime was blooming in pink and white and green. It couldn't be! Could it? Was I a...*senior citizen?*

For unknown reasons, at that moment it was some shimmery, unidentifiable fragment of earliest adolescence—when all the yearning for life and the mystery of existence had first beckoned—that flickered and stirred incongruously within.

How strange and how remarkable—and unfair!—that trees get to be reborn, one season after another, their old gray branches bursting to life year in, year out.

That driver, was he young or old? I didn't notice! So maybe he didn't get a good look at me, either—maybe he didn't see me at all! And anyway, my birthday was still two months off! Bus drivers should know better—they should be trained!—not to ask *any* female if she qualifies for the reduced fare, especially one he's not sure of. If he needs to ask, then he shouldn't!

Because it's such a one as she who still occupies the indeterminate midlife zone where self-delusion flowers, forever young.

WHEN MY FATHER DIED in 1990, one condolence card especially comforted me, and I've saved it all these years. It's propped up on the shelf overlooking my desk, so I'm looking at it right now.

The picture is a black-and-white photograph of the Brooklyn Bridge, in mist and fog, vanishing into the distance, and it was from my friend Naomi Adir, in Brighton Beach. The note inside, written in her careful, deliberate hand, reads as follows: "I was shocked to learn of your father's departure from this life. He has crossed the bridge we must all cross one day."

That's all, a few words, yet they were like a rope of rescue, a line of light lowered into the sea in which I was thrashing wildly around, struggling in the wake of our cataclysmic disaster. I'd been aware, of course, that human lives come to an end, but hadn't known it could happen to one of my parents, and didn't know that I didn't know. My father's unanticipated "departure," as Naomi Adir put it, kept hitting me again and again as if for the first time, like some horrible aberration, an impossible reversal of the natural order, a horrific violation of the way things had to be. Without him, the world wasn't the world.

The card informed me of something: *we die*. It would take me four years to climb up onto dry land again and stand upright, but even today, decades later, her remarkably obvious observation—that death is universal and unavoidable—is something to hold onto. It contains, by implication, two unarticulated corollaries: first, that losing someone important has happened one way or another to anyone who's ever lived, and secondly (less than a promise, perhaps, but at least she was hinting), she was saying that death is survivable. One day, the earth would return to its normal orbit, and I to my life.

HOWEVER UNANTICIPATED my father's death from a heart attack, my mother's gradual transformation into an old lady ten years later, by way of illness, and her subsequent, precipitous fall into extreme old age were no less shocking. To see Mommy changing visibly from visit to visit—the strongest, most determined, most willful woman in the world growing frail in body and mind—was to finally start to fathom that the past had passed, and that I, too, must be getting older. The first information to this effect had actually reached me long before, in my early twenties, when one day, in our station wagon's brutally sunny rearview mirror, an odd little horizontal hyphen appeared on my forehead. I brushed it off thoughtlessly with the flick of a finger, then saw to my amazement that it was *imprinted in my skin...a wrinkle!*

Eventually, every birthday—especially the round-numbered turning points of the decades—would be like a bell tolling my name. *You call yourself an adult? What have you accomplished in life? How can you justify the year that's just gone?!* As a girl, I had assumed that getting married would prove my worth, and then, as a young woman, dreamed of the children who would be my redemption. Then the horizon shifted. I longed to get my writing published; my name in the *Jewish Observer* would tell me I was important. Later, I believed that grandchildren would create a real and enduring legacy...

The reality is something else. I have to keep starting over again from scratch virtually every day, sometimes moment by moment, losing and discovering my purpose in life between every dawn and dusk. There's no achievement, no state of well-being, that stays put. Happiness is never permanent, nor is self-respect. The *yetzer hara* fulfills his mission; he is a relentless destroyer.

Yet, as Rav Shimshon Pincus declared: the *yetzer hara* is the most beautiful thing in all Creation, because without it—without the endless opportunities to victoriously transcend it—life would have no meaning.

THE FEAR OF DEATH and the fear of aging are so closely intertwined; it's hard to distinguish one from the other. It's our underlying consciousness of death—that we're just dust, and ultimately shall return to dust—that lends to aging its quality of foreboding. After our mother's funeral, standing before our parents' graves where the two of them were together again, side by side, my sisters and I were overwhelmed by the realization that suddenly our childhoods existed only in the invisible kingdom of memory whose sole inhabitants were the three of us. And the memories that were mine alone were between me and G-d. To say goodbye to my parents was to let go of everything that had come before and to start in earnest to "number my days, so as to attain a heart of wisdom."

But there's one aspect of the fear of aging—the particular feminine expression of it, whereby a woman's specific focus is the progressive loss of youthful beauty—that can seem meaningless. Is the fear of losing beauty as natural an instinct, and as potentially beneficial and purposeful, as the fear of death? I'd like to think so. I'd like to think there's a spiritual definition, a dignified and face-saving explanation, for what on its face can certainly seem just plain silly: our perennial preoccupation with trying to stay young, and the absurd lengths to which we go, futilely trying to forestall the inevitable. As a Jew who recites her thanks to *Hashem* every morning "for returning my soul to me in kindness," and who believes (as I once heard from Paula Van Gelder, quoting Rabbi Jason Weiner of Los Angeles) that we don't *have* souls, but rather *are* souls, I'm ashamed of the extent to which I've actually identified through the years with my physical self, and the disproportionate impact my imagined external appearance has had on my self-image. It thwarts and confounds me—when the physical and spiritual lives of our people and *Eretz Yisrael* are in such incessant mortal danger—to have wasted so much of my allotted time on earth worrying vainly, and in vain, about my weight, my clothes...my this and my that, which translates increasingly into worrying about getting older. Lipstick, eyeliner, face cream...and above all, the religiously sanctioned *sheitel*...from feeble artifices such as these do we (or should I say *I*) erect dams against the flood...while time just keeps moving on.

Yet to doubt that any phenomenon in Creation is anything other than *gam zu l'tovah* is to engage in a form of *apikorsus*. So I have to trust that women's particular fears in this respect, like every other human tendency, were implanted in us by *Hakadosh Baruch Hu*, and that we can harness this inclination for its proper use by the *yetzer hatov*. After all, it was *Avraham Avinu* who *asked Hashem* for physical signs of aging, to distinguish him from Yitzchak. Human beings had always been mortal, but didn't turn gray, or shrink, or wither in their very bones. Adults were strong and healthy until the day they died, and parents and children could be mistaken for each other. Avraham's susceptibility to illness and infirmity made him the first human being to visibly age.

Would I mind being mistaken for my daughter? I doubt it. If I had a say in the matter—oh, if I had my say!—there are few things I'd rather do than expunge the signs. The loosened skin (which I never appreciated when it was firm), the wrinkles and crinkles, the torn cartilage that has me limping like an octogenarian, and eyesight that blurs the Big Dipper; the clichéd crow's feet and furrows out of some high school production's amateur makeup kit...Birthday presents such as these contradict the deeper, underlying knowledge, which we all have on some level, that we're souls untouched by time.

MUCH TO MY DISADVANTAGE, my values and self-perception have been distorted by the secular environment and culture into which I was born, and there's a way of thinking and talking about aging that to my mind has a distinctly American cast. Once you're old enough to have lost card-carrying membership in the younger generation, suddenly "age is just a number," "you're only as old as you feel," "it's all in your mind," "do not go gentle into that good night," "forty is the new thirty," and "life begins at fifty!" (or sixty, or seventy...wherever you're holding). Evidence of having aged is to be overcome if not by willpower then (if one has the money, and the audacity) by surgery, injection, or laser. The idea is to get control over one's physical form, in the American version of "Who is mighty? He who rules over himself," except that it's not one's *middos* over which one gains mastery but one's flesh and one's limbs. Physical fitness is seen as an equivalent for good character. Never mind that it's the sheer terror of growing and looking older that fuels America's immense cosmetics and cosmetic surgery industries; there's an underlying impatience and distaste for anything less than an outwardly cheery, can-do attitude, and to surrender to bodily decline is regarded as a moral failure. People come out proudly and happily with declarations such as: "I feel just the way I did at seventeen!" And the fact is, it's true, in many ways I do. But while seventeen was for me a time of wonder and purity, poetry, awe, and sincere spiritual searching (not to mention health and energy), it was also a passageway of blind, ignorant self-centeredness.

The prevailing attitude in secular society is one of Hellenistic identification of the human being with his physical self, but when it comes to aging, there's an insistence on *not* identifying with the physical self. A grandmother isn't expected to don an apron and knit one, purl two, but rather to don Nikes and attend her aerobics class.

It's easy to ridicule such an attitude, and to the extent that it constitutes the dogma of a secular religion, the more we make fun of it, the better. But the highest Jewish ideal is actualized when the physical and the spiritual are combined. To properly heed the injunction to "number your days, that you may acquire a heart of wisdom," developing a working perspective that will take us where we want to end up as Torah-true Jews is not something that will come about simply by deriding the poverty of other cultures' false beliefs.

Rabbi Avigdor Miller once said in a recorded *shiur* that anyone who's no longer in possession of a full set of teeth (he gave the specific number) should know he's already over the hill, as is anyone without a full head of hair, and anyone over the age of thirty-five. (I heard this particular tape years ago, when thirty-five was still a long way off, so I could be imagining that one.) He also said something to the effect that white hairs serve as an instant romance-killer, and that *Hakadosh Baruch Hu* designed us that way; and also, that a man should never try to hide his age; he should take the balding and graying and spreading as a personal warning that his time for acquiring Torah and creating his eternity is getting short; he has to get serious and get busy. In the same tape, Rabbi Miller advertised the benefits of daily walking, water drinking, and healthy food. After telling the men not to conceal their aging, he went on to remark, in what sounded like an afterthought (his audiences were mostly male), that for single women, it is not forbidden to try to look younger, and emphasized the necessity of a married woman's continued use of artifice and illusion to maintain her image in her husband's eyes.

Rabbi Miller was speaking and thinking in a politically incorrect manner (not, of course, that he cared). As usual, he was simply presenting the Torah perspective on the issue at hand, and according to Torah, the loss of youthful strength and beauty—like any other phenomena—is infinitely purposeful, and contains crucial messages for the human beings who experience or witness it. It makes it futile to rely for one's identity on the sort of self-image that is reflected in other people's eyes. Now our own eyes can do what they were created for: seeing! To *see* the incomprehensibly wondrous Creation of which we ourselves are the key component.

It's time to "lift up my eyes" and enter a larger life (but not, I hope, in terms of dress size!) in which other people's joys and accomplishments will be as gratifying to me as my own. As much as I've always feared, and fear still, growing old, there's something about it—now that I'm actually getting there—surprisingly akin to liberation, like that of a child (a child of six, perhaps...times ten) adventuring out onto her discovery of the bigger world, and finding herself not in her mother's arms, or her father's—for they're gone—but in G-d's.

PART II

I've always wondered how other Orthodox women handle the spiritual con-tradictions inherent in the experience of aging. So I conducted an unscientific little survey among a few friends and teachers from assorted backgrounds and life situations, some of them baalos teshuvah and some frum from birth, asking each one in turn, "What do you think about aging?" A few say all they had to say in a couple sentences. A few others speak at length.

A twenty-one-year-old special education teacher in Jerusalem, whose wedding took place ten weeks ago, replies: "I never really think about it. I guess it brings up mixed feelings. What do you mean? Like in my fifties? Or sixties?"

I nod.

"Well...When I was five, I'd look at a ten-year-old and he was huge. A fifteen-year-old was really cool. At each stage, the people who are farther along looked really old to me. Now if I look at older people, it's scary. Because life goes by so fast and I know that just like that, I'm going to be your age."

I feel myself smile.

"Oh, I don't mean it in a bad way!"

"Of course not!"

"So it's like a scary thought. Maybe when you get older and can look back and see you've had a fulfilling life—you helped people, you raised a good family...then you have satisfaction. You know yourself better. Who you really are. I guess you're more comfortable with yourself, not afraid of who you are. Not afraid anymore of what other people say. Is that it? Is it like that?"

A forty-six-year-old writer, married to a Breslover Chassid and the mother of a large family, answers my question with a gentle smile of pity, "Why worry about it? It's really irrelevant, don't you think?"

A married, well-off wife and mother, observant since her teenage years and longing for the spiritual inspiration she and the family experienced during her husband's sabbatical year in Jerusalem, says over the phone from London: "Hmmhh! This is my big thing exactly, looking ahead to the next stages. I don't like it one bit. I can't stand the thought. I keep having the feeling that life is passing me by, and so many missed opportunities. I'll never be able to really *feel* again, the way I did when I was young. To really feel human. It's scary. What's next? I don't look forward to the loss of youth. When I was twenty, the days you'd look into every car window as you walk by and like what you see...To regain yourself physically, all the effort you have to spend for the things you took for granted. Ever since I lost my father, I feel so old. I'm forty-four. Losing a parent makes a difference. What's frightening is not only looking old, but operations. Physical pain. One goes gray. Everything begins to wear out."

"Face cream is very important," replies a woman in her late fifties, a physical therapist who lives with her family in an Orthodox community in Brooklyn. "Your skin is the background for your features." She gives me the name of a so-called anti-aging product that she says is very good, then tells me about a *frum* friend of hers who just got a facelift. "I don't think it was very successful, though. It turned out like this." She places an index finger by the outside corner of each eye and pulls back the skin of her cheekbones. "She looks younger now, but you can tell she had surgery. It doesn't look natural. That's the risk. Also, the anesthesia. There's always a risk." She says the woman in question claimed that she had it done for professional reasons, "but it's a *she'eilah*, especially if you're just doing it for vanity." I ask if she would ever consider having a facelift herself. "I don't have the money for it, but if I did...I guess I'd do something to fix this, and this." She points to her jawline and neck, then draws up and back on the loose skin. "See? Don't I look younger?"

"What I think about aging?" This is a single American in her fifties. She gives me a perplexed look. "Well, I don't like it. When I see myself in photographs, I can't believe it's me."

I call Rebbetzin Tziporah Heller. "The negative side," she says, "is that there can be more and more self-absorption—going to the medical *kupah*; it becomes self-definitive. This sickness is who I am, this condition or that condition. We have to develop a different kind of self-definition, and keep creating a life.

"One of the ten curses of Chavah is that she doesn't age well. Women don't age as well as men. I don't feel pressure to be beautiful, but humans love beauty. It's only natural. The bad news is that bodies get worse and not better. We don't get more beautiful." She laughs. "Whether it's a large part of the picture or a small part of the picture, the good news is that the deterioration makes it easier. Makes us more serious. You're out of the rat race and can leave a lot of the nonsense behind. Put your head and heart into something of value. Many of the *Gedolei Yisrael* accomplished the most after age seventy. They were free of a lot of their earlier responsibilities and could devote themselves to what they really were. Women can do this, too, in a feminine style, but it's the same thing. Nonetheless, one of the difficulties for most people is the realization that comes about at a certain age that in terms of accomplishment, your life is not going to be radically different from whatever it is now. Men usually suffer more than women in this respect, but it's pretty universal.

274 *An Audience of One*

"I once took my mother to an exercise class, calisthenics for elderly women, and at one point the woman teaching the class said, 'Now you can live just for yourself.' Luckily, my mother was very clear about what this part of her life was for, but that was such a harmful message.

"My *mechutenista*, Miriam Succot, used to live in a downstairs apartment where the view outside her kitchen window was of a pedestrian bridge. So all day long, as she cooked and did dishes, she saw feet. When the children grew up and got married, Miriam and her husband moved to an apartment on a high floor, so now she sees the sky. That's very much what aging is about."

A poet in her mid-sixties, living in Jerusalem, replies: "Aging? It goes through my mind vaguely once in a while. The worries are not about aging per se as much as other things that happen *because* of aging. Not having strength. Not having the intelligence anymore or the emotional and physical stamina. That I won't be able to do the things I want to do, whatever they are.

"And there's the worry about *not* aging. You don't know how many years are granted to you. Maybe when I grow up, I'll discover what *Hashem* wants me to do, but will there still be time?"

"What do you want to do?" I ask.

"Whatever I was created to do."

"So if I were to ask your *neshamah*, what do you want to—"

"You *are* talking to my *neshamah*."

"So what are you supposed to do?

"I don't know. To answer without fakery, without any thought of how my words are going to sound...it's the minute-by-minute question that worries me: what does *Hashem* want me to do right this second? We're here to correct our character traits, so the main fear is, time is running out. Carpe diem, gather ye rosebuds while ye may. I was reading *Conversations with Yourself*, by Rabbi Zelig Pliskin, and there's a list of positive traits with the question, *Which would you like to improve?* Well, I had to improve every single one of them, a whole long list from A to Z, ending in *zerizus*.

"I know a woman around forty-five. She's so worried about losing her looks. And she's worried financially, making up this plan, that plan, for her future. Worried about the stress of *parnasah*, how it could affect her husband. Rightly or wrongly, I'm not very practical, but when I first got married, I was scared, I wanted life insurance. And I do worry about my husband's health.

"When I was seventeen, I felt the hourglass very strongly, but back then, all the sand was at the top. Now I've passed the halfway mark. My father at my age wasn't here anymore. I was thirty-one when he passed away. My mother said, 'I'm sorry he had so few years.' I was grief-stricken, but I thought to myself, *It's not like he was thirty or forty or fifty. After all, he **was** in his sixties.*

"I was anything but gorgeous when I got married, and as soon as I got married, I got fat. So in the early years, I used to ask my husband, 'Doesn't it bother you?' He was baffled. He'd say, 'Everybody is in the shape *Hashem* made him.' So I knew that's not what it was about. That wasn't my problem. The poet Robert Browning wrote, 'Grow old along with me, the best is yet to be.' So far, that really seems to be true, *bli ayin hara*.

"Aging is about trusting *Hashem* more and more and more. When I was a child, I didn't have to trust *Hashem*. I trusted my parents. When I was a young mother, my children were under my eye, then, as time went on, more and more I had to entrust them to *Hashem*. Now, my children are out of my hands...they're all married, *baruch Hashem*! I still worry about them, it's not that I don't worry, but they're not my responsibility. And my grandchildren...they're *completely* out of my hands. My daughter will call me up and say, 'Mommy, so-and-so has an ear infection but he's over the worst of it.' I love them so much, but I'm not responsible.

"And yet I haven't really experienced the ravages of old age. I have friends my age who have health issues that affect everything they do. Problems with eyes, and arthritis. Anything from small pains to really serious illness. I'm in my middle years—I have all the advantages and none of the disadvantages. And I have my mother, age ninety-seven in less than a month. Active, handling all her financial affairs, still volunteering.

"In childhood, I didn't understand anything of what was going on. Everything hurt me. I was playing and going to the beach and doing what children do, but I was in a lot of pain. The teenage years were agony, too. There were so many issues: *What do people think of me? Why is everyone else successful?* I kept wanting someone to tell me what it was all about. The first ten years of my marriage were also hard. The nature of the man and the nature of the woman—trying to merge. Pregnancy and birth...They were wonderful in many ways but still, the tremendous, tremendous responsibility. Am I going to keep these kids alive? Am I going to take care of them well enough so that no harm comes their way, to life or limb, until *Hashem* brings them under the chuppah? Will I raise them to be decent human beings, I who know nothing about raising children, not to mention the fear of not being a good enough wife, I who am so unsuited to handling a house. Then, in the forties, the *shidduchim* begin. Will my husband survive the stress? How are we ever going to do this? The fifties—more *shidduchim*, marrying everyone off. Did I give them a strong enough emotional foundation for them to establish a stable relationship?

"There's an old Yiddish saying: *'Nor di ehrshte hundert iz shveir.'* Only the first hundred years are hard. I was in pain because I didn't realize that things would pass. A two-year-old sees his father leave the room and cries. He thinks it will be forever. At each stage of life, I thought it would be forever.

"You get older and older and you understand more and more, and there's not as much pain. Now...*what do people think of me?*" She tilts back her head and laughs. "Who cares! I feel such joy at this time of life. I see younger women and want to tell them, don't worry about getting older! It's a wonderful, wonderful time when all that other stuff falls away. There's another Yiddish expression, the kind of thing a mother might stand off to the side and mutter to herself about a child who's doing something foolish, *'Vest elter vehren, vest kluger vehren.'* You'll get older, you'll get smarter.

"I don't hate myself anymore, as I did for the first fifty years."

"Would you say, then," I ask, "that you love yourself?"

"I don't know what that means, but I do know I don't hate myself. I had no self-acceptance. I used to think: 'I'm fifty and still haven't gotten my act together.' It was very hard not to fall into despair.

"Now I know that every moment is so valuable. The acquiring of wisdom is accelerating exponentially. When I was fifty, maybe I had one insight a day, or two insights a day. Now, it's every second. Now every day is constant insight and growth. Rebbetzin Heller once said that whatever your issues are, you'll live with the same issues all your life, but on different levels as the years go on.

"When the kids were little, the time took forever. Every year took forever. Now, no sooner do I buy a new little date book on Erev Yom Kippur, than, by the time I arrange the phone numbers, it's time to throw it away and buy a new one!

"Five years ago, I might have thought that my present age was old age, but now I feel I am just at the age of mellowing, of letting go of things. Once, the hourglass had a lot of sand in it. Now, it's counted. So each grain is very precious, and most of them are gone. I don't know how people without

Torah can manage old age. It's really scary. Because getting older is mostly about trust, *bitachon*, about trusting *Hashem* more and more and more."

A single woman in her early seventies, living alone in California and just beginning to find out about Judaism, says: "I think it's funny."

I ask why.

"Well, don't you feel the same way you always did, except for your body? So it's funny. We're not what we appear. People start relating to us as older people."

A sixty-seven-year-old mother of nine in Meah Shearim replies: "At a certain point the fragments of life start coming together. You don't necessarily understand every detail, but you get a sense of the whole, each part in perspective. And the main thing you understand now is that you only had your narrow angle on things. You never saw—it's impossible for a human being to see—anything in its entirety."

A single woman in her eighties, living alone in Florida and legally blind for the last twenty years, replies: "It depends on your health. The time I'm aware of the importance of health is when I don't feel well. I walk with a walker now, but I go very slowly, so it takes a lot of time to do anything, and I need help. Then when I get back to my apartment, I have to lie down. The time I have to lie down is getting longer, too. The *yeshiva bachurim* who usually help me haven't been able to come over as often. I used to listen to books on tape, but they haven't been putting out new Jewish books. They haven't been getting volunteers for the reading. But every day I look forward to the day. What's going to happen? Who's going to call me today?"

Dorothy Levenson from Rhode Island, a widow living at a senior residence in Jerusalem, made aliyah by herself when she was eighty-two. Her response: "Living with elderly people...you know, a lot of us are not all there anymore—it's not always easy. If you haven't resolved things in your life, it comes out when you're old.

"This morning the phone rang in my room, and when I got up to get it, I fell. But you know, I fell like a dancer! I almost fell with grace." She gives a big smile. "Sounds crazy but it's true. I am also aware that I have to protect myself from this happening, which I try to do to the best of my ability. When you're elderly, as I am, you need to accept the conditions. I accept them—not always lovingly!

"We're all in this universe to enhance the Al-mighty. *Hashem* has carried me from the very beginning. For me to be in Jerusalem now in my life is the most thrilling challenge. On September 24th I became eighty-nine."

"Really, Dorothy? Happy Birthday!"

"Well, you know, every day is my birthday. Sounds crazy but it's true. I know I could go any minute. The gift of being alive, and the added gift of being in Yerushalayim...I feel that *Hashem* is guiding me completely, past, present, and future."

Clara Hammer, elegantly dressed and coiffed, sits with folded hands in her Ramat Eshkol living room. Originally from Russia, where as a child she and her family were sentenced to a lengthy prison term for crossing the Romanian border while escaping pogroms and starvation, she is known around the world as "the Chicken Lady." It has been her self-appointed job for the past thirty years to raise *tzedakah* and distribute chickens to hundreds of poverty-stricken families in Jerusalem.

She hears my question and lifts her chin expectantly, as if waiting for more.

"That's the question," I tell her.

"Oh." Her blue eyes twinkle merrily "A fool doesn't get old."

"Your daughter tells me you had your ninety-ninth birthday party on May 19."

She grins broadly. "Would you believe it? I'll tell you, *baruch Hashem*, I guess that's part of my reward. I'm pretty safe. *Hashem* wants me to do it and helps me to do it. He made me capable to do what I do and gives me the energy and the ability. Anyone who puts out a hand, I put something in there, and I feel happy. The joy you get from giving. And now He gives my daughters the energy and the will and the ability to do all the things that have to be done."

TO THE SAME QUESTION, "What do you think about aging?" the last person I speak to is Rebbetzin Dena Weinberg—the wife of Rav Noach Weinberg. Mother of twelve and grandmother of more than a hundred, *bli ayin hara*, she replies: "I remember meeting an old woman in a store one time. She had a crinkled, crinkled-up face and she was buying face cream. Is that what life is all about? I don't think the *chevra kadisha* puts face cream on anyone.

"My sister had cancer for fourteen years. Every time she had a birthday, she celebrated that she was getting old. We should all feel excited about living another year. I once met a group of elderly women who weren't religious, and I asked them, 'If you had one week to live, what would you do with that week?' Some of them said, 'I'd want to be with my family. The children. The grandchildren.' One of them said she'd want to see the world. But none of them said anything about finding out what they had lived for, and where they were going now. They were eighty years old and up, and they said they'd never asked themselves that. It was a catastrophe. It can't be that we don't think of what will be after this world. We all go. Think of it. Even healthy people go. *So what are you thinking about?* One of my children once said to me, 'Ima, please don't think about it! You have another hundred years!' so I asked her, 'Are you saying that to make me relaxed?' The reality is that we're not here forever. Helping an elderly person live with this reality in mind, encouraging him or her to think about the next stage, energizes them. Think: What do I want to tell my children that I learned from life? If you're still young, speak to your grandmother. Get some wisdom from older people. One of the mistakes in our school system is that when you leave school, girls feel as if they're finished growing. Life is growth, right through to the very end. I started studying *Path of the Just* with my granddaughters. This is what I'd like them to know. A Jew should know what he was created for."

"Did you do that with your children, too?" I asked her.

"They had it for breakfast. It was their bread and butter."

"What about a woman who doesn't have children?"

"What G-d gives you in life is up to Him. How you use your life is your choice. If G-d gives you marriage, and children, that's what you need. If not, then that's not what you need. If He puts a woman in this world to have children, she will. It's painful. But children are by no means the only tool for a woman, and even if we have children, we have to go beyond that.

"You have to look at what you do have. If you only look at what you don't have, you don't build. You don't reach your personal potential for which *Hashem* put you in this world. Everybody has to ask himself the question: 'What should I accomplish in this life? What does *Hashem* expect of the people He created?' It can't be, 'I have children, so I'm OK.' One day, all my children were married.

"You have to know how old you are. Your body changes. You're not as thin as you want to be. Women lose self-esteem because of this, but your value is not in the externals.

"Many retired people get depressed. Why? Because they lose their identity. They don't know who they are. A terrific doctor I know had a stroke and couldn't practice anymore. He got deeply depressed. We cannot pin our value onto any particular role, cannot pin it on being there for our children. They have their own pleasures, needs, and accomplishments. We need a multiple identity. A woman who hasn't learned through the years will find it very difficult. *'Who am I? No one needs me.'*

"We have to lead a valuable life. A person should yearn to be like Sarah, Rivkah, Rachel, and Leah, to achieve that level of closeness to G-d. She should learn, *daven*, and do *chessed* every day. Dissatisfaction in life comes about from not doing these things. A flower that doesn't grow will die.

"How to do it? A little each day.

"In *Parashas Bereishis* it is written, 'And it was morning and it was evening, one day, and *Hashem* said: It is good.' But when it came to Friday, *Hashem* said: 'It is very good.' Why 'very good'? The midrash says it was 'very good' because on Friday, death was ordained.

"Take any setting—a business setting, or at home, any time a person has a project he wants to get done—if he has a deadline, a *dead* line, a sense of finality, that's when he gets to work.

"Old age is a very exciting time. That's when you can accomplish what you didn't accomplish in your youth.

"I knew a woman once who used to iron the draperies. When she got old, she regretted the wasted time.

"Plan for old age in order to keep growing. People can move away from G-d when they're in pain—or they can move closer. Come closer.

"As King David said, 'I ask one thing, to lead me to the House of G-d.'"

MY BIRTHDAY

For Rachel Greenblatt

I have a big new coffee cup
I have three big balloons
I have a piece of chocolate
in my living room

I have a brand-new coffee cup
I have three big balloons
I have a poem made just for me
in my living room

One balloon is silver
Two balloons are pink
The chocolate's very chocolate
in the cup, I think

My friend gave me a chocolate
My friend gave me a cup
They were waiting in the living room
when I got up

The pink balloons were floating
in the morning light
They'd been singing Happy Birthday
to themselves all night

When I came down this morning
they were waiting just for me
The poem, the cup, the chocolate,
and balloons, all three

My friend left me a chocolate
and a poem inside a cup
and three balloons that greeted me
when I got up.

AN EMAIL TALE

All Jews are responsible for one another.

Shevuos 39a

A fellow Jew—a onetime employee of my parents, of blessed memory, whom they had always regarded as a good friend—has been in touch with me lately by e-mail about an ongoing practical matter having to do with my father's papers. She and I had never hit it off, particularly, back in the days when my mother and father were here. There was a subtle friction with her I never understood or was able to diagnose; it really had no rational basis. Sometimes I've mused that it was a case of unconscious sibling rivalry, but if so, whether it was coming from her or from me, or was mutual, I couldn't tell. Maybe, as a devout secularist married to a non-Jew, she was hostile because I'm Orthodox? Or perhaps it was a simple matter of chemistry, like the natural antipathy between a dog and a cat, that by nature are oppositional.

In any case, while my parents were alive, our mutual, inexplicable unease with each other was kept politely under wraps, out of respect—I realize now—for them. But now, apparently, we're less motivated to maintain the pretense.

Last week, something in one of her e-mails elicited from me a coldly genteel retort. A minute or so later, back came her cooler reply, to which I responded in kind, unkindly.

At this point, a little voice inside me instructed me to reread her first email.

Much to my chagrin and embarrassment, I saw that I'd misunderstood. She hadn't said what I'd thought she said.

I quickly sent a note of apology. A few seconds later, there was the "ping" of an incoming message, but apparently our e-mails had crossed. In her own politely angry fashion, she'd turned the cool knife back onto me.

I immediately sent off another apology, and again waited. No answer. *Ah, right,* I thought bitterly, *forgiveness isn't her thing, neither the giving nor the accepting. Why couldn't* **she** *do some apologizing for once!*

I was obligated by halachah to ask three times for forgiveness, but to judge from experiences with her on a few other occasions long ago, why make myself vulnerable to someone with a track record of not respecting such gestures? Since she hadn't answered the second apology, and didn't know about the halachah, she'd just interpret this as weakness on my part.

The whole next day it was on my mind. This was a friend of my parents, and one of my father's oft-repeated lines was, "Life is an adventure in forgiveness." But every time those words intruded on my consciousness, I pushed them away. *Why torment myself? I made a mistake, I apologized twice and she still hasn't seen fit to reply, so I've done enough! Why would she reply if I apologize again? What more can I do?*

Last night at a *shiur*, the last quarter hour was devoted to the halachah governing *ona'as devarim*, so I brought it up. I wasn't expecting a solution; I was just hoping to understand this situation better, and to somehow get some advice about how to atone for my mistake in the absence of communication with the person herself.

The Rebbetzin replied that she'd once asked a *she'eilah* about a similar situation, and the rabbi had told her that indeed, she was obligated to ask three times for forgiveness. But the third time, he advised her, she could try apologizing in a different way. For example, if the first two times she'd written a letter, maybe now she could apologize on the phone. Or if before she'd apologized by phone, now she could send a gift.

Also, she said, the rabbi had told her to *daven*, to ask *Hashem* to make things right.

Well, I *harrumph*ed to myself inwardly, a gift would be going too far. And I could already imagine the chilly awkwardness of a phone call. But as far as *davening* was concerned, I took the advice sincerely, for my parents' sake as well as mine, then decided to try one more time, as follows:

−Original Message−
Sent: Sunday, January 01, 2012 10:17 PM

Dear ＿＿＿,
If you're open to it, I would like to talk. Not about the specific matter at hand−at least not for practical purposes−but as friends, or would-be friends. I feel there's a chance we can find our way out of the acrimony that has shadowed our relationship in the past, and which has resurfaced now.
Hoping,
Sarah

The reply flew in across the Atlantic two minutes later:

−Original Message−
Sent: Sunday, January 01, 2012 10:20 PM
Subject: Re:

Hi Sarah,
Yes, absolutely open to it and looking forward. My Wednesday and Thursday mornings are open if either works for you between 9 and 11 AM California time? If not let me know some other times that are convenient for you.
Best,

─────

We have a phone appointment, to my astonishment and joy.

SOMETHING TO READ

One spring day when suicide bombings and shootings and other assorted acts of satanic cruelty were at their height, and staying home for weeks on end had settled into a seamless cycle of cooking, eating, and cleaning up; and when boarding a bus to the Old City's Moriah Bookstore would have constituted a reckless act of self-endangerment and the one on Strauss had closed down for lack of customers—another casualty of the intifada—and going downtown to the Pomerantz, or my favorite second-hand place, Sefer V'Sefel (whose name, Book and Cone, harks back to its long-discontinued sale of ice-cream alongside the paperbacks) was out of the question, and the only excursion into the great outdoors that I could reasonably justify taking was the exciting elevator ride down four flights to the mailbox, to see if any new bills had arrived, followed by the two-minute walk to the neighborhood supermarket...when that's what life was like, last spring, I was standing absentmindedly before a bookshelf one afternoon, looking for something to read.

I urgently wanted...something or other. Something relevant to what was going on, or maybe...something irrelevant would be better. Something to help me understand, or enable me to forget.

The particular shelf I was looking at, just then, occupied less a spot in this room than a place in my heart. Souvenirs from the vanished land of childhood, reliable standbys, old and new favorites...and having them all lined up together like this—the way they stayed put there obediently on the fringe of my life—had always given me a tidy, if only half-conscious, sensation of autobiographical coherence and continuity, as if all the disparate, non-sequential fragments of my past actually shared some invisible underlying theme and internal historical logic, and had fallen inadvertently into a sensible progression of chapters adding up to one grand story in itself. Each of the books on this shelf had served me well at one point or another in my journey through time, as entertainment when I was bored or inspiration when down; as food for thought when my mind was running on empty or when nothing else was available (which was certainly the case nowadays). They'd put me to sleep when insomnia loomed, kept me company when I was lost, and had comforted me, again and again, with evidence that whatever might be happening to me "in the real world" at any given juncture, somebody somewhere had not only gone through it but had lived to tell the tale.

But the real world had become unreal. My brain strained in vain to either absorb it or ignore it. If there was something about being scared out of my mind that was wreaking havoc with my parenting ("No, you're *not* taking the bus to school!") and my household schedule ("OK! It must be dinnertime!") and had erased my natural inclination to feel well-disposed toward pregnant women ("That looks like an explosive under her chador!"), perhaps there was also something—*je ne sais quoi*—about murder that was robbing me of the written word.

Outside, terror was crossing and re-crossing the land. In the house, in limbo, we waited for it to go away. Back and forth, back and forth, the shadow kept passing over, like the darkness cast by a fiendishly spinning tornado. Breakfast was merging with lunch, lunch was becoming dinner, and I'd been turning behind my own back into somebody I didn't know. There I stood, gazing at the familiar titles like a vaguely hungry person holding the refrigerator door ajar, waiting for something to ring true.

> To make a prairie it takes a clover and a bee,
> One clover, and a bee,
> And reverie.

Since my first encounter with Emily Dickinson in Miss Sherry's ninth-grade English class, those lines had come to mind a thousand times. I'd be living somewhere in California or Manhattan, pining for just one measly tree to call my own (such as those with which my spoiled hometown had been over-generously endowed) when the thought of that little poem would remind me that to peer out a window at a rectangle of blue sky and cloud is to possess the whole sky. Decades later in Jerusalem, half a world away, the enduring lesson gleaned from those few words had, on countless occasions through the years, exponentially increased my enjoyment of the potted pink geraniums out on our own small porch.

So by all rights, it should have come in handy, especially nowadays, when we were stuck at home.

But with her *Collected Poetry* open in my hands, the poem stayed uselessly inert and flat upon the page. How pitifully detached she was from real life (meaning: our lives). Emily Dickinson was no stranger to suffering—she who had taken me on guided tours of my own heart—but I felt a jab of envy and resentment toward the ghostly image filed away in my mind of the nineteenth-century Protestant dreamer in her long white dress, in a garden, probably, in Amherst, Massachusetts, longing for reverie. That should be my biggest worry!

Maybe one of her death poems would suit me better. She had lots of those. In the index of first lines, I spotted the one that had articulated for me my own experience when my parents died.

> The distance that the dead have gone
> Does not at first appear.
> Their coming back seems possible
> For many an ardent year...

No echo, no mirror for me now in that one, either. *Emily, bubbele, you should never know from evil.* Back she went to her place on the shelf.

Merwin, Auden...too difficult. Maybe it was Edna St. Vincent Millay who could transport me magically right out of the Middle East.

> All I could see from where I stood
> Was three long mountains and a wood;
> I turned and looked another way,
> And saw three islands in a bay...

The incongruity of those elegant and exquisite cadences mocked my anxiety with sharp little knives.

Maybe E. E. Cummings?

> I thank you G-d for most this amazing
> day: for the leaping greenly spirits of trees
> and a blue true dream of sky

These lines didn't come sailing toward me now like a lifeline in a long loop of joy, as in times gone by. How utterly oblivious all these poets were to what was happening! They were ignoring us Jews completely! They wrote what they wrote on the other side of the moon, engaged in personal struggles that bore not even the faintest resemblance to the sort of blood-soaked war for survival against real, live enemies (make that anti-Semitic enemies) that we ourselves are forced to wage.

My eyes skimmed over into the shelf's Torah district. *L'havdil,* there was *Path of the Just,* mutely offering its ancient services. *The Two-Way Channel, Living Inspired, Man Is Not Alone.*

From *The Palm Tree of Devorah*:

> *There are people who are unworthy, and yet the Holy One, Blessed Be He, has mercy upon them. The Gemara explains the verse: "I will be gracious to whom I will be gracious."*

If a few seconds ago I couldn't stomach anything too far, then too near wasn't good, either. I had no interest in looking at myself this afternoon, didn't feel like being told that I should work on my *middos,* that the answer lay within. How about the world working on itself, for a change!

Their titles emanated silent reproach as my gaze passed by. *The Thinking Jewish Teenager's Guide to Life,* Akiva Tatz's mis-named masterpiece, that I had bought for my children and ended up consuming myself.

> *At the end of a lifetime, in the transition from this world to the next, three angels come to greet a person. One of these angels comes to search out: "Where is this person's Torah, and is it complete in his hand?" In other words, have you achieved what you were meant to achieve during your life?*

No...no...It was definitely escape I wanted. If only our neighbors were the type to have *People* magazine on hand! That would surely provide an hour or two of lowly distraction.

My eyes wandered back over to *Best Short Stories of 1992, Little House in the Big Woods, The Penguin Book of Interviews...*

How dare they speak their petty names!

Call It Sleep, Angela's Ashes. Their irrelevance irritated me.

The Denial of Death. There was Ernest Becker, still fretting about mankind's universal denial of mortality. Ha! Nobody around here has that problem.

But I paused. My heart softened. Taking it into my hands, the book opened of itself to an earmarked page much worn and underlined. "Most of us—by the time we leave childhood—have repressed our vision of the primary miraculousness of Creation."

There...the phrase that had served me once upon a time as a North Star. He was discussing the description by a medieval poet, from three centuries earlier, of a moment of epiphany in which "the world," as Becker put it, had appeared to him as it does "to the [pristine] perceptions of the child before he has been able to fashion automatic responses." He quoted from the poet's account:

> *All appeared new, and strange at first, inexpressibly rare and delightful and beautiful. The corn was orient and immortal wheat, which never should be reaped, nor ever was sown. I thought it had stood from everlasting to everlasting. The dust and stones of the street were as precious as gold...The green trees...transported and ravished me, their sweetness and beauty made my heart to leap, and almost mad with ecstasy, they were such strange and wonderful things...Boys and girls tumbling in the street, and playing, were moving jewels. I knew not that they were born or should die...The city seemed to stand in Eden...*

The primary miraculousness of Creation. In his last years, Ernest Becker, with his intensely Jewish sensibility, had embarked upon a more explicit search for G-d; I'd read somewhere that not long before he died, he had started exploring Judaism. But in the harsh, no-frills light of *ha'matzav*, "the situation," Becker's whole quest for truth and authenticity seemed to turn its back on us, his people. *The Denial of Jewishness*, how about that for a title. And the quoted passage, that I had reread and savored so many times, suddenly rankled for resembling some kind of pagan worship of Creation, rather than of the Creator, as if all that worldly magnificence and wondrousness and perfection were a lucky fluke of nature in an impersonal and neutral Void. I, too, longed to perceive the magnificent, wondrous, perfect world that was right before my eyes, longed as much as I ever had for the sheer miracle of existence to make itself visible in my sight. But the portrait of a beautiful Creation I embraced would have to include and lend meaning to the evil that figured in it so prominently.

At least *Escape from Evil*—another one by Ernest Becker, written in 1975—referred to the issue at hand.

> *[T]he point I am making is that most of the evil that man has visited on his world is the result precisely of the greater passion*

*of his denials and his historical drivenness. This leads us directly
from problems of psychoanalysis and…*

Oh, Dr. Becker, get with it. You're a few decades, a few centuries, behind the times. Islam's not even listed in your index, much less Eisav.

At James Agee's *A Death in the Family*, I stopped short. This was the book whose tender, astounding prose had imparted to me, as a teenager, a beautiful hint of what life, and death, had in store. Certainly, it would have some bearing on our current catastrophes.

*We are talking of summer evenings in Knoxville, Tennessee, in the
time that I lived there so successfully disguised to myself as a child.*

What was happening to me? Upon glimpsing that beloved opening line, I caught the groan of a disgusted inner complainer: "Tennessee? Oh, come on, spare me!" What a self-centered reader I'd become! Since when did the religion of Literary Criticism stipulate that a work of literature had to be specifically about your own life in order to have relevance for you? Since when did a work of art have to be precisely congruent with your own experience in order for it to have meaning? When it came to art, universal truths had always succeeded in transcending the gaps between me and other cultures, other peoples, but now that the chips were down, there was a bitterness in me like heartburn over the vast chasm.

Out of respect for all that this novel had given me since first coming my way back in the 1960s, I gave it another try, opening the dear, frayed, fragile paperback to the passage in which the child Rufus asks his mother if he and his sister are orphans, now that their father has died in a car accident.

"Mama, are we orphans now?"

"Orphans?"

*"Like the Belgians," he informed her. "French. When you haven't
got any daddy or mamma because they're killed in the war, you're
an orphan, and other children send you things and write you
letters."*

*She must have been unfamiliar with the word, for she seemed
to have to think very hard before she answered. Then she said,
"Of course you're not orphans, Rufus, and I don't want you going
around saying that you are. Do you hear me? Because it isn't so.
Orphans haven't gòt either a father or a mother, you see, and*

nobody to take care of them or love them. You see? That's why other children send things. But you both have your mother. So you aren't orphans. Do you see? Do you?" He nodded; Catherine nodded because he did. "And Rufus." She looked at him very searchingly; without quite knowing why, he felt he had been discovered in a discreditable secret. "Don't be sorry you're not an orphan. You be thankful. Orphans sound lucky to you because they're far away and everyone talks about them now. But they're very, very unhappy little children. Because nobody loves them. Do you understand?"

He nodded, ashamed of himself and secretly disappointed.

I turned pages, looking for a particular conversation between the grandfather and his newly widowed daughter.

"Something I've got to tell you," he said.

She looked at him and waited.

"You remember what Cousin Patty was like? When she lost George?...She ran around like a chicken with its head off. 'Oh, why does it have to be me? What did I ever do that it happened to me?'"

[Mary's] eyes became cold. "You needn't worry," she said.

"I don't, because you're not a fool. But you'd better, and that's what I want to warn you about...See here, Poll, it's bad enough right now, but it's going to take a while to sink in. When it really sinks in, it's going to be any amount worse. It'll be so much worse that you'll think it's more than you can bear...And worse than that, you'll have to go through it alone, because there isn't a thing on earth any of us can do to help, beyond blind animal sympathy."

She was gazing slantwise toward the floor in some kind of coldly patient irony; he felt sick to death of himself.

"Look at me, Poll," he said. She looked at him. "That's when you're going to need every ounce of common sense you've got...You've got to bear it in mind that nobody that ever lived is specially privileged; the ax can fall at any moment, on any neck, without any warning or with regard for justice...You've got to remember that things as bad as this and a lot worse have happened to millions

*of people before and they've come through it and that you will,
too. You'll bear it because there isn't any choice—except to go to
pieces. You've got two children to take care of and you owe it to
him...It's a kind of test, Mary, and it's the only kind that amounts
to anything. When something rotten like this happens. Then you
have your choice. You start to really be alive, or you start to die..."*

Beloved James Agee. So close and yet—like the others—so far from
life as we know it. Far removed in both time and space, from the Jews in
Netanya and Tel Aviv, Haifa and Afula, and Jerusalem; removed as if by
veils behind veils behind veils from the mad, mad, mad, mad Middle East
on this magnificent spring day in the first years of the twenty-first century.
For it wasn't general truths about death or loss or pain or grief, or, on the
other hand, the evasion of same, but rather our truth that I needed. Our
Jewish truth. The Jewish belief that there is indeed such a thing as Divine
justice and kindness, that, indeed, the fabric of the universe is composed
of it, and that everything is meant to be. That neither justice nor kindness
is random. I needed truth that would endure amid flames, as people run
between bombs as if between the raindrops, when fingers and hands and
feet were being severed, and parents and children were being separated,
murdered in each other's sight, and there were people consciously aiming
to maximize our suffering *because we were Jews*. It was a mystery. It was
what I'd read about in Holocaust books, yet the Holocaust had always
seemed like such a weird, unbelievable phenomenon

My eyes sought out something farther along the shelf.

*When the second guard's chance came, he grasped the club with
an expression of combined reverence and joy—such as a Jew
exhibits in taking the four species on Sukkos. He flailed with such
ardor that the first guard was jealous...When the time came to
get up, my feet simply would not obey. Unable to straighten up,
I could not help thinking of the axiom coined by our Sages: "You
live despite yourself."*

It was *Slingshot of Hell*, by Rav Yechezkel Harfenes. I turned at random
to another page.

*The following week I became more daring. I traded [my bread] for a
ration of tobacco. This time, however, luck was against me...When
I went back to fetch the...tobacco ration—it was gone! Shlomo*

> *HaMelech said, "Bread is not to the wise" (Koheles 9:11). I had been too clever.*

And another:

> *In passing, I must devote a few lines to that exalted and noble soul from the city of Dej, Reb Benzion Weinstein...I noticed how he always gave away part of his ration to the person next to him. I asked him the reason for this and he explained that since he did not have the opportunity to keep any of the practical mitzvos, he devoted his efforts to that which he could do, in this case the giving of charity. Besides, when he lived at home he always felt that he had not properly fulfilled the commandment of charity, which means providing the necessary form of aid to the one who really needs it. Here [in the camp] everyone needed food; he could not go wrong. From each meal, therefore, he gave away food joyfully, even before tasting it himself. I do not know how long this precious Jew held out. I could only exclaim, "Blessed is the nation with men like him!" A pity he had to die.*

And another.

> *It was by now late afternoon and the heavenly gates were about to be sealed shut. I did not return to my minyan for the Ne'ilah service. I did not have the strength. This had been my most difficult day in Auschwitz, not because of the fast but because...I had not sat down all day. I now turned my face to the wall and said the closing prayer. I muttered the few words from the liturgy that I could remember, but those were garbled and confused. I skipped other parts out of restlessness. How empty, cold, and worthless it was! I can only compare my prayer to the gasping of fish on land; they open and close their mouths—in the hope of wetting them—while their very life escapes.*

I had sat down upon my bed. It was late afternoon here, too. If it was relevance I was after, and incongruity that offended, this should be my cup of tea. How could I have guessed, just a few short years ago—I never imagined such a possibility—that I'd soon be looking in this book's darkness for a mirror of our own circumstances. This beautifully written, wonderfully truthful memoir had always struck me as so bizarre, unfathomable, and nightmarish that it had belonged to a different world; I'd always had to remind myself: *This happened.* It really happened, to real people, like us, my brethren, because they were Jews.

> *After the order to disperse was given, I went over to my son. His eyes were closed, as if he wanted to sleep. I didn't know whether to disturb him or not, but finally, unable to contain myself, I blurted out a question asking how he felt. He opened his eyes and looked pityingly at me, like one sorry that I had to suffer for his sake. I asked him if he wanted anything. He didn't. He summoned up his strength and said, "Father, you must soon go to work...Give me your parting blessing before you go. Kiss me once more. Who knows if we will meet again?" His condition was critical. I looked at his eyes whose light was already half-extinguished. His cold, dry lips sought mine. It was the last physical contact I had with my cherished, beloved son. I wished him a speedy recovery and an au revoir.*
>
> *With heavy heart and eyes lowered with shame, I left. I cannot recall if he shed any tears when he uttered that last sentence of farewell, but I do clearly remember that I did not weep. My heart screams out at the animal indifference and callousness that blurred my senses and feelings on that terrible day...Now, years later...I am shocked at this inexplicable emotional treachery. I am stunned. I can only say that even this was a product of Divine Providence. For had I allowed my heart free expression of its grief over this horrible misfortune, I would not have survived...*

I stopped. It was getting too dark to continue. Outside my window, the light had dwindled. I needed...

Hope.

Slingshot of Hell went back to the shelf, with my love.

It must be somewhere...Where could it be? I hadn't used it in years. Other editions, less archaic; other translations, not as awkward, had taken its place. The last time I could recall—it must have been that time in my sister Candis's house on Leroy Street, in Berkeley, California. It must have been the early '70s. I was visiting. I remember the blue corduroy shirtwaist I was wearing. I couldn't have moved to Israel yet. We'd been sitting in her kitchen after dinner, or I was sitting and she was cleaning up. We were talking, laughing...when suddenly we both fell silent, and were looking into each other's eyes. From far off a sound was approaching that I'd never heard before, an unfamiliar roaring, like an echo spreading underground, under the world, and then...the floor was...unbelievably...rocking under us, as were the walls and the ceiling...and the strange sound was getting louder, and broader, like a hundred or a thousand subway cars coming at us. It was also silent. We were clutching each other and probably scream-ing, or maybe uttering not a sound, but the next thing I knew, my book of *Tehillim* was gripped in our four hands.

The earthquake in that kitchen turned our lives upside down and inside out, and the sisters—both daughters of the American suburbs; it was just recently that one of them had heard, for the first time, that G-d had a Jewish Name—clung to each other and to that book as if the survival of Berkeley depended on it. The universe as we knew it had in a few seconds been transformed into something we couldn't rely on. The aftershocks rumbled and rocked in the ground beneath our feet and outside in the starry sky, murmuring in the walls, trembling up and down our bones. The book didn't shut and our eyes didn't close; that life raft kept us afloat all night long until the break of day. No matter what page we turned to, the words were precisely our own, articulating in our own voices what was hidden in the crevices of our own minds. The words took us up, up, up in an infinite lifeline, crying perfectly for us to G-d in that moment and that moment alone, as if no other moment and no two other girls had ever existed in history.

It took about a minute. There it was, a beat-up old black volume, pushed over into the corner. *The Psalms: Translation and Commentary by Rabbi Samson Raphael Hirsch.* Feldheim Publishers, 1973.

> *I called Thee, O save me...Early at dawn I stood and implored; I hoped for Thy word. My eyes forestalled the night watches...Hear my voice according to Thy loving-kindness, give me life, O Lord, as is Thy way to do...I will not give sleep to my eyes nor slumber to my eyelids; Until I shall have found the place for the Lord, dwelling places for the Elevating Power of Jacob...That He will deliver you from the snare that is laid, from deadly pestilence...you will take refuge beneath His wings. His truth is a barbed shield...The trees of the Lord also have their fill; the cedars of Lebanon which He has planted. Where the birds make their nests; where the stork builds his nest upon the trees...My enemies taunt me all the*

time...For...my heart is dead within me...Help me, O Lord my G-d, save me in keeping with Thy loving-kindness, That they may know that this is Thy hand, that Thou, O Lord, hast done it.

Something relevant to what was going on, but out of this world.

To Him Who leads His people through the wilderness, that His loving-kindness endures forever.

To help me understand, and enable me to forget...

Who remembered us in our lowly state, because His loving-kindness endures forever...

To keep me company now that I was lost, and remind me that no matter what might be happening, the poet had gone through it and prevailed, because evil and goodness are given in kindness by one and the same Hand. Neither too near, nor too far. Neither easy, nor difficult. Precisely congruent. Designed uniquely for "the real world" at this unique moment in history, for this modern era, and the sweetness and beauty made my heart to leap.

The nations will fear the Name of the Lord, and all the kings of earth Thy glory...He has turned to the prayer of the solitary, and has not despised their prayer...

The lifeline came sailing toward me now in a long loop of joy.

Then our mouth will fill with laughter and our tongue with exultation; then they will say among the nations: "The Lord has done great things with these."

All of a sudden it dawned upon me that it must be dinnertime! I had to go get dinner ready!
Well.
At least I'd found something to read.

ESTATE OF THE MIND

The black-and-white photograph looks like something out of an idyllic childhood dream—this must be how childhood is supposed to look. Two long-haired, delicate little girls age seven or eight—one dark, one light—sit beside each other on a sun-dappled marble bench, and in the background shimmers a leafy, shady congregation of trees. The child on the left, gazing off to one side, holds an old-fashioned shawl over her shoulders with two small hands, and the fair one leans toward us engagingly with a winsome smile.

Were you to notice it in passing, in its silver frame on the corner of my desk, you wouldn't briefly close your eyes as do I, recalling the elusive fine-woven softness of my mother's orange-and-brown plaid mohair shawl, nor pause—with a keen, bothersome pang of nostalgia—to seek, in the darkness behind your closed lids, the sunlit image of the woman taking the picture, standing on the grass a few yards away, head lowered, green eyes focused intently down into her Nikon viewfinder. You wouldn't know she was the fair one's mother, and that it was toward her that my little friend was leaning.

Nor—unless you happened to have been one of the countless guests who frequented the dark-haired child's home during the many years we lived there—would you be aware of the big old ivy-covered house looming up over to the left, just out of view; nor guess that what was being recorded here for posterity was a game of dress-up, since both little girls were so serious about disguising their childishness that their game was more in earnest than in play. The costumes they'd finally settled on, after a morning spent rummaging furtively through various wardrobes in various closets inside the big house, had been chosen in hopes of conveying a long, loose, stylishly "offbeat" impression—not the quaintly comical look of dresses simply ten sizes too big for their pint-size inhabitants. The lipstick they'd confiscated from the bureau drawer of an older sister had been applied with studied self-restraint. And though they were no longer so naive as to imagine they'd actually be taken for adults, the two of them did meagerly harbor half a hope that maybe, for the duration of an afternoon, they'd be accorded some version of the respect that they mistakenly imagined any adult, by definition, ordinarily commands.

For looking older than they were was these little friends' most dearly held ambition, even though they knew they couldn't manage any such thing, and were as pitifully young as ever. They yearned to be seen as important, and significant. They wanted dignity, though that's not the way they would have put it. They just wanted to be treated more like grown-ups.

On second look, you might notice that the fair one's smile was something of a smirk, but would have no way of knowing it was less akin to innocence than irony, or an attempt at irony; wouldn't know she was straining to affect a casual, conspiratorial air of camaraderie, a lofty, sophisticated amusement whereby she'd signal to her mother that she understood perfectly well this was all a joke; that all this dress-up stuff was really babyish, and the important things were photography, and literature, and the Museum of Modern Art, and classical music. She inclined toward her mother as a flower leans toward light, but not with pleasure, or trust, but in futile search of that maddeningly precious, necessary, invisible something or other that was never to be had: her mother's stamp of approval. She wanted her mother, who could never be wholly pleased, to smile back with a look that would say, *You're just fine the way you are.*

What neither child knew was that the critical remarks and humorous putdowns that came the fair one's way had their source not in any genuine scorn on her mother's part, but rather, its opposite: an unarticulated longing for her own buried innocence. It was the very thing that, in their eagerness to gain entry into what they thought of as "the world," the little girls themselves were so eager to conceal; not only to conceal but to annihilate. All that droll, tongue-in-cheek belittlement was seen by observers (if they paid it any attention at all) as the harmless, affectionate maternal ribbing of an unsentimental mother who didn't look at her children through rose-colored glasses, through the prism of her own vanity; she was seen as an intelligent woman who knew better than to emotionally coddle and spoil her kids. Who could have guessed that all the wit and cleverness arose in reflexive, involuntary response to a sense of loss on the mother's part so profound that it passed under her own radar, and couldn't be acknowledged or understood.

It was the loss of simple aliveness, akin to the life enjoyed by flowers, and grass, and all natural things. Her child's aliveness made that mother feel like a bump on a log. It kept unearthing the tip of her own childhood—that dimly recalled era—when she herself was young, growing, and wholly alive. When the sky up ahead had promised a life full of love, and everything wondrous was possible.

Before walking past, maybe you'd notice something else, too, staring you in the face...

Or maybe not. Only those who were there in those days, in that place, which no longer exists, would recognize easily now what we all missed, somehow, back then: Emily's future, fast approaching, casting a shadow over her smile.

I WAS PUSHING EMILY, with her long blond braid and her long pale limbs, on the hammock, which was strung up between two gray trees, or rather, *the* two gray trees. Because, like everything else on our property, those two gray trees were well-known to me, completely familiar. No surprises from those two gray trees, that's for sure, nor from the ground beneath my feet. There was the ground with its grass, and the big irregular oblong of packed gray-brown dirt under the hammock where my feet and Emily's feet had braced and dragged themselves a thousand times to stop the hammock's wild swinging; and the section of old gnarled gray root that disturbed our feet from dragging, sticking up out of the ground right in the middle of the smooth packed dirt. Up over behind us, some ten yards off, stood a tall tree, the oak, and the rope swing hanging from it was probably dangling around slightly, on its own, in the autumn breeze. The ground sloped down before us to the rocky, gravelly driveway.

My mother had just gotten home from Safeway and was going back and forth between the car and the house, carrying bags of groceries into the kitchen. The black Ford Falcon station wagon was parked out by the back porch.

I could hear the screen door slamming shut a few times.

It was my turn to do the pushing, so there I was, standing there lethargically in the muggy heat as the hammock swung to me, away from me, to me, away from me, and my glance was wandering around the woods in the distance, out to the old barn, up around the sky, when it stopped suddenly at one of the gray trees. The one on the left. Then something happened.

My eyes opened. My eyes and my stomach and my heart.

Tree.

Sticking up out of the earth.

Earth, the one next door to Venus in the science books, third from the sun in the row of planets. The little blue and white circle. This tree is standing right now upon its surface.

The texture of the gray trunk, rough and ridged and variegated, seemed suddenly like some sort of moonscape, seen from above, from a great distance.

This tree right here is emerging from the surface of that very planet in those books, the one and only Earth. This brown dirt beneath my own feet is on the actual, the very edge of that one and only famous Earth, which is moving through outer space. Earth, which is pressing its one and only face right up against the atmosphere, which starts right here at my sneakers and goes on without end.

The tree

Exists.

I...

Am.

I must have stopped pushing because Emily said, "I've got seven more swings, I counted them. You've only done thirteen."

ONE COLD, WET AUTUMN Sunday morning when I got to their house, Claudia told me that Emily was in her room. The Elliots' KLM stereo was on, a vocal jazz rendition of Bach. I walked through their cozily warm living room with its understated modern Danish furniture, looked out their sparkling-clean, wall-length plate-glass window onto their apple tree and lawn, all in mist, beyond which a small field of high grass was blowing in the light rain and wind. I passed by Claudia's oil portrait of Emily's older sister Jana, who was away at Vassar, and her large charcoal line drawing of Emily's brother Christopher as a small boy. Every object in that room was a gem of some sort; every surface itself a thing of beauty, and displayed for the observer some small treasure of art or of nature that Claudia had created or discovered. A primitive American watercolor framed in warm gold and set off against the wall's whitewashed brick; over the fireplace, a black iron weather vane of a wild-maned, elegantly slender-hooved galloping horse, plucked from the roof of an old New England barn and purchased in some out-of-the-way antique store along Route 7. Smooth polished stones and curving shells salvaged along the North Carolina beach near Charles's ancestral home, where they summered annually. Some object colorful and bold and brazen, such as a nineteenth-century fireman's hat, whose purity of line could be perceived by the rest of us only because Claudia's prescient eye had recognized its inherent artistry. Atop the piano or coffee table, an arrangement of subtly colored dried wildflowers in a dainty ceramic vase from the Pottery Corner outlet in Westport. A row of charming antique teddy bears atop a bookshelf. Objects of rare and formerly concealed beauty all, which acquired value by having been placed in the circle of light cast by Claudia's perspicacious glance. Elsewhere these objects might have seemed ordinary, nothing special, but here they were exquisite things.

As for me, the whole thing said that I wasn't important. And as for Emily, she seemed to be the one thing in that house that didn't find favor in Claudia's eyes.

I walked through the living room into the hallway and knocked on Emily's door as I pushed it open. She was sitting on a chair near, but not at, her desk, facing the bedroom window with her back to me. She turned around, greeted me, and crossed her arms atop the back of her chair. We talked a few minutes.

Then she said, "I was thinking today about this plant." She pointed with her chin toward the windowsill, at a delicately crafted ceramic vase, glazed royal blue, from which one long, thin stem rose up with a few heart-shaped leaves, and bowed its flowered head beneath the single burden of its own small white blossom.

"I was thinking," she said, "that since I'm alive and it's alive, there's a connection between us." She sat there, pensive, arms crossed on the chair, regarding the flower. "That there's always a connection between two living things."

I didn't think about things like that. An ugly little feeling of my inferiority wriggled around in some dark place deep inside me, like a little gray worm.

I thought to myself: *Claudia and Charles have no idea.*

ONE SUMMER NIGHT while cleaning out my desk, I came across the black-bordered white card that had notified friends and family of Claudia's death years before, and got a yearning to speak to Emily. I had no idea where in the world she was these days. I dialed Charles, in North Carolina.

"Emily's number?" he said. He sounded so old. "Why do you want Emily's number, darling?"

"I want to talk to her. Is there a number where I can reach her?"

"Darling. Emily is not available, I'm afraid, for a phone conversation. Nor will she be for the foreseeable future."

He finally gave it to me.

It was a number with a different area code. A man answered with what sounded like a Midwestern twang. "Wilmington Mental Health. How may I help you?"

"Emily Eliot, please."

"That's a patient?"

I nodded.

"Ma'am? Is that a patient?"

"Yes. She's a patient."

There was a silence as he transferred me to another extension. Could it be that in one moment Emily herself would get on the phone?

"B Level," said a voice. It was the same kind of accent.

"I'd like to speak to Emily Eliot, please? I'm calling long-distance from overseas. From Israel."

"Who's calling, please?"

"Her friend Sarah." I was about to say my last name, but realized Emily might not recognize my married name.

The woman put me on hold. Around a minute went by. I started worrying about how much this was going to cost. Then someone got on the line, and for a second I thought it was Emily, but it was the woman again. She said, "The party you want to speak to doesn't wish to come to the phone."

"What! Did you tell her it's her friend Sarah?"

"Yes, I did, ma'am."

"Are you sure she knows who this is? Tell her it's her best friend Sarah! From childhood! We're like sisters! We grew up together!"

She paused. "One minute, please."

About three minutes went by, then someone got on and my heart jumped, but it was the woman again. "She says you cannot speak to her."

I wasn't sure I'd gotten that right. "What?"

"She says you cannot speak to her."

"What do you mean?"

"That's what she says, ma'am."

"But why not! I can't believe she—"

"She says—" The woman cleared her throat. "The party says you cannot speak to her until there's a Palestinian state.

"Ma'am?

"Ma'am, are you on the line?"

"Yes."

"So why don't you write a letter to her."

"Yes."

"So you take care now. And have a nice day."

"Goodbye."

She hung up. I hung up. I sat on my bed for I don't know how long. Then I looked at myself in the third person. *This is probably a significant crossroads in a person's life.*

A couple of minutes went by.

Sooner or later I'm going to have to get up and turn off the light.

So I might as well do it now.

SCHOOL HAD BEEN CANCELED, *and I was at Emily's house. We'd played outside all morning building a snow tunnel. The opaque winter daylight came in overhead, right through the white ceiling of this little transient home we'd created all by ourselves.*

We patted and patted the icy sides of the tunnel with our wet, frosted-up gloves until the packed snow was hard and smooth. As the afternoon light got softer and more shadowy we started shivering uncontrollably. How cozy it was inside that cramped, hidden, cold space! We looked at each other and grinned.

When we got back inside the house, red-faced and exhilarated, after we'd taken off our boots and changed into dry clothes, after her mother had served us hot cocoa and we were sitting on the high stools in their kitchen (I always wished we had a kitchen like that), Emily's mother said, "I want to read you something."

We sipped the cocoa as she sat down—it was strange. How old could we have been? Ten? Eleven? Nine? Not very old, in any case, but she was talking to us as if we were adults.

What made her think we'd understand?

"It's a poem," she said. "Listen. It's called, 'Estate of the Mind.'"

> *The house on the hill, where all of them played*
> *The ivy-covered house on the hill.*
> *All is silent now*
> *In the house on the hill.*
> *It exists nowhere*
> *But in their minds.*

Q&A WITH…CINDERELLA!

Q: *On behalf of the whole newsroom, Cinderella, I'd like to say how excited we are to have you here with us this morning.*

A: It wasn't easy, you know, getting here. With one slipper.

Q: *Wait…but…didn't the Prince find the other one? I thought…*

A: Don't believe everything you read. Life's complicated.

Q: *I see…well…anyway, Cinderella, we've all heard so much about you, and personally speaking, I never really expected to meet any of the characters I read about in fairy tales. To tell you the truth, when we heard the voice-mail, we all assumed it was a hoax.*

A: A hoax?

Q: *Yes, well, of course, you wouldn't believe how many of those quack calls we get. A few weeks ago, someone called saying she was Mother Nature! And it was a collect call!*

A: I was with her when you didn't accept the reverse charge. It hurt her. You think that just because we're figments of your imagination, we don't have feelings?

Q: *Oh! My goodness, I'm so sorry. I had no idea—Please! Here's a tissue!*

A: It's all right. I'm just sensitive because…well, you know, it's no picnic. I get so sick and tired of people thinking I'm not real. Even if I'm not.

Q: *On the contrary, Cinderella. Rabbi Avigdor Miler once said that even if you just visualize something in your mind's eye—for example, let's say an enormous red apple the size of a house—well, that apple is real, and can't be destroyed. Thoughts exist forever. All the more so, someone imaginary like yourself. The influence wielded by you, and your stepmother, and your stepsisters, your whole mishpachah—the untold impact you've had on generations of women down through the ages is inestimable. In my opinion, you're even too real.*

A: Too real?

Q: *Oh! My goodness! Here's a tissue! All I meant was, generations grew up with distorted ideas about what it is to be a human being, and a female, based on your life story.*

A: I never had a life.

Q: *But Cindere—*

A: Please. *Your Royal Highness.*

Q: *Of course. But, Your Royal Highness, you just said you get so tired of people thinking you're not real. And then a second ago, that you never had a life. Here, I brought along a copy of Grimm's Fairy Tales. It's right here in black and white, "And they lived happily ever after."*

A: Time froze for me with that last line. For both of us. Have you ever stopped to think what it's like, imprisoned in one dimension? Not only for me and the Prince, but for Sleeping Beauty, too, in the castle. The Beast feels the same way. So does Peter. We're trapped in our stories.

Q: *Peter?*

A: Pan. In Never-Never Land. He never grows old. Little Red Riding Hood's grandmother has the opposite problem—she was never young. Snow White, and the Queen, the whole "Mirror, Mirror on the wall" complex. Always worrying how they look. To dwell in a fairy tale is to be stuck eternally in meaninglessness. Like Oklahoma. No ups and downs. Everything's always the same. It bores me to tears! Human beings are so lucky! You're able to change your stories!

Q: *Cinderella, I had no idea this interview would be so upsetting for you. Let's change the subject! So how's the family?*

A: My wicked stepsisters are eternally jealous of me, and there's nothing I can do about it.

Q: *Why don't you apologize?*

A: For what? They're the ones who need to apologize, not me! It's not my fault the Prince chose me. I'm pretty. They're ugly.

Q: *Hmm. So. And how's your husband doing?*

A: Not so well. He has no memory of anything after that last line.

Q: *Well, you look fantastic. Just the way I imagined you. And your complexion! Peaches and cream, after all these years! You look eighteen.*

A: I *am* eighteen. And I'm sick of it already! Can you imagine what it's like, to never get any smarter or better or wiser or kinder than you were at eighteen! I'm still as immature and self-centered as I was then! After all this time!

Q: *I see. So let's see...tell me, is this your first visit to the Holy City?*

A: No, not the first—there've been a few girls here and there who've read my story—but generally speaking...and I don't know whether this is just my insecurity...but I really don't feel welcome here.

Q: *Well, there's some truth to that, Cinderell—*

A: Your Roy—

Q: *Your Royal Highness. But please don't take it personally. It's just that you're the creation of a gentile German culture—the Hellenistic darkness where social Darwinism and physical externals reign supreme. In the hearts of Jewish girls all around the world, for at least the last three hundred years, you and your ilk have wreaked real havoc in our lives, even though you're not real. Or because you're not real. Oh! My goodness! Here take another one. Your mascara's all smudged now. Look, Cin—Your Royal Highness, how about telling our readers what prompted you to get in touch with us like this, out of the blue?*

A: I don't mean to be rude, but it's the other way around. As a figment of your imagination, I found myself on *your* mind. It's I who should be interviewing *you*. What made you think of me?

Q: *Well...you're right about that. I was about to deny it, but you're right, it's true. The other day I made some mention of you to my granddaughter in Jerusalem who's eight, and she had no idea who you are. It was so wonderful. You and everything you stand for have been extinguished in her life. Oh! Cinderella, I'm so sorry! Here, take the whole box!*

THE KOHELES ERA: IN THE
REALM OF NOT KNOWING

In November 2018, *Hamodia* published "My Well Has Run Dry," by Rabbi Avraham Twerski, *shlita*. That painfully frank, straightforward personal essay about aging—his own—was followed a few weeks later by several pages of letters to the editor.

I, TOO, WANTED to put in my two cents.

I wanted to say:

> *Since Rabbi Twerski himself states flat out in his essay that respectful and kind reassurances about the huge value of his past contributions—and the strong likelihood of his continued achievements in future—are not a source of comfort to him anymore, then we who have been inspired and educated by him through the decades can honor him now by taking him at his word. To passively observe the dying embers of your inborn fire, looking on as if from the sidelines at your own weakening self...is to suffer an inevitable fact of life, if you live long enough to suffer it. And the only comfort that rings true to him, Rabbi Twerski appears to be saying, comes from knowing that this suffering is precious, if not to us than to our Creator, Who designed the system.*

That's basically what I intended to say, along with another idea I once heard somewhere, something about "who we become when we're no longer ourselves."

At the time, however, I was immersed—"up to the eyebrows," as my mother, *a"h*, would have said—in a different task, one I'd set for myself at Rosh Hashanah, a month or so before. And it was overwhelming, preoccupying me to such an extent that many, many other things were falling through the cracks.

For I'd made up my mind: I'd finally start going through the messy old cardboard boxes—boxes upon boxes upon boxes—of papers and miscellanea, stacked up unsteadily one atop the other, in the small room of our small apartment that's meant to serve as our guest room. Looking timidly into the boxes' unknown, unexplored depths, I'd get glimpses here and there of things I knew would be of great personal value, once extracted from the chaotic darkness. But first I'd have to design some kind of filing system, and devise a way to categorize everything before extracting them, so there'd be somewhere to put them. Some items I'd catch sight of were very important in my eyes, but then others seemed more important, as new items—remembered and unremembered details from my life on earth—appeared and offered themselves for contemplation. Things that should be saved for emotional reasons, or practical purposes…or for the sake of family history. Science articles clipped from the *New York Times* that my mother had sent me through the years. "Are We Alone in the Universe After All?" asked one of them in the year 2000, written by an astrophysicist. Found amid those articles were my mother's handwritten letters to me when I, age nine, was homesick at summer camp. Several MRIs of my brain, taken in 2006, after a series of migraines. The images looked like a lily pond, or a lady's flowery sunhat. Things scattered among obsolete bank statements and phone bills, incomprehensible blood test results dating back twenty and thirty years, Social Security documents, an X-ray of somebody's ribs (mine?) and all kinds of other old and current medical records. Fascinating family photographs and memorabilia, from my parents' and sisters' childhoods, and my children's childhoods, and mine, and my grandchildren's, and pictures of identified and unidentified forebears. Dozens of journals and diaries from all the eras of my life.

The mental frame around the entire collection of details—in other words, around my life—kept getting larger, and more unwieldy, and increasingly less subject to categorization. If I could classify by the date or by the family member, separate past from present, find the thread that holds the years together, placing details in their correct context and perspective, then my life would be at my fingertips, spread out before me like a wide, simplified landscape, with landmarks signifying major crossroads and turning points. What was important would obviously look important, and what was not important would become self-evidently disposable. Report cards from elementary school—amazing how to this day I remember what was written in the assigned space for each year's Teacher's Comments; only now can I see how much their words built my self-image, for better and for worse.

Letters that brought to mind my most significant mistakes and regrets. A handwritten letter from Dr. Willis, a Connecticut pediatrician, instructing my mother how to make a formula for her newborn (me). A large box full of my mother's typewritten stories, written in her eighties, about her life, and her parents' lives as Russian immigrants on the Lower East Side. Articles by my father, a writer, and his one unpublished, unfinished manuscript—his first and only venture into fiction. Drawings by my children, and my grandchildren—all mixed up together indistinguishably. More precious letters to and from my parents, more photographs, letters from relatives who have died, letters from friends in my own generation—many of whom are gone now, too, amazingly. So many people...young, tall, laughing, strong...got old, or didn't get old, and passed away.

One, two, three, four, five alphabetized accordion files stuffed with the precious writings I'd saved from writing workshops, from 1992 on. Writings by Rebbetzin Shaindel Bulman, *a"h*, and Malka Adler, *a"h*, and Lily Dubner, *a"h*...

Documents from a court case that stirred within me now the old bitter rancor. Should I preserve the whole record, or just its happy ending? Would I ever do something with the legal papers? Prove something, if it ever became necessary? Will I be more inclined to look through them in the future than I am now?

Throw them out!

Throw them out?

The guest room was unusable. A friend in California sent me the best-selling book by a Japanese author on "the magical art of tidying up," which advises readers to unclutter their living space by throwing out anything that doesn't "spark joy."

If I ever have to prove why I wasn't born Japanese, that book could do it, because as far as I'm concerned—and I associate this with my being a Jew, thank G-d, and to our People's exultant, tragic history of persecution and despair and joyful rebirth—sadness cannot be disentangled from joy. If something dark "sparks" grief, guilt, regret, bitterness, then so be it!

That doesn't necessarily indicate that it's something that can or should be forgotten and discarded. Whether or not we believe it, we know that everything comes from the Creator and is therefore good. Even though following vines to their roots may be humanly impossible, what makes a thing unworthy of being saved? It's my life I'm holding onto!

How to say goodbye to the X-rayed ribs? Maybe the image would come in handy someday.

No, throw it out.

The magazine with Rabbi Twerski's article went missing at one point in the guest room, and eventually resurfaced. I sat down with a cup of coffee and read again:

> *...I did a fair amount of writing in my active life, both books and many articles. As a psychiatrist, I gained many insights from my patients, which provided me with material for writing. My current condition not only greatly limits new ideation, but the aging process has also affected my memory for events beyond my youth. Whereas I always had ideas to address, my well has now run dry...*

HERE I HAVE TO STOP before going further, to do the dishes and put in a load of laundry.

Dishes are great. *Fleishig, milchig.* Dirty, clean.

But the darks cause self-searching. I'll separate darks from lights, and face the kind of moral issues that are mine these days.

Socks and stockings, my husband's and mine...Which wrongdoing is worse: to expose bath towels to bacteria from the street, or to discolor white towels by washing them with dark items? Since most of the time it's only two in our little household, then were I to not compromise on such distinctions of sanitation and good housekeeping and thrift, it would take too long each time to accumulate enough wash for a load. But too-small loads waste water. My mother would disapprove. On the other hand, holding on to dirty laundry until there's enough for a bigger load causes a smell in our little apartment from the hamper.

The dish towels: most of them are white, as are most of our bath towels...Would my mother have said they shouldn't be washed in the same load? Undergarments: it's unsanitary to wash them together with towels used in the kitchen.

Doing colored kitchen towels with dark socks...not OK. (No children's clothing in our hamper; our children are in charge of the new generation's weekly wash, in their own households, near and far.)

My delicate pink-and-gray Shabbos sweater would fare better at the dry cleaner's...but my mother always said that the chemicals used by dry cleaners are, G-d forbid, carcinogenic.

My mother died in 2001. She used to say, "Time flies," but the longer she's gone, the more present she becomes.

OLD MR. SHALLER, who lived in a ramshackle, weather-beaten, old nineteenth-century farmhouse facing Comstock Hill Road, was a daily component of our childhood. I never met him, never even saw him up close. He sat on his rocking chair, out on his broken-down front porch, and my mother would tell us to wave hello to Mr. Shaller as we hurried by in the car. We'd wave to him gaily out the windows of the station wagon. He'd hold up one slow hand in response.

It would be early morning, and she was trying to catch up with the school bus that we'd missed, or early evening, on the way to my father's 6:10 p.m. commuter train from New York. Or summertime. She was driving us to swimming lessons, or piano lessons, or to a friend's. She'd be on the way to the supermarket, or doing the million other things that being the young mother of a young family entails.

That Mr. Shaller sat out alone on his porch all day, every day, rain or shine, wasn't a mystery to me, because to my mind, that's just what he did. If I thought about it at all, it was because my mother said that his wife had died a long time ago, but he had two married daughters who took turns coming to cook for him. I wondered how an old man could sit out on his porch all day, not reading, not doing anything, and not get bored. I was glad I wasn't Mr. Shaller. I was glad to be a child.

So far, there are no photographs of Mr. Shaller that I've come across in any of the boxes, but his image is preserved in my mind's eye, indelibly suspended in memory. He'd probably be surprised that a child who used to pass by in a neighbor's car—now a Jewish woman as old, or maybe even older, than he himself was in those years, and living in Yerushalayim in the twenty-first century—is thinking about him: she can't put her finger on it, but she learned something from him.

SO...I CONTINUED TRYING to sort things out and fit pieces of the jigsaw puzzle together, but too many thousands upon thousands of pieces were missing from the boxes for any kind of coherent picture to emerge from the darkness.

Some important files did get organized, among them the writings in my possession by other *frum* writers, and one day, in the midst of my awful sense of futility about the project that had consumed so much time and effort, and left me perplexed about my life and what it all added up to, and did not add up to, from birth to my approaching seventh decade, I called Sudy Rosengarten.

Sudy, a generation or so ahead of me, is a wonderful, wonderful writer, "the real McCoy," as my mother would have said.

"Sudy," I said. "Hello!"

"Who is this?"

"Wow, we haven't spoken for so long. You don't even recognize me anymore. It's me, Sarah! How *are* you?"

"*Baruch Hashem*. How are *you*?"

"Oh, I don't know. Trying to figure out what my life is about. And what I should be doing with the rest of it. I don't know what *Hashem* wants of me now."

"Are you writing?"

"No, not really. Not for a long time. A few months ago, there was a letter to the editor I wanted to write, but I never got around to it."

"Look, Sarah, I'm going to tell you something. You're not the only one who goes through this. Things change. We change. The feeling you have now doesn't last forever, and whether it does or doesn't, there are other things in life we can do, other things we have to do, and are able to do. You're not alone. It happens to everyone. We all go through it."

"Who's we?"

"For many of us, it happens about being mothers, when that era of life passes. It happens to anyone who's always identified with his work, not only writers. If a person identifies with whatever it was he did earlier in life, and there comes a time you don't have the same passion for it because a good deal of what was motivating you was ego. And by the time you start getting something down on paper, it doesn't seem that important anymore, because our perspective on life has changed. Our perspective gets much wider. It's not a bad thing. Look, did you see the article by Rabbi Twerski, about the well going dry?"

"Yes! That's the article I wanted to write a letter to the editor about! But listen, Sudy. What I'm calling about is I found a bunch of stories by you. Some of them are typed up on that old kind of computer-roll paper, remember? So it must have been from a long time ago."

She gave a laugh. "Oh, yeah, I remember that paper."

"They're just wonderful, Sudy. If you don't have copies, I can send them to you."

"Oh, I don't know. I think I have copies of just about everything I wrote back then. What are the titles?"

"There's one I just finished reading, called 'Waste.'"

"'Waste?'"

"Right, 'Waste.' Do you remember it?"

"I don't remember anything with that title. No."

"Can I read it to you?"

So that's what happened. And Sudy—who in fact didn't remember at all having written that story about her father—laughed and marveled, as if someone else had written it. I heard her laughter on her end of the phone, at her home in Bnei Brak, and through her laughter I'd hear her murmuring "It's true. That's the way he was. That's the way he was."

By the time I finished reading Sudy her story, I knew what I was living for, even though I had to find another purpose in life the next morning…and again the next afternoon, and night. Which is one of the aspects of the *Koheles* era of a person's life: we have to create the meaning and purpose; it doesn't just find us automatically anymore, fueled and powered by our passions.

I can brace my feet against my childhood bedpost—as Mommy would say—"until the cows come home," refusing to let life go by, refusing to say goodbye.

But it does. And I will.

After 120 years, the picture will be restored in its entirety, inside the frame and beyond the frame of a lifetime. I need to trust that the One Who made me will know what's missing and where things belong and will show me what I need to see, in correct proportion. For now, it's all right to not know. To know nothing. The truth of life continues to unfold, relentlessly and incomprehensibly. I just have to be patient, and know that every small mitzvah brings us closer, step by step.

Step by step.

As it is written in *Koheles*, there is "a time to be born, and a time to die…"

A time to weep and a time to laugh...

A time to keep and a time to discard...

A time to be silent and a time to speak...

I have observed the task that G-d has given the sons of man to be concerned with:

He made everything beautiful in its time;

He has also put an enigma into their minds,

so that man cannot comprehend what G-d has done, from beginning to end...

The sum of the matter, when all is considered:

fear G-d and keep His commandments, for that is man's whole duty.

WHO CREATES DARKNESS

My sister Candis, maybe twelve, and I, around eight, are lying awake at night under the slanted ceiling of our converted attic bedroom, staring into the dark, unable to sleep, terrifying ourselves by imagining an unimaginable thing. Overhead and all around is the drumming, pounding downpour of a Connecticut summer thunderstorm—thunder rolling and crashing and cracking open the night with split-second weird lightning flashes that light up the tree outside our window, the whole huge sky illuminated electrically outside like an X-ray, an instant here, an instant there...like a darkroom negative...a horrible unearthly fluorescence and then the cracking and rolling angry thunder. We can't fall asleep. Our parents haven't come back home yet from New York City, even though they called Mom at dinnertime to say they were starting out. Such a long time ago! Hours! Mom, our grandmother, who's downstairs, is very strong, but she's of no help at all during such a scary night, at least in my opinion, because (also in my opinion) she loves Candis and not me. It's Mommy and Daddy who stand permanently smiling and big and strong and confident, capable and good at the center of the world. Beyond them, Outer Space is just empty miles of nothing, an impersonal sphere of reckless indifference, neutrality, an immense realm of random forces and tiny cold diamond stars...wielding power to destroy insignificant humans; whether they're grownups or children doesn't matter. Down here on insignificant Planet Earth, there's falling electric wires and flooding and car crashes on the Merritt Parkway...atomic bombs in Japan...German concentration camps for Jewish people (and that was me! Candis and I were Jewish people!)...a TWA plane crashing into a United plane over Long Island...months later the postman delivered some black-charred stamped envelopes and Happy

New Year cards addressed to us at 160 Silvermine Road, that had fallen out of the burning plane with the people! We don't know about G-d, my sister and I—how could we think G-d's any more realistic than the giant in *Jack and the Beanstalk*? No one had ever claimed to me that G-d was real, or could be spoken to, or that He would know if a human being talked to Him or didn't talk to Him.

I must have drifted off, still in the cold grip of Outer Space, because the next thing I remember is...*voices*.

Daddy's and Mommy's voices!

They got home!

Mommy's voice, "Norman, I'll put in a sweet potato, would you like that?"

Daddy's voice, I can't hear what he's saying and it doesn't matter.

Their voices downstairs! I can hear them talking and my mother's footsteps, footsteps from kitchen to dining room. My father in the living room playing the piano, "Blue Moon." It's still raining, still thundering once in a while, and lightning. It's cozy. I look over in the dark at Candis's bed. In the bluish moonlight from the window, the sheets had been thrown back and the bed's empty. She must have gone downstairs to Mom.

The wind...

Mommy and Daddy.

They're home.

The feeling in my mind, one thought in my heart: *G-d's in His Heaven, all's right in the world.*

THE OPPOSITE OF NIGHTTIME

Awakened by thunder, I lie in the dark
Yet here in the dark I cannot lie.
All that by day was dim, is stark
when here in the dark by night I lie.

There was a dream but I can't recall
what I was doing there at all.
I was in a dream but lightning caught fire
on the hem of the dream and I awoke.
I tried to remember, but no longer tired,
forgot the dream as the thunder spoke:

"What are you doing? Where do you stand
among all the dreams that by day you planned?
There was a day but you can't recall
what you did yesterday at all.
Thousands of words in a drift of sand.
Thousands of deeds in a drift of sand."

The clock ticked its questions, the skies told time.
The stars behind clouds called my bluff, and this rhyme
got twisted up in my blankets. All asunder
went my plans for tomorrow.
     Continued the thunder:
"Your dreams are but dreams, by day or by night.
How is your wrong all that different from right?
Wake up! Go to sleep! It's all the same thing.
You dream you're awake and awake when you dream.
Your days fly by on ego's wings,
Your days are filled with empty things.

Thousands of thoughts in a drift of sand.
Thousands of moments in a drift of sand."

I switch on the lamp and *Reader's Digest*
fills my mind with American dreams.
At last, determined to get my rest,
        I turn it off.
It's strange. It seems
that what in the light is easily denied
in the night's too bright for me to hide:
The only kindness I do that's kind
is the kindness I do with You in mind,
my only words less false than true
are those I know are heard by You,
the only ground that does not slide
away from my feet like sand on either side
        is the ground I walk in search of You.

The hours drag by, but at last—what's this?
The darkness is blowing a goodbye kiss,
and now at the window a tentative dawn
is whispering greetings.
        The stars are gone.
As morning gropes softly with long pale gloves,
I linger back to the sleep my heart loves,
and when I awake, curtains lifting on a breeze
inform me the day has arrived.

        Oh, what a tease
that darkness! How heartless thunder's anger,
caring me like that
when there was really no danger.

WRITING THE WAVES

As someone who has used writing ever since childhood to prove to herself that she exists, typing this sentence is already making me feel better. It's as if after five months of semidarkness. I'd been plugged into an electric outlet.

Here at my computer, pleased to have finished that opening sentence but not knowing where to go from here, I just checked the word-count. It's forty.

Forty.

Forty is how old I was when my father died. That's how I learned that there's such a thing as death. I'd heard of death, of course, and had always feared it. But only when it happened, impossibly, to my father, did I begin to grasp that it could, and had. As he himself used to say, "No one gets out of this world alive."

Even if this particular piece ends up forgotten in my computer files, to describe this moment is to catch the butterfly and make her stop, so I can get a good, long look, and engrave her in memory. To find words is to turn an experience into something tangible, that you can save. Words can turn time past and time future into the present, and can make this fleeing fraction of a second last as long as you want—in theory, even forever.

This whole long corona pandemic of the year 2020...*first wave, second wave...no wave...a new phase...quarantine, restrictions lifted, lockdown reimposed, the end is in sight, and no end in sight...*has been characterized by a sense of weird unpredictability, vagueness, inscrutability, uncertainty. But no sooner do you describe shapelessness than it instantly takes on form, and acquires an edge *Not knowing* becomes recognizable as an underlying condition of human life, a condition from which we constantly strain to stay distracted. Now the human race has been forced to *stop*. Stay home. Stop running.

WHEN I WAS EIGHTEEN years old, I once attended a lecture by Dr. Nathan Adelson, in which he said that we human beings seek some sort of Seal of Approval from…one's fellow human beings. He likened this comical state of affairs to a long line of empty vacuum cleaners, attached to one another by their hoses like elephants tied by theirs tails to one another in a circus. Each vacuum cleaner is trying to absorb approval from the empty vacuum cleaner in front of it, just as the vacuum cleaner in back of it is trying to suck up approval from the one before.

There's nothing to do but open our eyes to who and how we are. Staying home and opening our eyes means all kinds of things. A recent article in the *New York Times* reports that tailors are getting a significant increase in the number of orders for alteration.

> Sourdough is making me feel good right now," [says one of Mr. Moon's customers.] "I'm not going to stop eating bread—I need to feel good right now." Elsewhere in [Mr. Moon's] shop, five pairs of Theory slacks and a blazer were awaiting enlargement. Mr. Moon, 49, said he was dubious that lockdown weight gain is solely to blame.
>
> "[Clothes may have been] a little tight before, but we were so busy…we didn't really feel that," he said. "Right now, you have a lot of time, and a lot of thinking going on."

IT WAS A PHONE CONVERSATION with my daughter that unblocked some channel, which I hope remains open long enough for me to finish writing this.

"Mommy, hi! How are you?"

I suddenly forgot how to not say how I am. "I'm so depressed, Yehudit."

"Mommy, you are? I'm so sorry!"

"I've been drifting around the house, not doing anything. *Davening Shacharis* is just about the only thing I do on a schedule. I keep puttering around from one room to another. I keep expecting an end to this, as if real life were on vacation and we'll be going home soon to normal. Until then, I sit around waiting for life to click back on."

"You know, you're not the only one."

"Of course, I'm not! I know!" (Feeling irrationally defensive is an occupational hazard of depression.)

"Mommy, did you think I meant something critical? What I'm saying is that it's the people at your stage in life who are really having it the hardest, I think. For people my age who have a job, even if it's different now working at home, or for people like me who are mothers, at home practically all the time anyway, life isn't that different from usual. I'm on my normal schedule. I'm so busy, Mommy, morning to night. I have a friend who was just telling me before Shabbos about her mother. Her mother's going through something that sounds so similar to what you're saying, Mommy. Her mother misses everyone so badly. She's not the kind who can sit at home. She's a doer. The kind of grandmother who's always helping, and taking out the grandchildren, and having everyone over for Shabbos. Her parents always have all kinds of guests, and friends, and she's always been busy helping, and doing for everyone, and going places. The two of them take a walk at night around the neighborhood, with masks, but both her mother and father are in the high-risk category. So they can't even go to the store. They have to order for deliveries."

"Well, I've never been that active a grandmother, you all know that. And now I'm basically just sitting around gaining weight, waiting for this whole strange time to come to an end. I haven't reorganized my life."

"So, Mommy, why don't you do whatever you *can* do?"

"Easier said than done."

"Why don't you write about what you just told me? Because I think a lot of people feel the same way."

I was about to give her the reasons, *why not*. Then it occurred to me: *why not?*

So here I am, looking out the living room windows at the trees, rocking on the old wooden rocking chair that my mother gave me before she died, with the sky out there high above, and crows and doves and littler birds flying around all over the place.

I'll look back over my shoulder at the last five months—the most basic sort of outline—and take stock.

LIKE MANY OF ITS OTHER turning points, corona's earliest appearance on the world stage is indistinct in my mind. Contradiction, concealment, and reversals have reigned from the start.

Was it in February 2020 that we first noticed news of a scientist in faraway China who was in trouble with his government for having warned his brethren about a new, unfamiliar virus?

He died.

When the pandemic was still getting underway—not yet known by that term—a physician here in Jerusalem told my husband that people were panicking unnecessarily. This was simply a new strain of flu, in his view—albeit stronger and more severe than what twenty-first century people are used to—yet nonetheless, a flu. He advised frequent handwashing.

I couldn't help but relax when I heard this.

The rabbinical consensus at that early juncture was that we should maintain Torah learning at all levels, even as we heed medical recommendations to avoid exposure to the virus.

I have no idea how long it was before my son asked me on the phone, "Mommy, what do you think about this corona thing?"

I didn't know how to answer. I wanted my children, all of whom are now adults with young families—to err on the side of caution.

Sometime not too long thereafter, we were told about this unfamiliar phenomenon called "social distancing," and that children and grandchildren must not hug grandparents, and that each family unit should have the Seder by themselves. Our own Seder at home, just the two of us, was lovely. I opened an old notebook at random in my bookcase, of notes from a *shiur* I attended in the 1980s, and read: "The biggest test *Hashem* gave Am Yisrael during the plagues was of our *emunah*."

Time passed.

We received an email from our son-in-law of a *psak halachah* issued by another respected Rav, which ruled that men are required to *daven* at home. I'd only seen my husband miss minyan twice, while in hospital after an operation.

When Jerusalem was first ordered into lockdown, I found myself liking it. It was one of the first times in memory that I didn't feel pressured to accomplish anything. Competition with my fellow man, and even with myself, dissolved. Life was easier, and quieter. Guests are wonderful, yes, but I could do without them for a few weeks. I'd enjoy it.

The jokes started pouring in, too, via email. It was fantastic. Not even one comes to mind at this moment, but they were wickedly funny at the time. All around the globe, people were cackling away at this weird temporary situation. My husband says he would hear me chuckling and giggling to myself in the next room. All mankind all around the globe was playing the game called Lockdown, and we were entitled to jovial self-pity. What a scream!

Then…all within a brief span of time, the jokes seemed to wane. Once in a while, a good laugh would still come my way, but something had shifted, as if mankind had all at once understood that this isn't funny. Corona comedy had made its exit; humor was irrelevant. Mankind's mass abuse in modern times of the privilege of social closeness is undergoing correction. From behind tall curtains whose uppermost heights we can't see, a panoramic tragedy—many of whose characters are our own—has taken center stage.

MY DAUGHTER YAEL called tonight. "Mommy, how are you?"

"I'm fine, how are *you*? How's everyone? Is Elchonon in the corona hotel?"

"Yes, Mommy, he is. But he's feeling fine. I just spoke to him. And Shlomo's out of *bidud*. We're all fine, thank G-d. But Mommy, I wanted to tell you: something. Yechezkel and I went to Bnei Brak after Shabbos to Rav T—. We wanted to hear from him what we could take on, what *avodah* we should do, what *chumrah* we can take on. Because so many people in Beitar have it now, Mommy. People are suffering. Many wonderful people, many *tzaddikim*, We wanted to know what we should be doing. Rav T—was wearing a mask and so at first it was hard to understand him, but you know what he told us?"

"Please! Tell me!"

"He said that the best *avodah* now is just to be happy. Because everything that's happening now is from *Hashem*. It's good."

DEAR DADDY

*D*ear Daddy.

As I type that standard opening, it already feels so good, so right after all these years, to be addressing myself to you. To turn myself again toward you—the way any personal letter, by definition, intrinsically entails—is to turn my attention simultaneously inward, toward my own most deeply implanted ideals. It's to reexperience instantly, after thirty years of your absence, the person I want to be in your presence.

The air you breathed was your respect and love for words, and your words bring you so easily back to life, even while offering proof, inadvertently, of the irrevocable distance increasingly separating us, with time's incessant onward roll. Once upon a time I couldn't have imagined engaging in a contrived exercise such as this without fighting off a turbulent undertow of mourning.

Yet here I sit, dry-eyed and tranquil. Remembering.

DEAR DADDY.

When an Orthodox magazine invited a group of writers to contribute to a feature entitled, "A Letter to My Mentor," my initial reaction was to retort proudly: "I never had one."

"Really?" probed the publication's emissary. "Never?"

"Well," I answered, "not if by 'mentor' you mean someone who thinks there's such a thing as teaching how to write. Maybe the closest thing I had to a mentor were the various books that I loved when I was growing up, which made me want to write."

I was thinking of the stories that kept me company through childhood, that I'd read over and over again, and can reread until today, marveling at the authors' mastery. How did they create whole worlds that as a little girl I could occupy in utter innocence of the creators' expertise, worlds more real to me back then than the alternate reality of my actual hometown? **A Little Princess**, *by Frances Hodgson Burnett,* **The Long Winter**, *by Laura Ingalls Wilder.* **Charlotte's Web**, *by E. B. White. In high school it was* **Our Town**, *by Thornton Wilder, and James Agee's* **A Death in the Family**, *and Agee's* **Let Us Now Praise Famous Men**. *And Edna St. Vincent Millay's sonnets, and Emily Dickinson's poetry.*

No sooner had the magazine called back with acquiescence to this proposal than suddenly I realized: Of course I had a writing mentor.

DEAR DADDY.

You didn't tell me there was a right way to write, as some authorities unfortunately are inclined. Nouns are better than adjectives. Develop your characters' personalities. Decide at the outset on a good plot. Active tense better than passive.

And so on and so forth.

What you gave over, Daddy, was not how to write but how to live. What you taught—you who were a most wonderful writer, and wonderful editor, someone for whom writing was at the center of his life until the end—was that a work of literature is only as good as the noble ideals it serves. Without saying so explicitly, you gave me to understand that writing well is not about style, not about method, not about technique. It's about the integrity of the writer himself, and whether he's writing something for worthy purposes, in his own voice, from his unique life's perspective, with ideas he has earned the right to use.

Good writing is about words that promote good in the world, by telling the truth as the writer sees it. Just as everything in nature, with no exception, serves a good purpose—every cell, leaf, flower, cloud, every animal, star and atom—so, too, does everything an individual experiences, by the hour and by the day, and through the years. So, too, everything that mankind experiences.

So, too, must our words serve good purposes.

Style, and sometimes beauty, will follow.

YOU DIDN'T DISHONOR the phenomenon of language by using speech for lowly purposes, Daddy. To the best of my knowledge as your daughter, you did not lie. You found lying repugnant, beneath human dignity, and gave your children to understand, by extension: beneath ours.

In all my life, I never once heard you use crudities.

You were not the address for put-downs. Gossip bounced off of you; it would not stick.

Is it only in my imagination that you said, "Optimism is realism," or was that a principle you nonverbally imparted?

In all my life, you never broke a promise. A man of your word, literally.

"For Sarah Kit," reads your penned inscription to your teenage daughter, on the title page of my copy of the 1964 edition of March's Thesaurus, for which you served as editor-in-chief. "For everything begins with the right word. With love, Daddy."

THE MOTHER'S RETURN

I have no memory of her leaving, but do remember her coming back. Mom, my grandmother, was standing on my right, in her long polo coat. She'd been taking care of us while our mother and father were on a trip to Japan.

We were at the train station to pick them up, but my father, for whatever reason, is not included in this memory, this most ancient of memories, when I was less than three.

My parents had been away. The words I remember are "gone for a month."

A long train came in on our left, and then, far off down the long platform: the woman we were waiting for. She stepped down onto the platform and appeared. She had gotten off the train.

She was walking, coming toward us, then she stopped, and looked.

She was in something long and blue. Her head was tipped down, she was drawing in her chin. She was looking at me.

I knew that smile. Who was she? I didn't like it!

That's when I was born.

Those twinkling eyes smiling at me from where she was standing far away, standing still, knowing I was about to…Taken aback that I was turning away from her…her feelings a little hurt? That red-and-white smile: this was my first introduction to the thing called beauty, and it was maddeningly stronger than myself. I had been wanting her for so long, more than myself, but had adjusted to Mom, whom I didn't particularly love because I didn't think she loved me. She liked my older sister. I'd drifted, had gotten unhinged from that face…but now I was losing myself. I was getting smaller. How dare she just come back, all of a sudden!

She was looking at me from far away with those eyes...smiling! A reddish wavy hairdo cut close around a soft face, short bangs cut high on the forehead. Beauty, more than I could bear. Warmth, more than I could resist! I turned into the beige cashmere of my grandmother's coat and hid my eyes. I hugged the leg of my grandmother, whom I didn't love; she loved my older sister.

That smile was the warmest thing in the world. I didn't like it. No!

Mom tried to pry me loose, but I held on tight, until suddenly...*Mommy!*

I was running! The world had been empty. Now I was swept up again into the arms of the world, and I dissolved, and didn't need to see myself again for a long, long time.

GLOSSARY

The following glossary provides a partial explanation of some of the Hebrew, Yiddish (Y.) and Aramaic (A.) words and phrases used in this book. The spellings and explanations reflect the way the specific word is used herein. Often, there are alternate spellings and meanings for the words.

a"h: a Hebrew acronym for "May she rest in peace."

achdus: unity; brotherhood.

al kiddush Hashem: for the sanctification of the Divine Name; martyrdom.

aliyah: lit., ascent; immigration to the Land of Israel.

am ha'aretz: a person who is ignorant in Torah knowledge.

ani ohev otach: I love you.

apikorsus: heresy.

at shamaat: "Did you hear?"

Avinu Malkeinu: our Father, our King.

avodah: service of G-d.

Avraham Avinu: Abraham, our forefather.

b'ahavah: with love.

b'emet: truthfully.

Baal haTanya: Shneur Zalman of Liadi, an Orthodox rabbi and the founder and first Rebbe of Chabad, a branch of Hassidic Judaism.

baal (fem.–baalas) teshuvah: a penitent; a formerly non-observant Jew who returns to Jewish practice and tradition.

bachur (pl.–bachurim): a young, unmarried man; a yeshiva student.

baruch Hashem: "Blessed be G-d"; "Thank G-d."

berachah: a blessing.

bidud: quarantine.

blech: (Y.) a metal sheet that covers a heat source, used to keep food warm on the Sabbath.

bli ayin hara: "May there be no evil eye!"

boker tov: "Good morning!"

bris: a covenant; the ritual of circumcision.

chacham: a wise, learned person; a Torah authority.

chareidim: a group within Orthodox Judaism characterized by strict adherence to Jewish law and tradition.

Chassidic: belonging to a group within Orthodox Judaism, which follows the teachings of the Baal Shem Tov.

cheder: lit., a room; a Jewish primary school for boys.

cheshbon: reckoning; accounting.

chessed: lovingkindness; acts of kindness.

chevra kadisha: (Y.) lit., the sacred society; Jewish burial society.

chillul Hashem: desecration of G-d's name.

chinuch: Jewish education.

Chumash: [one of] the five books of Moses.

chumrah: stringency.

daven: (Y.) pray.

derech: the way or manner of doing something.

Eidah Chareidis: the Charedi Council of Jerusalem, a large ultra-Orthodox Jewish communal organization based in Jerusalem.

ein mah la'asot: "Nothing can be done."

emunah: faith in G-d.

emunas chachamim: faith in the words of the wise, learned ones.

Eretz Yisrael: the Land of Israel.

fleishig: (Y.) made of, prepared with, or used with meat or meat products.

frei: (Y.) lit., free; non-religious.

frum: (Y.) religious; observant.

Gadol Hador: a great Torah sage and leader of the generation.

gaivah: pride; arrogance; egotism.

gam zu l'tovah: "This too is for the good."

gan: preschool.

Gedolei Yisrael: sages and leaders of the Jewish people.

gedolim: Torah sages and leaders.

ger: a convert.

glatt kosher chessed: pure acts of kindness.

ha'kol hevel: "All is vanity."

hachnasas orchim: hospitality.

Hakadosh Baruch Hu: the Holy One, blessed be He.

halachah: the entire body of Jewish law(s); a specific law.

Hashem Echad: the One G-d.

Hatzolah: lit., rescue; an emergency medical service.

Havdalah: lit., separation; the ceremony marking the conclusion of the Sabbath and of festivals, separating the holy day from the other days of the week.

hishtadlus: the human obligation to make efforts to alleviate a situation, with the realization that the result of these efforts is ultimately in G-d's hands.

ich veis: (Y.) "How do I know?"

ima sheli: my mother.

intifada: (Arabic) an uprising; a rebellion.

kapparah: atonement.

kartisiyah: a bus ticket.

kavod: honor; glory.

kelalah: a curse.

kiddush Hashem: the sanctification of G-d's name.

Klal Yisrael: the Jewish nation.

kollel: a center for advanced Torah learning for adult students, mostly married men, who receive stipends for their studies.

Kupat Cholim: an organization that provides health services to its members.

kushi: a black person.

l'kabel yissurim b'ahavah: to accept suffering with love.

Lag Ba'omer: the thirty-third of the forty-nine days of the counting of the Omer, a joyful day interrupting a period of semi-mourning.

le'at: slowly.

levayah: a funeral.

lo aleinu: "May it not happen to us!"

mammale: (Y.) lit., little mama; endearing term.

mechanech (fem.–mechaneches): an educator.

mechutanim: parents of one's son-in-law or daughter-in-law.

mechutenista: (Y.) the mother of one's son-in-law or daughter-in-law.

megillah: a long, involved story.

mehadrin: a strict level of observance.

menschlich: (Y.) with integrity.

meshuga: crazy.

meshulach (pl.–meshulachim): lit., an emissary; a fundraiser; a messenger or charity collector.

middos: character traits.

milchig: made of, prepared with, or used with milk or milk products.

min haShamayim: from Heaven.

mirpeset: a porch.

mishpachah: a family.

mitzvas asei: a positive Biblical commandment.

Motzaei Shabbos: lit., the departure of the Sabbath; the evening following the Sabbath; Saturday night.

Mussar Movement: a Jewish ethical, educational, and cultural movement.

mussar: ethical teachings; Torah ethics and values aimed at character improvement.

neshamah (pl.–neshamos): a soul.

neshamah Yehudi: a Jewish soul.

nisayon (pl.–nisyonos): a test; a trial.

parashah: the weekly Torah portion.

parnasah: livelihood.

peyos: sidelocks.

pigua: a terrorist attack.

Rabbeinu Yonah: Rabbi Jonah ben Abraham Gerondi; a rabbi and moralist, best known for his ethical work, *The Gates of Repentance.*

ram kol: a loudspeaker.

Ribbono Shel Olam: Master of the Universe; God.

ruchniyus: spirituality.

sefer (pl.–sefarim): a book; a holy book.

Sefer Devarim: the book of Deuteronomy.

shadchan: a matchmaker; a marriage broker.

Shechinah: the Divine Presence.

she'eilah: a question on a halachic issue posed to a Torah scholar; a halachic question.

sheitel: (Y.) wig.

shidduch (pl.–shidduchim): a marital match.

shiur: a Torah class.

shlita: a Hebrew acronym for "May he live long"; "May he live a length of good days, Amen."

shemiras halashon: lit., guarding one's tongue; i.e., watching one's words to make sure not to say anything forbidden.

shemittah: the Sabbatical year.

shomer Shabbos: one who is Sabbath observant.

shuk: a marketplace.

simchah: a joyous occasion.

siyata d'Shmaya: (A.) Heavenly assistance.

tachanah: bus stop.

talmid: a student; a disciple.

Tanach: a Hebrew acronym for the Holy Scriptures: Torah, Nevi'im (Prophets), and Kesuvim (Writings).

Tehillim: Psalms.

Tishah B'Av: the ninth day of the Hebrew month of Av, which is a fast day commemorating the destruction of the Temple in Jerusalem.

tzaddik (pl.–tzaddikim) (fem.–tzaddekes): a righteous, holy person.

tzanua: modest in dress and behavior.

tzniusly: modestly.

tzuris: troubles.

yemach shemo: "May his name be blotted out."

Yerushalayim sheli: my Jerusalem.

yetzer hara: the evil inclination or impulse in human nature.

yetzer hatov: the good inclination or impulse in human nature.

yevarech otach: "will bless you."

Yidden: (Y.) Jews.

Yiddishkeit: (Y.) Judaism.

yiras Shamayim: fear of Heaven.

yishuv (pl.–yishuvim): a settlement.

zeh sheli: "It is mine."

zisselah: (Y.) sweetie.

zt"l: a Hebrew acronym for "May the memory of a righteous person be for a blessing."

MOSAICA PRESS
BOOK PUBLISHERS
Elegant, Meaningful & Bold

info@MosaicaPress.com
www.MosaicaPress.com

The Mosaica Press team of
acclaimed editors and designers
is attracting some of the most
compelling thinkers and teachers
in the Jewish community today.
Our books are available around
the world.

HARAV YAACOV HABER
RABBI DORON KORNBLUTH